**Approved by OCR for the new CLAIT**

# new CLAIT
## LEVEL ONE
### IT User Qualification

## Student Workbook

# ALAN CLARKE

Orders: please contact Bookpoint Ltd, 78 Milton Park, Abingdon, Oxon OX14 4TD. Telephone: (44) 01235 827720, Fax: (44) 01235 400454. Lines are open from 9.00 - 6.00, Monday to Saturday, with a 24 hour message answering service. Email address: orders@bookpoint.co.uk

British Library Cataloguing in Publication Data
A catalogue record for this title is available from The British Library

ISBN 0 340 846984

First published 2002
Impression number10  9  8  7  6  5  4  3  2  1
Year                          2005  2004  2003  2002  2002
Copyright © 2002 Alan Clarke

Cover created by Stewart Larking
Typeset by Stewart Larking
Printed in Italy for Hodder & Stoughton Educational, a division of Hodder Headline Plc, 338 Euston Road, London NW1 3BH.

# Contents

# Acknowledgements

To my wife and sons for their help and support during the writing of the book and particularly to Christine for improving my grammar and spelling and Peter for checking the technical content of the book.

The publishers would like to acknowledge Life File photographic agency for the use of their photographic images: © Life File/Emma Lee for laptop computer, floppy disk and computer mouse; Life File/Jan Suttle for the computer keyboard.

The author and publisher wish to acknowledge the following for use of on-screen images: CorelDRAW, Altavista Europe, Atomz.com and the Microsoft Corporation.

**OCR does not endorse the use of one software package over another, and all CLAIT qualifications are written in generic form. This book is written using the Microsoft Office suite as examples, simply to provide clear support to the majority of candidates who will be using that package. The use of any other form of software is equally appropriate and acceptable to OCR.**

# Introduction

New CLAIT is an initial information and communication technology course and does not assume that you have any prior experience of using computers, applications (e.g. word-processing) or accessing the Internet. It is suitable for people new to computing and is a qualification offered by OCR, who are a major qualification awarding body. The qualification conforms to the National Qualifications Framework.

The OCR Level 1 Certificate for IT Users (New CLAIT) is composed of a mandatory unit "Using the Computer" and optional units. In order to achieve an overall Level 1 certificate you need to successfully complete the mandatory unit and four other units of your choice.

The book is based on Microsoft Office 2000. However, the exercises have been selected so that they are in many cases suitable for Office 97. Only the Computer Art unit employs an application not based on Office. This is the drawing package CorelDRAW 10. All ten optional and single mandatory units are covered within the book. The BBC's Becoming WebWise can also be used as a unit. You can find out more about WebWise by visiting the BBC's Website at www.bbc.org.uk. If you choose to study Becoming WebWise then you cannot include unit 2 Electronic Communication as part of the five units which make up the New CLAIT certificate. The two units have similar content.

The assessment of each unit is based on a practical test which places an emphasis on undertaking a task by accurately following instructions. The assessment is provided by a local assessor who will arrange a convenient date and time with you. The exception is Unit 1 which is externally assessed. If you do not achieve all the assessment crieria you will receive feedback on what you have to improve on and a chance at a second attempt.

You must not make any critcial errors. These include failing to provide all the requested printouts of your work, not saving using the designated file names or making more than three accuracy errors.  An accuracy error is making a data entry mistake or failing to fully carry out an assessment objective.

Data entry errors vary according to the unit being studied so that they are not tested in unit 1 Using a Computer, but are based on a word in Unit 2 Word-processing. If you make mistakes in four words in the word-processing task you will fail the assessment. A word is defined as the characters that make it up plus any associated punctuation and the space following the word. A numerical date (e.g. 13/02/52) or a string of numbers (e.g. 1234) would be judged as a word.

Your local tutor will be able to provide you with detailed guidance about the nature of the assessment. However, following the assessment instructions and being accurate are essential. It is important to read the assessment instructions carefully and follow them completely.

# Using a Computer

This chapter will help you to use a computer and to manage your data.
You will be able to:

identify and use a personal computer, monitor, keyboard
and mouse

access and locate data on a computer

input small amounts of unformatted text, numbers
and symbols

print a document using the default printer settings

manage documents and data

The chapter covers the contents of the New CLAIT mandatory unit. It
contains information and helps you practise skills which are essential to the
successful completion of the optional units. We would therefore recommend
that you start by studying this chapter. You are then free to select which of
the optional units to study. In a similar way many of the optional units provide
opportunities to practise the variety of skills and knowledge that this chapter
introduces to you.

## Assessment

This unit does not assume any previous experience of using a computer. After
studying Unit 1 your skills and understanding are assessed during a 2-hour
practical assignment. This is set by OCR and externally assessed by an OCR
examiner-moderator.

## What is a computer?

A computer consists of two main components; **hardware** and **software**. The
hardware is the physical element of the equipment that you can see when you
look at a computer. Figure 1 illustrates a desktop computer and Figure 2
shows a tower computer. These are the two main variations of personal
computers. In both cases you will see a monitor which resembles a television,
a box that contains the electronic heart of the computer (Central Processing
Unit), a keyboard (Figure 6) and a mouse (Figure 8). The views of the
computer may seem complicated and you may wonder what the purposes of
all the parts and connections are. For OCR New CLAIT you do not need to
know but if you are interested you will find an explanation in the summary
section at the end of the chapter.

All computers are different so when you look at your own computer it will be similar but not identical. The on-switch is often positioned on the front of the computer but in many models there is a second switch on the back of the computer. The second switch is usually the power supply control so it needs to be on in order for the front switch to operate. When the computer is switched on a small light near to the on-switch is illuminated.

**Software** is the set of instructions that controls the hardware. It controls the operations of the hardware such as saving information, electronic communications, word-processing and many other applications. Software is divided into two main types.

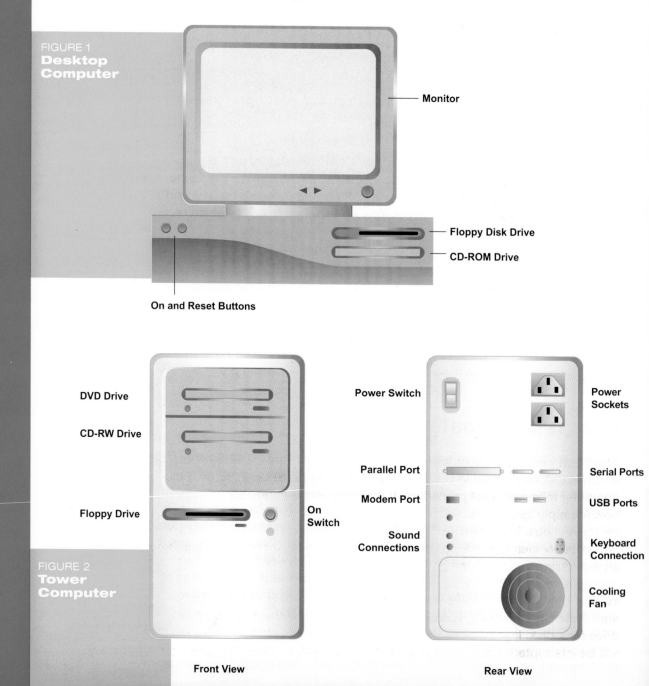

FIGURE 1
**Desktop Computer**

Monitor

Floppy Disk Drive

CD-ROM Drive

On and Reset Buttons

FIGURE 2
**Tower Computer**

DVD Drive

CD-RW Drive

Floppy Drive

On Switch

Front View

Power Switch

Power Sockets

Parallel Port

Serial Ports

Modem Port

USB Ports

Sound Connections

Keyboard Connection

Cooling Fan

Rear View

**Operating system –** this is the program that controls and connects the application software and hardware. It provides all the standard features of the computer (e.g. saving information, printing and display of information on the monitor screen). This book is based on the Microsoft Windows 98 operating system. However, there are other versions of this product and also other completely different systems (e.g. Linux).

**Applications –** these are programs which help you to carry out specialist tasks (e.g. word-process, draw pictures, communicate and design presentations). The later chapters consider applications in considerable detail.

# Exercise 1

## Investigate the hardware

**1.** Before you switch on your computer, and with all the hardware disconnected from the power supply, carry out a visual inspection of the equipment. Observe the different connections and pieces of hardware.

**2.** Identify if the computer is a desktop or a tower, locate the printer, keyboard (Figure 6) and mouse (Figure 8). These are the main components of a computer system's hardware.

**3.** Inspect the back of the computer and you will observe a number of connections and cables. These link the different parts together and allow information to pass between the different elements (e.g. the computer sends information to the printer so it can produce a document).

**4.** Locate the on-switch or switches.

## Switching on

When you switch on a computer you are instructing the operating system, which is software stored in the computer's memory (**hard disk**), to start the computer following a set procedure. If the computer is connected to the power supply then you will hear the hard disk making noises while searching for instructions. The monitor will display some of the instructions but these are probably meaningless to most computer users except those who are at an expert level.

You may notice that the light on the floppy disk drive is illuminated. The standard start up (called **'boot up'**) procedure involves checking the floppy drive for a disk. If you have left one in the drive then the start up sequence will be interrupted. This seems unusual but is actually a safety feature – if you have a hard disk failure it allows you to investigate the problem.

After a few moments the Microsoft Windows logo will apear on the screen. The system will continue to make noises until eventually the logo disappears and is replaced by what is known as a dialogue box in the middle of the screen. This will ask you for your Ußer name and Password. You can change both once you have access to the computer. Once you have entered the correct name and password you click on to the OK button using the mouse pointer. This will present you with the Microsoft Windows desktop (Figure 3). This illustration has been kept very simple and on many desktops there will be many small pictures (known as **icons**) representing different software applications.

Figure 3 shows some icons on the main desktop area. Two important ones are:

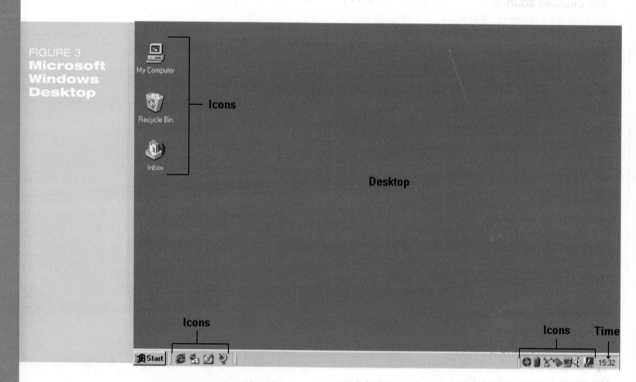

FIGURE 3
**Microsoft Windows Desktop**

**My Computer –** this links you to the areas of the computer where information is stored (known as drives). Drives include the hard disk which stores the bulk of the information as well as CD-ROM and floppy disk drives which allow information to be placed in portable form. My Computer also links you to resources connected to the computer such as printers
**Recycle Bin –** this is a place where deleted files are kept so that if you make a mistake you can reclaim them

At the bottom of the desktop there is a grey bar – the **taskbar**. At the right end of the taskbar is an area called the status area in which a range of small icons are shown. These represent programmes which are currently working.

Other icons are also on the **toolbar** which allow you to access the applications they represent while on the left end is the button called Start. Clicking on this provides access to a range of applications and other services and is also the way to switch off the computer.

# Exercise 2

## Switching on (booting up) your computer

**1.** With the computer, monitor and other hardware connected to the power supply, press the on-switch on the front of the computer and on the monitor. In both cases a small light will be illuminated and you will hear the whirring and clicking sounds of the computer starting.

**2.** If nothing happens then check that the power switch at the rear of the computer is in the on position.

**3.** Observe what happens – the time to start (boot) the computer can vary considerably depending on what is connected to the machine and how it is configured, so do not be concerned if it takes a few minutes.

**4.** Eventually you will see the dialogue box requesting your User name and Password. Once these have been entered you will see something similar to Figure 3 appear.

## Switching off

Switching off a computer must be done in the correct way or you run the risk of damaging your system. To switch off a computer using the Microsoft Windows operating systems requires you to click on the Start button. A menu (list of options) will appear (Figure 4) and if you select the Shut Down option then a small box entitled Shut Down Windows will appear (Figure 5).

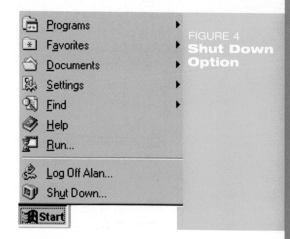

FIGURE 4
**Shut Down Option**

The Shut Down Windows box provides several options and in most cases you will want to select Shut Down. You select an option by clicking in the small circular area and a black dot will appear in its centre to indicate that it has been selected. If the dot is already present you do not need to select it. If you now click on the OK button then the computer will begin to shut down. If you click on the Cancel button you will return to the desktop.

FIGURE 5
**Shut Down
Windows**

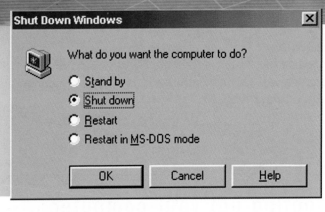

The process of shutting down involves the computer making noises and the screen showing a variety of images. The time required to complete the shut down process varies but does not take very long. When the shut down is complete the light on the computer will be switched off. However, the light on the monitor will still remain on and you need to press the manual switch.

## Input

Users communicate with computers using input devices such as:

a desktop keyboard (Figure 6)
a mouse (Figure 8)

There are many input devices depending on how you need to interact with the computer system. When you input information into the computer it responds by displaying the information on the monitor screen.

FIGURE 6
**Keyboard**

A keyboard is similar to a typewriter and is designed to allow you to enter text into the computer. Both a keyboard and a typewriter have alphabetical keys which are laid out identically. There are also other keys which are common to them both, e.g.

space bar
capital lock
shift
punctuation keys

The major difference, however, is that the keyboard has many more keys than a typewriter. These are:

**a row of number** keys towards the top of the keyboard and a separate number pad on the right

**enter keys** which are used to confirm that you want to enter information into the computer

**a top row of keys** labelled F1 to F12 which carry out particular functions

**a number of other special purpose keys** whose role will gradually emerge as you work through the book

# Exercise 3

## Exploring the keyboard

**1.** Work your way across the keyboard. You will notice that it is divided into four main areas:

function keys across the top of the keyboard

number pad on the right of the keyboard·

main alphabetical keys – notice the QWERTY layout (this is the sequence of alphabetical keys along the top left of the keyboard)

various other keys sandwiched between the QWERTY and number pad areas (e.g. Enter)

**2.** Identify the following keys: Ctrl, Alt, Home, Pg Up and Num Lock. These are the special purpose keys, and eventually you will learn their purpose. For the moment you simply need to know where they are. This will help you once you start to use applications.

**3.** To enter uppercase letters requires the shift and character keys to be pressed together. This is also the way symbols of the top half of some of the keys are entered.

**4.** Some keyboards have a small Microsoft Windows symbol on a key. This is a shortcut equivalent to pressing the Start button on the Microsoft Windows desktop. This might not seem useful at the moment but its importance will become apparent later.

There are other types of keyboard and many specialist ones have been devised for particular tasks.

Figure 7 illustrates a laptop computer keyboard. This is smaller and so suitable for a laptop computer which is designed to be portable. The main difference from a desktop keyboard is the lack of a number pad.

A mouse is a small palm-sized device which is connected to your computer by a cable. The mouse is linked to an on-screen pointer which normally appears as an arrow and mirrors the movements made by the mouse. Figure 8 shows a two-button mouse which is the type most widely used, but there are also single and three-button mice available. This book will only discuss a two-button mouse.

FIGURE 7
**Laptop Computer**

FIGURE 8
**Two-button Mouse**

If you move the mouse the on-screen pointer moves in the same way as the mouse. If you move right the pointer goes right, if you move down then the pointer goes down and so on. The buttons on the mouse allow you to communicate with the computer.

There are other input devices which will also control the screen pointer. A trackball works by your manipulating a ball and clicking buttons to control the pointer and make selections. Laptop computers have a variety of devices using touch buttons, pads and thumb balls to control on-screen pointers.

**Note**
The mouse normally sits on a small mat which is, not surprisingly, called a mouse mat. This helps the mouse move smoothly across the surface.

# Exercise 4

## Using a mouse – right handed users

1. Place your right hand with your index finger on the left-hand button and your second finger on the right button.

**2.** Move the mouse and watch how the pointer responds on the screen.

**3.** Practise using the mouse until you are comfortable – move the pointer up, down, left, right and diagonally until you can accurately control the pointer. Notice where you move the mouse to achieve the desired result.

Alternative
# Exercise 4

## Using a mouse-left handed users

**1.** You can adjust the mouse to make it suitable for left-handed people. This involves clicking on the Start button, Highlighting <u>S</u>etting and another menu will appear on which you chose <u>C</u>ontrol Panel and then double click on Mouse icon. This will reveal the Mouse Properties window and you can select the left-handed option which you select by clicking on the radio button and then the OK button.

**2.** Place your left hand with your index finger on the right-hand button and your second finger on the left button.

**3.** Move the mouse and watch how the pointer responds on the screen.

**4.** Practise using the mouse until you are comfortable – move the pointer up, down, left, right and diagonally until you can accurately control the pointer. Notice where you move the mouse to achieve the desired result.

**Note** – remember that if you select the left-hand mouse options then you will need to take this into account when reading the instructions in this book.

It is very important that you learn to use a mouse accurately and effectively. This will take practice. The main skills are:

**accurately moving the on-screen pointer** when the point touches objects on the screen. Often they will be animated or a text box will appear to explain their purpose

**single clicking the left mouse button** as this communicates a command to the computer to start a process

**single clicking the right mouse button** to communicate a command to the computer to show some extra features such as revealing an extra menu of choices

**double clicking the left mouse button** which communicates a command to the computer to start a process

**clicking and dragging** (if you press the left-hand mouse button but do not release it while the pointer is resting on an object on the screen and then you move the mouse, the object will be dragged across the screen until you release the button)

# Exercise 5

## Practising your mouse skills

**1.** You can practise your mouse skills in many ways but a fun way is to play a game which is supplied as part of the Windows operating system. This is called Solitaire and is a card game played using the mouse pointer to move the cards.

**2.** To load the games program requires using the mouse and can be quite a challenge if this is the first time you have used a mouse – but do keep trying.

**3.** The first step is to single click with the left mouse button on the Start button. A list of options will appear above the button. This is called a menu and is a standard way of presenting an option in Microsoft Windows and in applications.

**Step 1:** Slide the mouse up the menu and you will see that as the mouse pointer crosses an option it is highlighted (the background changes to a new colour). Continue until you highlight <u>P</u>rograms.

**Step 2:** At the end of the word <u>P</u>rograms you will see a small pointer (triangle) which tells you that there are more options available. If you leave the mouse pointer over <u>P</u>rograms a new menu will appear to the right.

**Step 3:** Slide your mouse pointer in a straight line to the right until you highlight an option in the new menu, then move the pointer up the menu until you reach the option Accessories.

**Step 4:** If you leave your pointer over Accessories another menu to the right will appear. Again, in a straight line slide your pointer to the right until a new option is highlighted. Move the pointer until it is now over the option Games and a final menu will appear containing the option Solitaire. Once again, slide to the right in a straight line and move the pointer up or down until the Solitaire option is highlighted.

**Step 5:** With the option highlighted, single click on the left mouse button and you will see the Solitaire game appear.

It will provide you with an opportunity to practise moving and controlling the precise direction of the mouse pointer.

**4.** Figure 9 illustrates the Solitaire game after a few cards have been played. The game has the same rules as the card game. You turn cards over by single clicking on the pile. Move cards by clicking the left mouse button on the one of your choice and holding the button down and dragging the card to its new location.

**5.** Try to play a game. If you find that every time you drag a card to a new location it returns to its original position, it is because you are making an illegal move.

**6.** Keep playing until you are confident about dragging and dropping and clicking with the left button. These are key elements in using a mouse but leave out two other important actions. These are double clicking and single clicking with right mouse button. There will be many opportunities to practise these skills in other parts of the book. However, double clicking which is clicking the left mouse button twice rapidly needs practise. People often find it initially difficult to click twice quickly enough. If you find that after double clicking no action results it is probably because you are leaving too large an interval between the clicks. Keep trying to click twice as quickly as you can. You will eventually get it right.

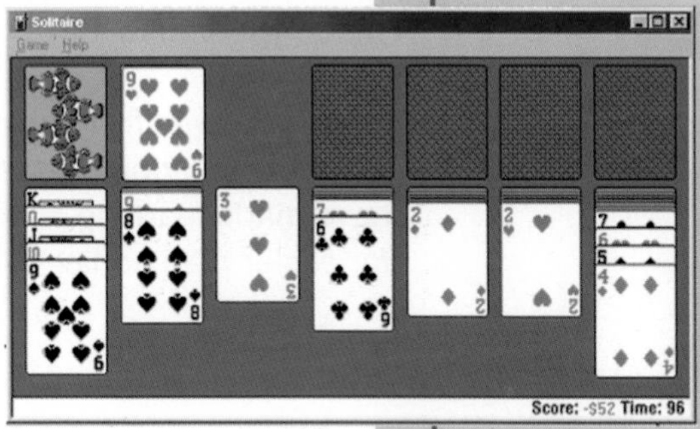

**7.** To close the Solitaire window you need to single click with the left mouse button in the button marked with an X in the top right-hand corner of the Solitaire window. Figure 10 shows the three buttons which appear in the right-hand corner of the window. The buttons allow the window to be minimised to a button on the Desktop taskbar, maximised to fill the entire display, and closed. Experiment with expanding the window to fill the whole display and minimising it to a button. When the window is maximised you can reduce it in size by using the same buttons. Figure 10 shows how the three buttons change in appearance when the window is maximised (fills the whole screen) (i.e. right-hand image).

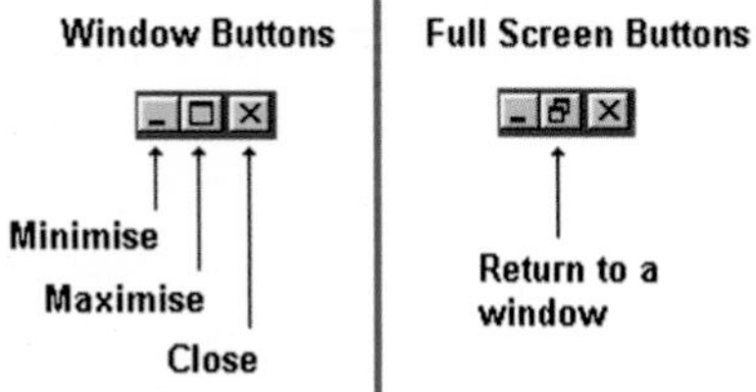

**8.** These controls appear on all windows. Applications can be displayed as a window ( a rectangular area, the whole display or a single button on the taskbar). It is a standard part of the operating system.

**9.** When you have finished playing Solitaire, close the window.

FIGURE 9
**Solitaire**

FIGURE 10
**Windows Controls**

Window Buttons

Minimise
Maximise
Close

Full Screen Buttons

Return to a window

# Graphic User Interface

Microsoft Windows and the vast majority of modern software uses a Graphic User Inteface (GUI). GUI are a highly visual interface which combines the use of a pointing device (e.g. a mouse) with visual links to applications, commands and options. The visual links take the form of small pictures called icons, buttons (small rectangles) or menus (i.e. list of options). GUIs are easy to learn and to use since you do not need to remember a large number of commands, but only to recognise them when they appear on the screen. Most GUIs are consistent so that you can work out what to do even when you are using a new part of the system.

A key feature of a GUI and Microsoft Windows and Office is the **window**. This is a rectangular enclosed area in which applications, files and messages are displayed. Windows can be moved and resized (i.e. a window can fill a whole screen or be reduced to small picture on the edge of the display). Windows can be stacked on top of each other and at first you can sometimes lose your window because it is hidden under another one.

While you are still learning about Windows, using a mouse and GUIs you probably feel confused and uncertain but this will change with practice. GUIs have made learning about using information and communication technology far easier than earlier computers based on command interfaces.

## Storing and locating information

FIGURE 11
**Floppy disk**

Computers have a permanent store for information, programs (applications) and data. This is called the **hard disk** or **hard drive** and it can store an enormous amount of information. It is often designated by the letter C with a colon, so drive C: is the hard drive. Information can be stored in far smaller amounts on **floppy disks**. A floppy disk is a portable storage device that you can carry from one computer to another. The hard disk is normally a permanent part of the computer. There are computers which allow you to remove a hard drive but these are relatively rare. The floppy drive is often designated as the A: drive.

Figure 11 illustrates a floppy disk. The disk is inserted into the drive with the label on the top, the metal slider entering first. The disk is firmly pushed into the drive until it clicks. It is not possible to insert a disk the wrong way round so if it does not go in, you are holding it the wrong way up.

# Exercise 6

## Inserting a floppy disk

**1.** Try to insert a floppy disk into the drive (Figure 1 and 2). Remember to firmly push the disk into the drive, but if it will not enter then check you are inserting it the right way (i.e. label on top and metal slider first).

**2.** The floppy will make a noise when it is in place and will be inside the computer so that you cannot reach it. To remove the disk you need to press the button which is located near to the drive. This button will pop out as the floppy disk is pushed in.

**3.** Press the button and see the disk emerge.

**4.** Repeat the action of inserting and removing the disk until you are confident.

The Windows operating system provides you with the means to search the hard disk and floppy disks when they are inserted into the drive. Windows Explorer lets you view the contents of the computer drives. Figure 12 illustrates Windows Explorer showing the contents of the C: drive (hard drive). Information is stored in a computer in what are known as files. These each have a unique name and are normally grouped with related files and stored

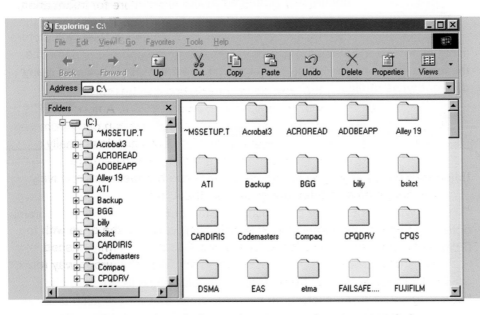

FIGURE 12
**Windows Explorer**

within folders. This is rather similar to the storage of paper records in cardboard files and it is intended to help you locate them again when you have a large number of files. In the computer it is also possible to store folders within other folders. In Figure 12 you will notice many small plus signs

1    2

FIGURE 13
**Folders**

billy    GAMES    My Briefcase    it4all

in the left-hand area of the display. This indicates that these folders contain other folders. Clicking on the plus sign will open up the folder to reveal what it contains. These are shown in the right-hand window. Figure 13 shows a group of folders each with a unique name.

FIGURE 14
**Files**

Figure 14 shows the files stored within a folder. Files store different types of information and take on different forms or formats depending on the information they contain. Here we see examples of picture files (e.g. PhotoSuite Image), documents (e.g. Microsoft Word Doc) and spreadsheets (e.g. Microsoft Excel Wor).

| Name | Size | Type | Modified |
|---|---|---|---|
| formatexcelmenu.b... | 294KB | Paint Shop Pro 5 Im... | 03/06/01 17:30 |
| games.bmp | 735KB | Paint Shop Pro 5 Im... | 30/06/01 17:27 |
| Image3.gif | 4KB | PhotoSuite Image | 30/06/01 13:40 |
| Image4.gif | 3KB | PhotoSuite Image | 30/06/01 13:40 |
| Image5.gif | 6KB | PhotoSuite Image | 30/06/01 13:40 |
| Image6.gif | 4KB | PhotoSuite Image | 30/06/01 13:40 |
| Image7.gif | 2KB | PhotoSuite Image | 30/06/01 13:40 |
| Insert excel.bmp | 123KB | Paint Shop Pro 5 Im... | 02/06/01 15:22 |
| Interesting World ... | 28KB | Microsoft Word Doc... | 29/04/01 12:10 |
| Invasion of Russia... | 22KB | Microsoft Word Doc... | 19/05/01 22:37 |
| keyboard.bmp | 289KB | Paint Shop Pro 5 Im... | 01/07/01 15:22 |
| New Bold Garage.... | 14KB | Microsoft Excel Wor... | 02/06/01 15:59 |
| NewBold.bmp | 1,123KB | Paint Shop Pro 5 Im... | 02/06/01 16:03 |
| Open.bmp | 378KB | Paint Shop Pro 5 Im... | 28/05/01 12:46 |
| Page Setup.bmp | 444KB | Paint Shop Pro 5 Im... | 28/05/01 12:32 |
| Paint.bmp | 641KB | Paint Shop Pro 5 Im... | 25/06/01 21:01 |
| Paragraph.bmp | 510KB | Paint Shop Pro 5 Im... | 28/05/01 12:39 |
| powerpoint.bmp | 792KB | Paint Shop Pro 5 Im... | 25/06/01 20:10 |

Windows Explorer provides you with the functions in the File menu to delete or rename your files. You highlight the file you need to work on by single clicking on it, then select File menu and the options Delete or Rename. In the Edit menu you are also provided with options to copy (Copy and Paste) or move (Cut and Paste) the file to another folder. To locate a file you need to click on the folder to reveal what other folders or files are stored within.

It is not always easy when you first start to use a computer to distinguish between different types of files. Applications (e.g. word processors) are stored as files, documents produced by the applications are also stored as files and so on. In a way everything is a file. You distinguish between files by considering the small picture (icon) in front of the file name and the extension at the end of the name (i.e. the letters following the full stop – .bmp, .gif, .doc and .txt). There are many different types of files.

# Exercise 7

## Windows Explorer

**1.** Open Windows Explorer by clicking on Start button, highlighting Programs option and clicking on Windows Explorer item. This will open Explorer (Figure 12).

**2.** Explore the application by clicking on the plus signs to open up the folders structure. Keep clicking on new plus signs that are revealed and observe what changes.

**3.** Highlight folders in the left-hand list and observe what changes in the right-hand area of the window. This area shows what a highlighted folder contains. You can also click on folders in the right-hand area to open them. Again notice any changes this causes.

**4.** When you click on a folder in the left-hand list you will notice the picture of the folder itself changes to look like an open folder.

**5.** Use Explorer to investigate what is stored on the computer's hard disk. However, do not select Delete or Rename or any option within the menus since you may cause changes that harm your computer.

**6.** When you have investigated the structure close Explorer by clicking on the close button in the top right-hand corner of the window or select the File menu and the Exit option.

If you use a computer regularly, you will find that you have many hundreds of folders and files. Although they all have individual names, in order to find them you will need to remember the name of the file and in which folder you stored it. This is further complicated by storing folders inside other folders. The Windows operating system provides you with a way of finding files and folders, if you cannot remember a particular file location.

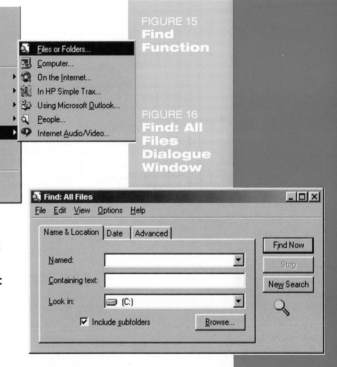

FIGURE 15
**Find Function**

FIGURE 16
**Find: All Files Dialogue Window**

If you click on the Start button, a menu will pop up containing an option called Find. If you highlight Find, another menu appears. Slide the mouse pointer on to this menu and click on Files or Folders (Figure 15). The Find: All Files dialogue window will appear (Figure 16)

# Exercise 8

## Finding a file

**1.** Load the Find: All Files dialogue box and enter Windows into the Named box and click on Find Now button. The Find function will now search the drive which appears in the Look in box. You can change this by clicking on the down arrow at the end of the box and select from the list of options which appears by clicking on it. Explore this option but search the C: drive.

**2.** Observe what happens and you should see the dialogue box extend (Figure 17) and a list of files or folders appear. These all have the word window in their titles. At the bottom of the box you will see the message that the Find function is searching. This message will rapidly change as it searches the different parts of the C: drive (i.e the hard disk)

**3.** When the search is completed the message at the bottom of the box will tell you how many files it has found. A list of files and folders is presented in the extended box. You need to review the list to identify the particular file you are searching for. If you want to open the file you need to double click on the chosen item. The file will open inside the application which created it (e.g. text files in a word-processor).

FIGURE 17
**Find Files**

**4.** Explore the search by entering new names and see what you can find. You will notice that there are two other tabs in the Find: All Files box – Date and Advanced. Explore these two tabs and you will find that they allow you to search for a file by the date it was created (Date tab) and to search for a particular type or format of files and even by its size.

**5.** Continue until you are confident in locating files. Try locating files on a floppy disk as well as on the hard disk (C:).

**6.** Close the function by using the Close button in the right-hand corner of the window.

# Creating and printing a document

The Windows operating system includes several applications which are built into its structure. These include:

**Paint** – a straightforward drawing application
**WordPad** – a basic word processor
(Figure 18)
**Calculator** – an on-screen calculator
**Address Book**

These can be accessed in a similar way to Solitaire by using the Start button, the Programs and Accessories options on the menus and then single clicking on the application of your choice. In the next exercise you are going to use WordPad (Figure 18) to create a short document, save it to a floppy disk and print it.

FIGURE 18
**WordPad**

# Exercise 9

## Creating a document

**1.** Open WordPad by clicking on Start button, highlighting <u>P</u>rograms and Accessories and single clicking on WordPad. The application will open (Figure 16). Maximise the window using the control buttons in the top right-hand corner of the window.

**2.** On the first line of work area you will see a flashing upright line. This is called the cursor and indicates where any text or numbers that you enter will appear on the screen. Press any letter or number on the keyboard. You will see your selected character appear and the cursor move one space to the right, indicating where the next one will be entered.

**3.** Move the mouse pointer around the display and you will see that it changes shape. It is no longer shaped liked an arrow when it moves across the work area but is like the letter I.

**4.** Using the keyboard enter:

My name is ...................... I live in ............... and I am .... years old.

Fill in the blanks with your own details – name, town/city and age.

To enter a capital (upper case characters) you need to hold down the shift key and then the letter of your choice (Figure 19). If you want to enter everything in upper case press the Capitals Lock (i.e. Caps Lock) key once. To return to lower case you need to press Caps Lock again. For the current exercises you only need to enter single upper case letters.

Capitals Lock

Shift Key

**5.** If you make a mistake then you can remove it using the backspace key. This is located on the top row of the keyboard (Figure 20) and will delete any character to the left of the cursor. There is another delete key which removes characters to the right of the cursor (Figure 20).

Backspace

Delete

**6.** When you have entered the text then move your mouse pointer until it is immediately in front of - I live in ..... and then single click. You will see the cursor move to this new position. This is how you move the cursor using the mouse, although there are other ways such as using the arrow keys on the keyboard.

**7.** If you press the enter key (Figure 4) then the text will be broken into two parts as shown below.

FIGURE 19
**Shift Key and Caps Lock**

FIGURE 19
**Backspace and Delete Keys**

My name is ......................
I live in .............. and I am .... years old.

The Enter key inserts a new line but if you continue typing text, the words will automatically go to the next line when you reach the end of the previous one.This is called text wrapping. If you hold down any key you will see the character appear many times and will wrap around when it reaches the end of a line.

**8.** If you single click on the menu item File (Figure 21) a menu will drop down. This provides many standard features which if you click on them give you access to useful functions such as:

FIGURE 21
**WordPad
File Menu**

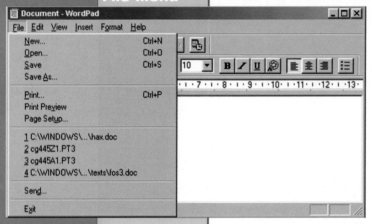

New – creates a new document

Open – opens an existing document so that you can amend it

Save – allows you to save your document to the computer's store on the hard disk or on a floppy disk

Save As – allows you to save an existing file under a different name

Print – allows you to print your document on a connected printer

Exit – an alternative to using the Close button

**9.** Close WordPad by selecting File menu and Exit option unless you want to progress immediately to Exercise 10.

## Printing

Printers provide you with the means to output your computer work to produce letters, reports and other paper documents. There are several different types of printer. Three widely available printers are:

monochrome laser printer

monochrome and colour inkjet printer

colour laser printers

A laser printer uses magnetic toner to produce text and images on paper. Inkjet printers work by squirting small drops of ink onto the page. They can provide both black and white and colour printing. Laser and inkjet printers are widely used in the work place and at home. Colour printers are more expensive than monochrome ones but the price of colour inkjets is now in reach of most computer users.

Printers are manufactured in a variety of sizes and shapes. Two key features of any printer are the on-switch and the paper holder. The on-switch is positioned in a range of locations including the back corners, front panel and the sides of the printer. In a similar way the paper holder can be located in a pull-out drawer or pushed into an opening. Each manufacturer has their own design and it is important to study the printer's manual before using it.

# Exercise 10

## Printers

**1.** It is important to familiarise yourself with the printer you are going to use, so in this exercise you are going to explore your printer.

**2.** First make sure the printer is not connected to the power supply. Inspect the printer and see if you can locate the on-switch and where the paper is loaded.

**3.** Remove the paper and inspect it. In most cases the paper is A4 size and is loaded as a block. Replace the paper carefully. When you load paper it is useful to fan the edges of the block since this will help stop it sticking together. A problem with all printers is that the paper will sometimes jam inside the printer (rather like a photocopier).

**4.** Connect the printer to the power supply and switch the printer on. Each printer will start in its own individual way but you are likely to hear the printer's setup and any control lights flash. If you are using a large laser printer it will have a display panel and you are likely to see a message appear such as Warming Up. When the printer is ready this message will change (e.g. Ready). Smaller laser and inkjet printers will often have only a few lights. Inspect the labels near the lights and you may see error, paper and data lights. The meaning of the lights being illuminated depends on the type and model of your printer.

**5.** Observe the printer's start up process.

**6.** Some printers have a demonstration or test function. This is indicated by a button labelled Demo or Test. If your printer provides this function press the button and see what happens. Often a short document will be printed. In some cases this provides background information about the printer.

**7.** Once you are confident that you know how to switch the printer on and load the paper switch the printer off if you are not going to use it.

# Exercise 11

## Create, save and print a document

**1.** Open WordPad by clicking on Start, highlighting Programs and Accessories and single clicking on WordPad. The application will open (Figure 16). Maximise the window using the control buttons in the top right-hand corner of the window if the display does not fill the screen.

**2.** Enter the following:

This is a short passage to help me understand how to create, save and print a document. The keyboard has many keys to enter text and numbers. The number keys are 1,2,3,4,5,6,7,8 and 9. The symbol keys are =-/#.,:@?!£&%+*.

Observe how the text wraps around at the end of each line and the movement of the cursor. Remember to use the shift key to access symbols on the top of keys and to insert upper case letters.

**3.** Once you have created a document you can save it as a file by selecting the File menu and the Save option. The Save As window (dialogue box) opens (Figure 22). This shows a view of a folder called My Documents in which is stored four other folders (i.e. Alan, Chris, My Pictures and Peter) and a variety of files (e.g. Document.doc).

FIGURE 22
**Save As Window**

To save your work you need to enter a file name in the box File name and then click on Save button. Your file would then be saved in the My Document folder. If you would like to save your file elsewhere you need to change the name in the Save in box. You change this box by clicking on the down arrow button at the end of the box and a list of other choices where you can store your file appears (Figure 23).

**4.** Insert a floppy disk into the drive. Enter your file name as Document and select Save in as Floppy (A:) and click on Save button. You will hear the disk drive and see the mouse pointer turn into an hour glass for a few moments. This tells you that Windows is working on a task.

**5.** If you now change your document by adding more text and want to update your saved file all you need to do is select File menu and option Save. The Save As window will not appear since the system assumes you want to update your file Document stored in the same place (i.e. floppy disk).

**6.** Add this is extra text to test saving again. Your passage should now read:

This is a short passage to help me understand how to create, save and print a document. The keyboard has many keys to enter text and numbers. The number keys are 1,2,3,4,5,6,7,8 and 9. The symbol keys are =-/#.,:@?!£&%+*. This is extra text to test saving again.

**7.** Select the File menu and the Save option. You may hear the drive start up but the Save As window will not appear. It is good practise to save your document early and then to update it at regular intervals. Some applications can be set to automatically save your work every few minutes. However, you should establish the habit of saving at regular intervals. There are few things worse than losing all your work due to a problem with the computer or an electricity failure because you have not saved your work for a few hours.

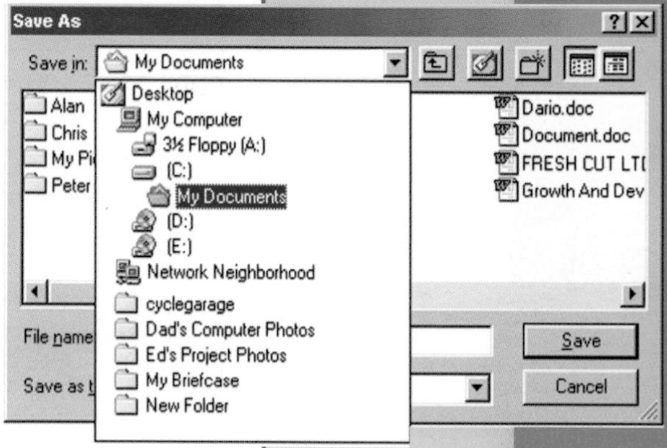

**8.** Another useful feature of saving in Windows is that you can save the same document many times under different names. If you select File menu and Save As option then the Save As window will appear and you can chose to save the document again under another name and in another folder. In this case save your document as Document2 in the floppy disk. You should see the original Document file (Figure 24).

FIGURE 23
**Save As Folders**

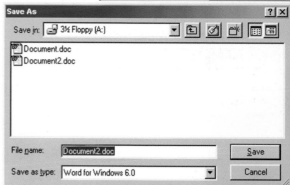

FIGURE 24
**Saving several files with different names**

**9.** You can repeat this operation as many times as you like and it is useful as a means of keeping an original document while revising its contents for another purpose (e.g. using a letter to the electricity company as a template for one to the gas supplier).

**10.** Having created a document you can print it by selecting File menu and Print option. A Print window will appear and you can print immediately if your printer is connected by clicking on the OK button. This will print your document using the printer's default settings. These are the standard settings which establish factors such as the number of copies, which pages to print if your document is longer than a single page, orientation of the paper (i.e. portrait or landscape) and quality of the printing. In many cases it is the defaults which produce a perfectly acceptable printed document.

**11.** Print your short document using the default settings. Repeat the printing actions until you are confident you understand the process.

**12.** Close WordPad by clicking on close button or by selecting File menu and Exit option.

## Retrieving a file

Once you have saved a file you can use the application you used to create it to retrieve it in order to print extra copies or change its contents.

# Exercise 12

## Retrieving a file

**1.** Open WordPad by clicking on Start, highlighting Programs and Accessories and single clicking on WordPad. The application will open (Figure 16). Maximise the window using the control buttons in the top right hand corner of the window if the display does not fill the screen. Insert your floppy disk into the drive.

**2.** Select File menu and Open option. This will reveal the Open window. Chose Floppy disk by using the down arrow button at the end of the Look in box. This should reveal the files stored on your floppy disk. (Figure 25)

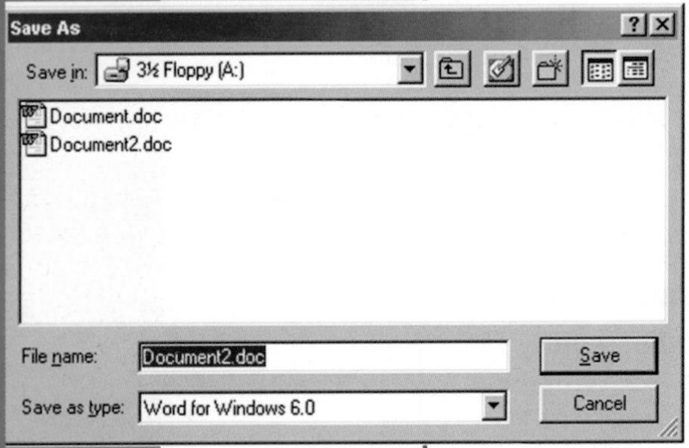

**3.** Highlight the file you want to retrieve by single clicking on the file and you will see the file's name appear in the File name box. Click on Open button and you will see the contents of the file appear in WorkPad work area.

**4.** Close the application by clicking on the close button or select File menu and the Exit option.

**5.** Repeat this exercise until you are confident that you can retrieve files.

FIGURE 25
**Open Window**

## File management

You have now created two files on your floppy disk. Windows provides you with a range of functions to copy, move and delete files and folders. If you double click on the My Computer icon on the Windows desktop a window will open (Figure 25A) showing the different drives within the computer system. You can open each drive to view the files and folders stored on them in a similar way as when using Windows Explorer.

If you double click on the floppy icon, a window will open to reveal your two files. If the window does not fill the display you can use the maximise button (i.e. in the top right hand corner). If you are content with a smaller display, you can, if you wish, move the window by clicking on the bar at the top of window. Holding down the left mouse button, you can drag the window to anywhere in the display using the mouse.

To copy your chosen file, you need to highlight it by single clicking then selecting the Edit menu and clicking on the Copy option. Highlighting is the standard way of identifying the file or folder you want to operate on. You will probably hear the disk drive and see a small hourglass appear. This tells you Windows is carrying out an action (i.e. copying your file). When the hourglass disappears, Windows is ready for you to choose where you want your file copied. You can copy it to any drive or folder on the system (e.g. on the C: drive). You move to that drive or folder, select the Edit menu again and the Paste option. If you stay in the same folder then the file is named as a Copy of .... to show it is different from the original. If you copy the file to a new folder then it retains its original name. Windows provides you with a quick way of undoing any mistakes. If you select the Edit menu and the Undo copy option then everything returns to the state before you started to copy. You may see a message appear that asks if you are sure you want to delete the copy. Click on the OK button if you do.

FIGURE 25A
**My Computer**

Windows allows you to create new folders by selecting the File menu, highlighting New and clicking on Folder. A new folder will appear. The cursor will flash inside the name box to indicate you should enter a name using the keyboard. You can move files into the new folder by clicking on them and holding down the left mouse button. If you drag the file over the folder and release the button, it will disappear. The file is now stored in the new folder. You can see what is inside a folder by double clicking on it to open a new window. Mistakes can be corrected by selecting the File menu and the Undo Move option.

To delete a file or folder you must initially highlight it, then select the File menu and click on the Delete option. A message window will appear to check if you are sure you want to delete the file or folder. There is a further layer of protection in that files and folder are not automatically deleted but stored in a special folder called the Recycle Bin. You can restore files or folders by opening the Recycle Bin which is available on the Desktop.

# Exercise 13

## File management

**1.** Insert the floppy disk on which you have stored the two WordPad files into the drive and click on the My Computer icon to reveal the system drives and folders (Figure 25A). Select the floppy drive by clicking on it.

**2.** Copy the file Document2 by highlighting it then selecting the Edit menu and the option Copy. You should place the copied file on to the floppy by selecting the Edit menu again then the Paste option. Observe what happens. A message window appears telling you that the file is being copied from drive

Using a Computer

A: to drive A:. The copied file will be named Copy of Document2.

**3.** Create a new folder by selecting the File menu, highlighting New and clicking on Folder. Observe a new folder appearing with the cursor flashing in the name box. Enter the name CLAIT using the keyboard. You now have a new empty folder and you should move files into this folder.

**4.** Click on the Copy of Document2 file and holding down the left mouse button, drag the file over the new folder and release the button. Observe what happens. You should hear the drive work and see the file become transparent then disappear. It is now stored in the CLAIT folder. Double click on the folder and a new window will appear showing you what it contains (Figure 25B).

**5.** You will notice that the new window overlaps the original one and may obscure parts of it. You can drag the windows around by clicking on the bar at the top of them and holding down the left mouse button. Experiment with moving them around the display.

FIGURE 25B
**CLAIT
Folder**

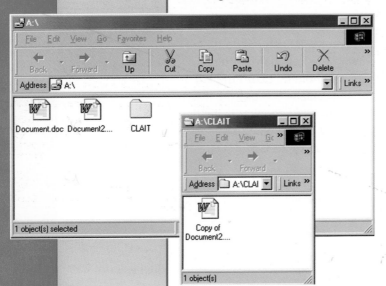

**6.** The windows appear to be stacked on top of each other. To bring a window to the top you simply click on it. Experiment by clicking on the different windows. If you cannot see one of them then it is probably underneath the top window so drag this to another part of the screen to see what is beneath it. Explore until you are confident that you can move and select windows.

**7.** Highlight the Copy of Document2 file and select the File menu then the Delete option. Remove it from the folder. A message window will appear to confirm whether you want to delete the file. Click on the OK button.

**8.** Close the folder window by clicking on the Close button in the top right-hand corner of the window.

**9.** Highlight the CLAIT folder and select the File menu then the Delete option. Remove the folder. A message window will appear to confirm whether you want to delete the folder and its contents. Deleting a folder is a way of removing all the files and folders it contains. Click on the OK button.

**10.** Close the Floppy Disk folder by clicking on the Close button in the top right hand corner of the window and then close the My Computer window in the same way.

## Changing a password

Computer security is extremely important for both office and home users. In the office, making sure systems are secure through the use of passwords is vital for protecting data from unauthorised access. At home, although you may not have data which you wish to keep secret, good security protects against misuse be it accidental or malicious – a child can easily cause a great deal of damage to an unsecured computer.

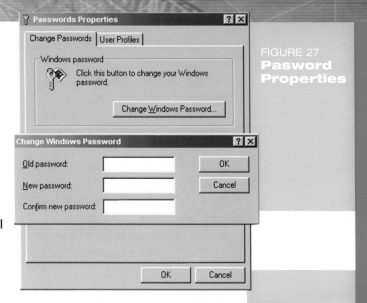

FIGURE 27
**Pasword Properties**

FIGURE 26
**Control Panel**

Microsoft Windows and many other suppliers offer a wide range of security systems. Whatever security software you use it is important to understand the need to use original passwords and to change them regularly. Try not to use your name or anything obvious. Good practice is to either pick a word at random from a dictionary and add some numbers either within or at the end of the word, or to use a completely random series of numbers and letters.

To change your Windows password you need to access the Control Panel. This involves clicking on the Start button, highlighting Settings to open a menu and clicking on Control Panel to reveal the Control Panel window (Figure 26). In this window there is an icon called Passwords and is shown as a bunch of keys. When you double click on this icon it will open the Password Properties window. Clicking on the Change Windows password button will open another window (dialogue box). Both Password properties and Change Windows Password are shown in Figure 27. To change the password you need to enter the old password, the new password and then confirm the new password. This ensures you do not enter a password with a small mistake which will leave you locked out of windows.

## Safe working practice

There are a number of straightforward actions you can take to reduce the risk of injuring yourself when you are using a computer. One of the key problems is Repetitive Strain Injury (RSI) in that by using the computer incorrectly you place a strain on your body (e.g. hands, wrists and arms) which may result in permanent harm.

Some of the straightforward actions are:

**Space** It is important to give yourself plenty of space. You must give yourself sufficient space for your legs and body. There should be enough space around the computer for your papers and books so that you can reach them without stretching. You can use a paper stand to hold your papers to help you copy text without turning. You should be comfortable. Even a tiny need to twist or turn your body can be harmful over a long period.

**Breaks** It is good practice regularly to take breaks away from the computer.

**Chairs** Your chairs should be adjustable so that you can alter the height and backrest. The chair should support your lower back. Your feet should either be placed squarely on the floor or on a foot rest with your knees slightly higher than the chair to ensure good circulation of blood. Again it is important to be comfortable.

**Your eyes** should be aligned slightly below the top of the monitor and you should be positioned about 18 inches from the display.

**Reduce strain** When you are using the computer you must avoid placing any strain on hands and wrists by:

1. Keeping your wrists straight while typing (e.g. by using a rest)
2. Not resting on your wrists
3. Typing gently without excessive force
4. Taking frequent breaks and avoiding typing for long periods

**Light** Computer monitors are very susceptible to reflection. It is therefore important to position your screen so it does not reflect light from the sun or the room lights. You will probably need to experiment. Monitors are normally designed to allow you to change their angle and allow you to change their brightness and contrast.

## Short cuts

You may have observed that when you are using Windows or WordPad some of the menu options have a letter underlined. This is a keyboard short cut. They provide you with an alternative way of selecting the option other than clicking on the option with the mouse pointer. You press the Ctrl key and holding it down press the letter that is underlined (e.g. Printer). This has the same effect as clicking on the option. It is useful if you are entering text and can therefore select the option without taking your hands away from the keyboard.

# Help

Microsoft Windows has a help function. It is available by selecting the Start button and clicking on Help option. The Help window will appear (Figure 28). This provides help with many topics and introductions to Windows functions (e.g. Introducing Windows 98). You may wish to explore these introductions. They are accessed by clicking on the options which will reveal sub-topics and so on.

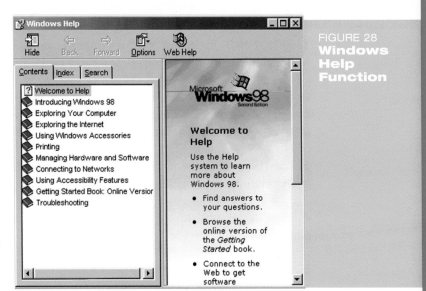

FIGURE 28
**Windows Help Function**

# Summary

**1. What is a computer?** A computer consists of two main components: hardware and software.

**2. Hardware** Hardware is the physical elements of the equipment that you can see when you look at a computer. These include a monitor, main box (containing Central Processing Unit), printer, keyboard and mouse.

**3. Software** Software is the instructions that controls the hardware. Software is divided into two main types which are operating systems and applications.

**4. Serial, Parallel and USB ports** Ports are the means of connecting peripheral equipment to the main computer.

**5. DVD and CD-RW drives** These are different types of drives which allow disks to be used with a computer. DVD disks allow the computer to read very large amounts of information which are stored on the disk. DVD disks are often used to hold the contents of an entire movie. CD-RW drives allow you to save information onto a special type of CD-ROM and to read the information stored on the disk.

**6. Mouse** The mouse allows you to carry out a series of actions including single clicking with left and right mouse buttons, double clicking and dragging and dropping.

**7. Keyboard** Keyboard allows you to enter text and numbers into computer applications.

**8. Window controls** In the top right-hand corner of the window are three control buttons. These are minimise, maximise and close.

**9. Storing files** Information is stored on disks (i.e. floppy and hard disks) in the form of files which are placed in folders to help organise them. Files have different formats depending on the nature of the information they store (e.g. documents and images).

**10. Windows Explorer** Explorer provides you with the functions to search the disks for files and folders. Other functions include deleting and renaming files.

**11. Find** Click on the Start button and highlight Find. Slide the mouse pointer on to the menu which appears and click on the Files or Folders option.

**12. Accessories** Windows provides you with several applications which come bundled with the operating system. These include WordPad (word-processing), Paint and Calculator.

**13. Load Wordpad** Open WordPad by clicking on Start button, highlight Programs and Accessories and single click on WordPad option.

**14. Save** Select the File menu and the Save option. The Save As window (dialogue box) opens. Select location (Save in box) and name your file (File name box) and click on Save button.

**15. Save As** Select the File menu and the Save As option. The Save As window opens. Select location (Save in box) and name your file (File name box) and click on Save button.

**16. Delete** Backspace key deletes characters to the left while the delete key removes characters to the right.

**17. Printing** Select the File menu, click on the Print option and OK button.

**18. Retrieve** Select the File menu and the Open option. This will reveal the Open window. Choose disk by using the down arrow button at the end of the Look in box and select the file to be retrieved.

**19. Change Password** Select the Start button, highlighting the Settings option to open a menu and click on the Control Panel to reveal the Control Panel window. Double click on Passwords icon and click on the Change Windows password button.

**20. Safe Working Practice** The straightforward issues to reduce the risk of harm are space, breaks, strain and light.

**21. Short Cut** Press the Ctrl key and holding it down press the letter that is underlined (e.g. Save).

**22. Help** Select the Start button and click on Help option.

# Word-Processing

This chapter will help you use a word-processor to:

identify and use word-processing software correctly

use an input device to enter and edit text accurately

select fonts and simple text formatting

format basic paragraph and document properties

manage and print word-processed documents

## Assessment

This unit does not assume any previous experience of word-processing. However, you may find it useful if you have previously undertaken Unit 1 (Using a Computer). After studying Unit 2 your skills and understanding are assessed during a 2-hour practical assignment. This is set by OCR and marked locally. However, the marking will be externally moderated by OCR. This ensures that the standard is being applied correctly across the many different providers of OCR New CLAIT.

## Microsoft Word

Word processors are one of the most useful and most used computer applications. They allow you to enter, amend, save and print documents of almost any size from a single word to the manuscript of a book. This chapter is based on Microsoft Word 2000 and Figure 29A shows the Word interface. Word is a powerful word processor. There are many other word processors available and applications such as text editors. The difference between a word processor and a text editor is mainly the degree of sophistication. Windows includes a text edition called Notepad which is shown in Figure 29B. This is loaded by selecting the Start button, highlighting Programs, Accessories and clicking on the Notepad option. Text editors are principally for producing simple messages while a word processor provides the tools for writing a wide range of documents (e.g. a letter to a book). Word processors provide powerful tools for presenting and formatting information, checking your spelling and grammar and are often WYSIWYG. WYSIWYG stands for What You See Is What You Get. This means that the way the words are presented on the screen is how they will be printed. It helps you to write by providing a wide range of features and functions such as spelling and grammar checkers. It provides you with considerable freedom to change your words, presentation, layout and appearance of your documents.

If you have never used a keyboard to enter text it may feel strange at first but you will rapidly realise how useful a word processor is.

It consists of three main areas:

**menus and toolbars** which provide you with access to the word processor controls

**the work area** is where you enter your words to create documents

**the status bar** (which reads from left to right) shows:

**Page 1** The page you are on (i.e. the first page).

**Sec 1** The section of the document you are on

**1/1** Shows you that you are looking at the first page of your document which is one page long

**At 2.5 cm** This tells you that you are entering text that will be 2.5 cms below the top of the page when it is printed.

**Ln 1** You are entering text into the 1st line of your document.

**Col 1** You are entering text in the first character position of the document.

There are several ways of loading an application such as Microsoft Word. The two most used are:

the Start button

the Microsoft Word icon on the Windows desktop

In the bottom left-hand corner of the Windows desktop (Figure 30) is a button called Start. This allows you to access many applications and standard features of the operating system. If you single click on Start, a menu will pop up which is shown in Figure 30. If you place the mouse pointer over the Programs item it will become highlighted (i.e. the background will change colour) and a new menu will appear alongside. This is shown in Figure 31.

The programs menu will vary in length and number of items depending on what applications you have installed on your computer. In this case all the

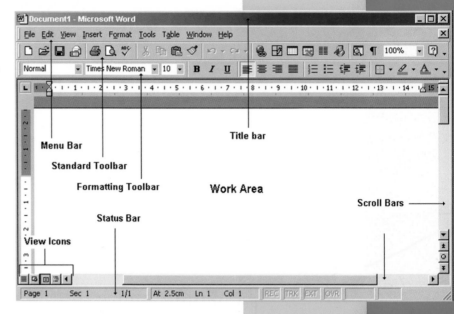

FIGURE 29A
**Microsoft Word**

FIGURE 29B
**Notepad**

FIGURE 30
**Start Menu**

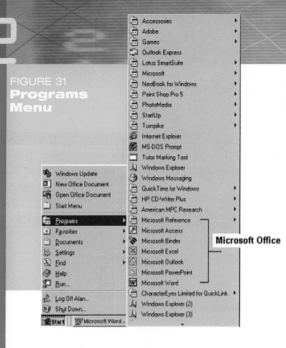

FIGURE 31
**Programs Menu**

Microsoft Office

Microsoft Office 2000 applications are available to you. You should notice that <u>P</u>rograms and other items sometimes have a small black triangle next to them. This indicates that if you highlight this item by placing your pointer over it, then another menu will open.

To load Microsoft Word you need to single click on the Word item on the <u>P</u>rograms menu (Figure 31). The Word application will open. An alternative way of loading Word is to double click on the Word icon on the Windows desktop shown in Figure 31.

# Exercise 14

## Loading and using Microsoft Word

**1.** Load Word by selecting the Start button, highlighting the <u>P</u>rograms option and clicking on the Microsoft Word item or by clicking on the Word icon on the desktop.

**2.** When the application is open you will notice that in the work area there is a small flashing vertical line in the top left-hand corner. This is called a cursor and it is here that your text will appear when you begin to enter it.

**3.** Using the keyboard, enter

Titan is the largest satellite of Saturn and was discovered by Christiaan Huygens in 1655. It is a large moon with a radius of 2575 km and is the largest moon in the solar system. Titan has a nitrogen and methane-rich atmosphere. This makes observing the surface of the satellite difficult. The Voyager spacecrafts used a variety of methods to investigate Titan. These suggest that Titan has an atmospheric pressure greater than the Earth and possibly has methane clouds which rain ethane.

FIGURE 32
**Enter Key**

**4.** Observe that the text starts a new line when it needs to without your doing anything. This is called word wrapping. If you have been trained as a typist it can often be difficult to stop yourself trying to create a new line.

**5.** Move your mouse pointer to the start of the text on the T of Titan. Click there and you will see that the flashing line has moved to the start of the text. If you enter text now it will appear at the cursor. This is the way you insert text into a document. If you press the enter key (Figure 32) you will create a new line. Press enter key twice and using the up arrow key on the keyboard move up the two lines you have just created. Enter the word Titan and you will have added a heading to your passage. The Enter key is sometimes known as the return key.

The text will look similar to Figure 33 which has been entered into Microsoft Word. Do not worry if in your work area you are not able to get the same number of words per line as in the example. This is a result of the settings within the word processor which you can change later.

FIGURE 33
**Entering Text**

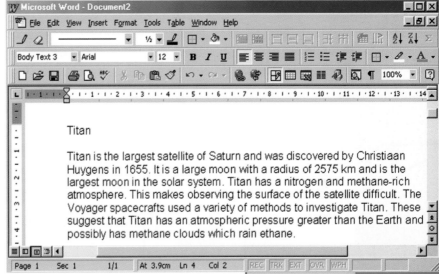

**6.** When entering text you will sometimes make a mistake. There are two main ways to remove or delete text.

**7.** Using the above example, the cursor should be flashing at the end of Titan. If you press the backspace key (Figure 34) then the cursor moves left and deletes the last character. If you continue to tap the key, you can delete your entry.

**8.** The other way to remove text is to use the delete key (Figure 35) which is located in the bottom-right corner of the keyboard near the number pad. The delete key works by removing the characters to the right of the cursor.

FIGURE 34
**Backspace Key**

**9.** Enter Titan again to replace your heading.

**10.** We will now save this passage onto a floppy disk. This procedure is the same in all Windows applications so you can save a spreadsheet, database or graphic image in exactly the same way.

FIGURE 35
**Delete Key**

insert a floppy disk into drive A:
click on the File menu item and a menu will open showing a list of options. Select Save and a window will open

**11.** Click in the box File name and Enter A:\Titan. Now click on the Save button on the right of the window. You have now saved your passage as a file called Titan. You may hear drive A: work during this process. An alternative approach is to select the location you want to save your document to by clicking on down arrow at end of Save in box (Figure 36). This will reveal a list of options. You can select your choice by clicking on it. In this case click on floppy disk. This will then appear in the Save in box. Enter the file name in which you want to save the document in the File name box but this time you do not need to give the drive letter (i.e. a:/ means floppy disk) so just enter Titan. Now click on the Save button on the right of the window.

FIGURE 36
**Save As**

**12.** In Figure 36 there is a box called Save as type. This informs you about the file format in which your document will be saved. In this case it will automatically default to Word. That is, the document (file) will be formatted as a Word file.

**13.** You can close Word now by clicking on the File menu item and choosing from a menu will appear with a list of options. At the bottom of the list is the option Exit. If you click on Exit then Word will close. An alternative way is to click on the close button in the top right-hand corner of the application window (Figure 37).

FIGURE 37
**Close button**

Minimise
Maximise
Close

## Manipulating text

You have already entered a short passage and saved it to your floppy disk. Microsoft Word and other word processors provide you with tools to insert, delete, move and replace text. There are three tools called Cut, Copy and Paste which are especially useful. They are available on the standard toolbar (Figure 38) and on the Edit menu (Figure 39). You can choose either option.

FIGURE 38
**Cut, Copy and Paste - Standard Toolbar**

The three tools operate in similar ways:

FIGURE 39
**Edit Menu**

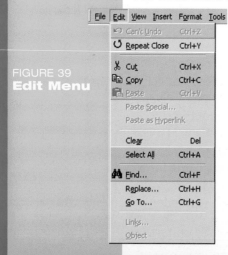

**The first step** is to highlight the text you want to manipulate. To do this, you move your pointer to the start of the text you want to work on and click, holding down the mouse button and moving the pointer over the words that you want to manipulate. You will see them highlighted (i.e. the background colour changes). When you have highlighted all the words you need, release the mouse button. If you have made an error simply click the mouse away from the highlighted area and the highlighting will disappear so you can try again.

**If you click on the copy tool or menu option** the text you have highlighted will be copied to a special area of the computer's memory – the Clipboard. You can now copy to another part of the passage. This process does not change the original text. You move the copied text by pointing to where you want to place it and clicking there. The cursor is now at the new location. If you then click on the Paste tool or menu option, the highlighted text is inserted into the new location. You can see that the Copy and Paste tools work together. You cannot paste until after you have copied.

**The Cut tool** or menu option works in the same way with one difference in that when you select Cut, the highlighted text is removed.

An alternative to Cut is to highlight the text and then click the left mouse button and hold it down. You can then drag the words to a new location using the mouse pointer. The standard toolbar contains two important tools for when you make an error - Undo and Redo (Figure 38). If you make a mistake you can reverse it by clicking on Undo. If you make an error in using undo then you can turn the clock back with Redo. This may sound confusing but we will practise these functions in the next exercise along with Cut, Copy and Paste.

# Printing

Printing documents is probably the single most used function of a word processor. Microsoft Word offers a range of functions linked to printing. One of these is an option to preview your text as a printed document without wasting any paper. Within the File Menu, Print Preview opens up the window shown in Figure 40. This allows you to check if the document is presented in the way that you want it to be. When you have completed the preview, click on the Close button to return to the Word document.

When you are ready to print click on the File menu then choose the Print option as displayed in Figure 41. You are presented with a number of options which you may find puzzling initially.

FIGURE 40
**Print Preview**

You must first select the printer on which your document is to be printed. This is shown in the Printer area at the top of the window in the box entitled Name. The Microsoft Windows operating system allows you to link several printers to a single stand-alone computer. The list of printers is shown when you click on the down arrow next to the Name box. You select your printer by clicking on it.

You can choose what you want to print.
**All** – whole document
**Current Page** – only the page on which

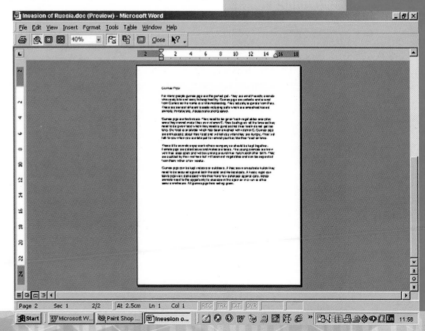

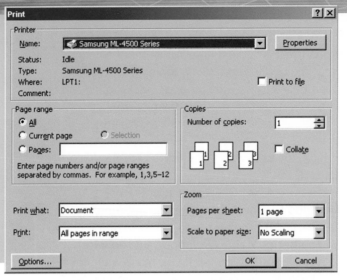

FIGURE 41
**Printing**

your cursor is flashing
**Pages –** you enter the page range you want to print (e.g. 23-34)

**You must decide** how many copies you want to print (Copies).

When you are ready you click on OK button to start the printer.

# Exercise 15

## Manipulating and printing text

**1.** In the previous exercise you saved a file called Titan. We are now going to load this file into Microsoft Word.

**2.** Load Word by selecting the Start button, highlighting the <u>P</u>rograms option and clicking on the Microsoft Word item or by clicking on the Word icon on the desktop.

**3.** You can load a file by single clicking on the <u>F</u>ile menu item to open up the menu which has an option called <u>O</u>pen. Click on <u>O</u>pen and a window called Open will appear (Figure 42). An alternative approach is to click on the open icon on the standard toolbar (i.e. it takes the form of an open file).

**4.** The Look <u>i</u>n box tells you what drive the window is looking at. You need to aim it at floppy disk. You do this by clicking on the small button with the down arrow at the end of the Look <u>i</u>n box. A menu will appear. Click on the Floppy Disk option and the details of the Titan file will appear in the main working area. To open the file, click once on the file to highlight it and then on the open button on the right-hand side of the window. An alternative way is to double click on the Titan file. In either case the text of the file should now appear in the working area of Word, similar to Figure 33.

FIGURE 42
**Open Window**

**5.** Enter the text below as new paragraphs below the previous text.

The Voyager spacecraft were not simply on a mission to survey Titan. They were taking advantage of the outer planets (e.g. Jupiter, Saturn, Neptune and Uranus) being aligned in the 1970s so that it was possible to visit several in one space trip. Two voyager spacecraft were launched a few weeks apart in 1977.

The Voyager-1 was to fly past Jupiter, Saturn and their moons while Voyager-2 was to visit Jupiter, Saturn, Uranus and Neptune and their moons. Both spacecraft had two cameras and took thousands of digital photographs of the outer planets and their satellites. The pictures were sent to Earth as radio signals containing the digital information.

**6.** Practise using the Undo and Redo icons so that you become familiar with how they work.

**7.** Practise using the Delete and backspace keys (Figure 34 and 35). Remember that the Delete key removes text to the right while the backspace key removes text to the left.

**8.** When you are confident about Undo, Redo, Delete and backspace keys then attempt these tasks:

a) Highlight

"The Voyager spacecraft were not simply on a mission to survey Titan"

This is achieved by positioning the mouse pointer immediately in front of the "The" and clicking the mouse button holding it down and moving the pointer over the sentence until it is all highlighted (i.e. background changes colour). You will see the sentence gradually highlight as you move over the text.

b) Copy

With the sentence highlighted then click on the copy icon. (If you place your mouse pointer over the copy icon you will see it animate and a small label will appear telling you it is the copy icon. This works with all the icons to help you identify their different functions.) You can also copy the text using the Edit menu which includes Cut, Copy and Paste functions. When you click on copy nothing will change and the sentence will remain highlighted.

c) Paste

To move the text you have copied (i.e. the sentence highlighted) you need to move the mouse pointer to where you want to copy the text to. In this case move your pointer to the end of the passage and click once and you will see the cursor flashing in the new position and the highlighting will disappear. Now click on the Paste icon and you will see the sentence appear at the end of the passage (Figure 43).

FIGURE 43
**Copy Text**

.............................................and took thousands of digital photographs of the outer planets and their satellites. The pictures were sent to Earth as radio signals containing the digital information. The Voyager spacecraft were not simply on a mission to survey Titan.

**9.** If you click on the Undo icon the pasted text will be removed and you can practise pasting again. Continue copying and pasting until you feel confident.

**10.** Now try the Cut function.

   a) Highlight the sentence below:

"The pictures were sent to Earth as radio signals containing the digital information."

   b) Cut

Click on the Cut icon and the sentence will disappear. You have not lost the text. It is simply saved to a special area of the memory called the Clipboard. Copied text is also saved here. Normally you can only paste the last item you have cut or copied. The clipboard does hold up to twelve items but to paste them you need to use the clipboard toolbar (select the View menu, highlight Toolbars then click on Clipboard to reveal the Clipboard window.

   c) Paste

Position your cursor at the location you would like to paste the cut text to by clicking once. If you click on the Paste icon then the text will now appear at the new position.

An alternative to using Cut is to employ the drag and drop technique. If you highlight the text you want to move and then click on it and hold down the mouse button you can drag the text to a new position. The pointer changes during the move to provide a guide bar to accurately position the text.

**11.** Practise using the copy, cut and paste functions. If you use Undo, Redo, Delete and backspace functions you will be able to return to the original passage.

Practise using the drag and drop technique. If you use the Undo function you will be able to return to the original passage.

**12.** Save your text when you have finished to the floppy disk. The file should be called New Titan.

**13.** Print your text after checking its appearance using the Print Preview option in the File menu.

**14.** Close Word.

## Replacing words and phrases

Obviously you can replace a word or phrase by simply deleting the one you wish to replace and entering the new word or phrase. However, Microsoft Word provides an automatic way to find and replace a word or a phrase. This is available within the Edit Menu (Figure 39) as the Replace option. If you select this option by clicking on it then the window shown in Figure 44 will appear.

Type in the text you want to replace in the Find what: box and the replacement text in Replace with:. The function will search for the text and either automatically replace it throughout the document (Replace All) or allow you to select which ones to change (Replace). In either case you start the function by clicking on the Find Next button.

## Appearance and layout

Word processors (e.g. Microsoft Word) have many functions which allow you to change the layout and presentation of text. These include altering the margins, changing the line spacing, justifying the text and emphasising words, phrases or whole passages. When you first enter a passage of text there is no need to get the appearance right first time since these functions allow you change it until you are satisfied.

Many organisations have a house style or a standard way of presenting their letters, documents and reports. This can take many forms but often it involves the use of a limited number of fonts and character sizes, leaving a space after each comma and two spaces after a full stop and using only main headings and one layer of sub-headings. This is intended to provide a common look and feel to all documents from an organisation. If you begin working for a new organisation it is important to know if they employ a house style.

### Margins
The margins of a word processor document are controlled by the Page Setup item under the File menu (Figure 45). If you click on File and then on Page Setup, the window shown in Figure 46 will be opened.

Figure 46 show you that you can change all four margins (i.e. top, bottom, left and right). You change the settings for each margin by clicking on the up or down arrow buttons. As you change the margin you can see the overall effect on your document by watching the Preview area. The changes take effect as soon as you click on OK button. If you make a mistake you can always use the undo icon to reverse the changes.

FIGURE 44
**Replace Function**

FIGURE 45
**File Menu**

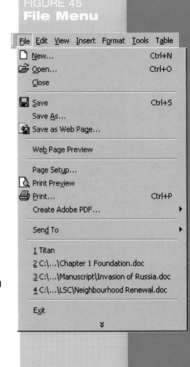

FIGURE 46
**Page Setup**

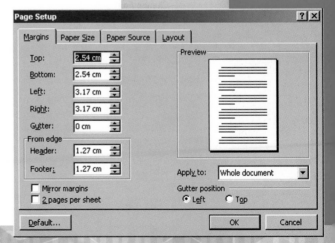

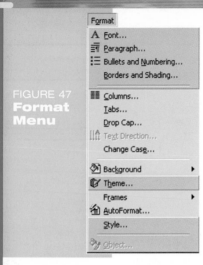

FIGURE 47
**Format Menu**

## Line spacing

Word processors allow you to adjust the line spacing of your document allowing you to double space either a single paragraph or a whole document. The line spacing functions are provided within the Paragraph item of the Format menu (Figure 47). When you click on the Paragraph item, the window shown in Figure 48 will appear. Towards the middle of the window you will see the Line spacing box which, if you click on the down arrow at the end of the box, you will display a range of options. These are selected by clicking on the one you want. When you enter text it will follow the new line spacing. To change existing text you need to first highlight the material you want to alter.

## Inserting a new paragraph

To add a new paragraph break you need to position the cursor by clicking with the mouse pointer at the desired position and then press the Enter key twice. The first key press moves the start of the new paragraph to the next line while the second press inserts a blank line between the paragraphs.

FIGURE 48
**Paragraph**

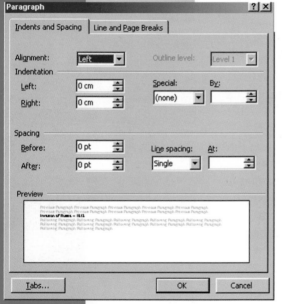

## Emphasise text

Microsoft Word provides you with a range of tools to emphasise your words. These include:

changing the font and character size of your text

emboldening your words

underlining your words

changing your text into italics

These functions are available on the Format Toolbar (Figure 49) and also in the Format Menu (Figure 47) within the Font item. If you select one of the toolbar options it will change to indicate that it is active and that everything you now enter is in the emphasised form (e.g. underlined). You need to click on the option a second time to de-select it. It can also be used to change existing text. The normal process of changing text, from a single character to a whole document, is to highlight your selection and then choose the functions icon or menu option.

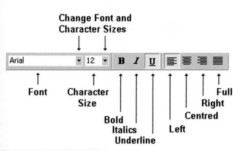

FIGURE 49
**Format Toolbar**

## Justification

There are four ways of justifying a document. These are:

**Left** – the left text edge is parallel with the margin and the right is ragged

**Right –** the right text edge is parallel with the margin and the left is ragged
**Centred –** text is aligned down the centre of the page with both edges ragged
**Double –** both left and right text edges are parallel with the Margins (this is called Justify on the Format Toolbar)

Justification functions are provided in the Paragraph option (Figure 48) of the Format Menu (Figure 47) and on the Format Toolbar (Figure 49). If you select one of the toolbar options it will change to indicate it is active and then everything you now enter will be in new line justification (e.g. centred). You need to click on the option a second time to de-select it. The process can be used to change existing text through once again highlighting the section and selecting the desired justification icon or menu option.

# Exercise 16

## Appearance and layout

**1.** Load Word by selecting the Start button, highlighting the Programs option and clicking on the Microsoft Word item or by clicking on the Word icon on the desktop.

**2.** Enter the passage below in Times New Roman and character size 12.

(Hint – select the font and character size from Format Toolbar before entering text)

Invasion of Russia – 1812

In 1812 Napoleon invaded Russia with one of the largest armies that had ever been assembled. Over 600,000 men had been brought together from all parts of Europe that formed the French Empire. Italians, Dutch, Belgians, Germans and Frenchmen marched across the frontier and the vast majority never returned. It was 700 miles to Moscow and the army had to march across a desolate landscape of forest and marsh where villages were days apart.

In past campaigns French armies had relied upon living off the countries they had attacked. Russia was not a rich land and a large force would not be able to subsist from pillage. The French knew that they could not use their old tactics so they had gathered stores to transport into Russia. Each soldier was heavily loaded with flour, bread, rice and biscuit to last many days. The army staff had planned to transport huge quantities of supplies to last through the normal fast and furious French assault to knock out the Russian armies.

Napoleon's army entered Moscow less than three months later having fought several major and minor battles but it had not destroyed the Russian army. In past campaigns the occupation of the capital city had followed the destruction of the opposing army. It was not long before the French army had to retreat through winter weather with a supply system that had completely failed.

**3.** Save the passage on your floppy disk as a file called "Invasion" (there is a save icon on the standard toolbar – a picture of a floppy disk or select the File Menu and the Save option). It is good practice to save your text as soon as you can and then to update the file as you make changes. When you select Save later you will not be shown the Save As window since the application assumes that you simply want to update your original file. If you want to save the altered text as a different file you need to select Save As option in File Menu. The procedure is then the same as you earlier undertook for saving a new file.

The Save As option also serves the purpose of allowing you to change the file name of your document. This is useful if you want to create a master document for a whole series of publications or if you want to keep copies of the document at the different stages of its development.

**4.** Change the margins of your documents so that:

left and right are 3 cms
top and bottom are 3.5 cms

By selecting the File Menu and the Page Setup option.

**5.** Change the line spacing to 1.5 by selecting the Format Menu and the Paragraph option.

**6.** Change the title Invasion of Russia so that it is in the Ariel font and in character size 14 and embolden the text (i.e. highlight the text, choose the Arial font and the character size on the Format Toolbar)

**7.** Change the justification of the Title to centred (i.e. highlight the title and select the centred icon on the Format Toolbar)

**8.** Change the justification of the rest of the passage to double (this is shown as Justify on toolbar). Highlight the text and select the Justify icon on the Format Toolbar.

**9.** Insert a new paragraph at *Each soldier was heavily loaded with flour, bread, rice and biscuits to last many days*. Position your cursor before Each and press enter twice to break the text and insert a blank line between the paragraphs.

**10.** Remember to save your finished text and print the document (select the

File menu, the Print Preview and the Print icon).

11. Close Microsoft Word by selecting the File Menu and the Exit option or use the close button in the top right-hand corner of the window)

## Practice

All computer skills and knowledge need to be practised to ensure that you both understand what you are doing and are competent in undertaking the task. The next exercise is intended to provide you with the opportunity to practise everything we have discussed in this chapter.

## More Practice

1. Load Word by selecting the Start button, highlighting the Programs option and clicking on the Microsoft Word item or by clicking on the Word icon on the desktop.

2. Enter the passage below in Tahoma font and character size10 by selecting the font and character size from the Format Toolbar before entering text.

3. Set the margins as follows:

  Left and Right – 4 cms
  Top and Bottom – 3 cms

Select the File Menu and the Page Setup option before entering text.

For many people guinea pigs are the perfect pet. They are small friendly animals who rarely bite and are easy to keep healthy. Guinea pigs are rodents and are not from Guinea so the name is a little misleading. They actually originate from Peru. There are several different breeds including selfs which are smooth haired animals, Himalayans, Abyssinians and Crested.

Guinea pigs are herbivores. They need to be given fresh vegetables every day since they cannot make their own vitamin C. Their teeth grow all the time so they need to be given food which they need to grind so that their teeth do not get too long. Dry food is available which has been enriched with vitamin C. Guinea pigs are enthusiastic about their food and will tell you when they are hungry. They will talk to you when you are late just to remind you they like their food on time.

Guinea pigs can be kept indoors or outdoors. If they are in an outside hutch they need to be secured against both the cold and the local cats. A frosty night can leave pigs very distressed while they have few defences against cats. Indoor animals need the opportunity to exercise in the open air in a run or other secure enclosure. All guinea pigs love eating grass.

**4.** Save the passage on your floppy disk as a file called Guinea Pig by selecting the File Menu and the Save.

**5.** Insert a title "Guinea Pig - Cavies" separated by one blank line from the rest of the passage in Ariel font and character size 14 (Use the Pointer to move the cursor, select the font and character size from Format Toolbar before entering the title).

**6.** Underline the title by highlight the text and selecting the Underline icon from the Format Toolbar.

**7.** Insert the new paragraph below so that it becomes the third one.

These little animals enjoy each others' company so should be kept together. Female pigs are called sows and males are boars. The young animals are born with their eyes open and will be running around their hutch soon after birth. They are suckled by their mothers but will soon eat vegetables and can be separated from them within a few weeks.

**8.** Change the line spacing to double by highlight the passage, selecting the Format menu and the Paragraph option).

**9.** Change the justification of the passage to left justify by highlighting the text and selecting the Align Left icon on Format Toolbar).

**10.** Replace 'guinea pigs' with 'guinea pigs (cavies)' throughout the passage – you should find five occasions ( Use the Edit Menu and the Replace option).

**11.** Save your changed file (File Menu and Save option or Save icon on the Standard toolbar).

**12.** Print your document by selecting the File menu, the Print Preview and Print options or print icon from within Print Preview).

**13.** Close Microsoft Word by selecting the File Menu and the Exit option or click on the close button).

# Summary

**1. Load Microsoft Word** Use either the Start button and the Programs menu or double click on the Word icon on Windows desktop

**2.  Close** Click on the File menu item and the Exit option or click on the close button in the top right hand corner of the application window.

**3. Save a file on a floppy disk** Insert a floppy disk into drive A: and click on the File Menu and the Save option to reveal the Save As window. Select the drive (floppy disk) and enter a file name.

Having saved a file once, you can update it by clicking on the File Menu and Save without the Save As window appearing again. It simple overwrites the original file.

An alternative is to click on the save icon on the Standard toolbar to update the file

**4. Insert text** You must position the cursor where you need to insert the text. Move your mouse pointer to the new position and click there. The cursor will appear as a flashing line and you can now enter your text.

**5. Delete text** You have two different keys which both work from the position of your cursor.

Backspace key – this removes text, character by character to the left of the cursor position.

Delete key – this removes text, character by character to the right of the cursor position.

There is also Undo and Redo. Undo removes the last action you have undertaken while redo carries out actions removed by Undo.

**6. Move text** Highlight the text you want to move. Select either the Copy or Cut icons on the Standard Toolbar or alternatively the Edit menu and the Cut or Copy options. Reposition the cursor at the place you want to move the text to and then select the Paste icon on the Standard Toolbar or Edit Menu and Paste option.

**7. Drag and drop** Highlight the text. Click on it and hold down the mouse button. Drag the text to the new position using the mouse. The pointer changes during the move to provide a guide bar to position the text accurately.

**8. Replace text** Using the Edit Menu and the Replace option. Replace window appears. Enter the text you want to replace in the Find what: box and the replacement text in the Replace with: box.

**9. Change margins** Using the File menu and the Page Setup item opens the window which controls the four margins (i.e. left, right, top and bottom).

**10. Alter line spacing** Using the Format Menu and the Paragraph option. The Paragraph window will open with the Line spacing function box.

**11. Justification** Select the Format Menu and the Paragraph option or the Format Toolbar.

Select one of the toolbar options (Left, Right, Centered or Justify). It will change to show it is active and then everything you now enter will be in the new justification (i.e. centered). You need to click on the option a second time to de-select it.

To change existing text, highlight it and then select the justification icon or the menu option.

# Electronic Communication

This chapter will help you to use electronic communication to:

identify and use e-mail and browsing software

transmit and receive e-mail messages and attachments

navigate the World Wide Web

use search techniques to locate data on the Web

manage and print electronic documents

## Assessment

This unit does not assume any previous experience of electronic communication. However, you may find it useful if you have previously undertaken Unit 1 (Using a Computer). After studying Unit 3 your skills and understanding are assessed during a 2-hour practical assignment. This is set by OCR and marked locally. However, the marking will be externally moderated by OCR. This ensures that the standard is being applied correctly across the many different providers of OCR New CLAIT. You cannot include this unit along with Unit 11, the BBC's Becoming WebWise, since the content of the two units is similar to your group of five units for the New CLAIT certificate.

### What is the World Wide Web?

The Internet is essentially a world-wide network of networks linking millions of computers. It was initially developed to allow communication between research organisations and provides users with a range of services including:

E-mail (electronic mail)

World Wide Web (WWW)

It is possible to send e-mail messages anywhere in the world to anyone who has an e-mail account. It is rather like being able to send a postcard almost instantaneously. It is fast and efficient and many people regard e-mail as one of the major benefits of the Internet.

The World Wide Web comprises an extremely large number of locations called websites which provide information about a subject or organisation using text and graphics. These sites are located on computers scattered all over the world. These computers are linked by telecommunication networks (e.g. telephone lines and optical cables). For many people the World Wide Web is the Internet in that there are now millions of websites offering information on almost every topic. Many users spend all their time visiting them. This is known as surfing the web and browsing websites.

To explore the World Wide Web you need to use a browser. A browser is an application designed to allow you to view websites. There are two main browsers:

Internet Explorer (Figure 50)

Netscape Navigator

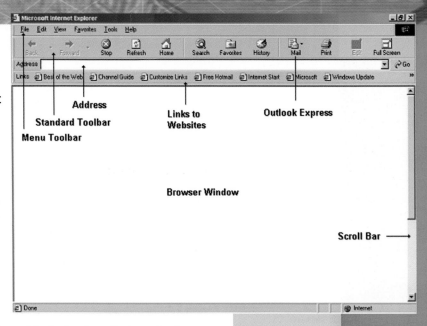

FIGURE 50
**Internet
Explorer**

But, there are others including ones developed to help visually impaired users browse websites by reading the site contents aloud to the users.

To send and receive e-mails requires access to a special application. Internet Explorer is linked to e-mail software called Microsoft Outlook Express (Figure 51) which provides the functions that allow you to send and receive e-mail. There are, however many other e-mail systems including those which operate from websites.

# Accessing the World Wide Web

The process of accessing the World Wide Web depends on where you are trying to communicate from. If you are at a college or at work then it is probably very straightforward, involving simply loading the e-mail application or browser. The college or work networks are often linked to the Internet automatically. However, at home you will probably need to carry out the additional action of connecting to the Internet through an Internet Service Provider that you have subscribed to. Once you have made your connection, you can then load the browser or e-mail application.

# Surfing the World Wide Web

To locate a particular website you need to know its address or URL (Uniform or Universal Resource Locator) when this is entered into the Address bar and the Enter key is pressed the browser then searches for the website which is then shown in the browser window.

Website addresses are unique and are structured in a similar way to a postal or street address. The address or URL for the BBC is http://www.bbc.co.uk. This comprises:

http – Hypertext Transfer Protocol – this tells the browser how to transfer the web pages across the internet so you can view it

**www** – World Wide Web
**bbc** – host of the website
**co** – company
**uk** – United Kingdom

The general form is thus http://www.host.typeoforganisation.country. However, websites in the USA do not use a country prefix. Other codes for some organisations and countries are:

| | |
|---|---|
| .ac | - university/academic |
| .com | - company |
| .co | - company |
| .edu | - educational institution |
| .gov | - government |
| .mil | - military |
| .net | - network |
| .be | - Belgium |
| .ca | - Canada |
| .dk | - Denmark |
| .nl | - Netherlands |
| .ch | - Switzerland |

**Outlook Express - alan**

File   Edit   View   Tools   Message   Help

New Mail   Send/Recv   Addresses   Find

Outlook Express

Folders
Outlook Express
Local Folders
    Inbox (1) ◄——— Received E-mail
    Outbox ◄——— Sending E-mail
    Sent Items ┐
    Deleted Items ├——— Records of E-mail
    Drafts ┘

Contacts ▼

There are no contacts to display. Click on Contacts to create a new contact.

Working Online

## Structure of a website

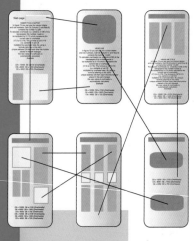

A website consists of a variety of pages each displaying content in the form of text and graphics. The pages can vary in length and you often need to scroll down them. Each page is linked to the others by hypertext links which when clicked on allow you to jump around the site. A website can be designed so that almost anything can be linked to something else. Links exist to connect items of information within pages as well as between different pages. This can sometimes be confusing since you may feel you have jumped to a new page whereas you have only moved to a new part of the same page. Websites vary in size and can be very large and complex. Figure 52 illustrates links between web pages. There can be links such as:

from an image to a text passage

from a word to the top of a page

from an image to another picture

from the bottom of one page to the top of another

between pages and within pages

Links often take the form of underlined words, areas of the screen that change the shape of the mouse pointer when it passes over them or of buttons.

The standard address of a website (e.g. http://www.host.type.country) usually links you to what is called the Home page of the site which is rather like the contents page of a book. It normally has links to the main parts of the site. However, it is possible to link to individual pages within a website by extending the address (e.g. htttp://www.host.type.country/nextpage/otherpages). This is useful when you want to direct people to a particular page but it can be confusing since by following a link you may suddenly find yourself in the middle of a new website. Links can be:

between pages in a single site

between pages in different sites

within a single page

Figure 53 illustrates a simplified structure of a website. This is presented as a series of layers but websites are often more complex than this with direct links from the home page to major parts of the site ensuring that you do not need to move through each layer. Although this is efficient, it is easy to get lost in a more complex website.

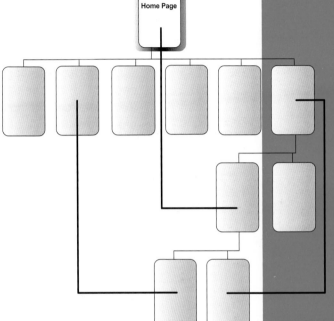

FIGURE 53
**Website
Structure**

Home Page

# Exercise 17

## Using the browser

Establish a connection to the Internet – this will depend on your location (i.e. home, work or college).

**1.** Using either the <u>P</u>rograms menu or by clicking on the Internet Explorer icon on the desktop, load the browser. The browser may appear either filling the entire screen or in a window. If you want to expand the window to fill the whole screen, use the maximise button in the top right-hand corner of the window.

**2.** Enter http://www.bl.uk/ (this is the website of the British Library) in the address bar and press enter. It is vital to be 100% accurate when entering URLs since any mistake will result in your browser giving you an error message suggesting there is no website at that address. When the page appears in your browser, scroll down the page and view the content. This is the home page so you should be able to locate a menu of the contents of the site.

3. Try to locate the links to other pages. These will take the form of underlined words, words in a different colour, areas that are highlighted when you move the pointer over them and the mouse pointer changing shape to become a hand.

4. Click on a link that looks interesting and watch what happens. You should see the page disappear and a new one take its place. Often the outline of the page will appear quickly but illustrations will take longer although a frame showing their location may be revealed almost at once. It takes time for the contents of a page to load. This changes depending on the size of the page (i.e. pages containing many illustrations are slow to load), how many people are visiting the site at the same time (i.e. the site gives equal priority to all visitors so if thousands of people are using the site at the same time it will be slow) and the number of people using the World Wide Web (i.e. the more people, the slower the access).

5. Explore the new page and again jump from this to another and so on. Investigate the site and see what you can find.

6. After a few jumps to new pages, it may be difficult to remember the route you have taken. However, you can retrace your steps using the Back button on the toolbar. This will move you back to the page you jumped from and you can retrace your steps. You can return using the Forward button.

7. Use Back and Forward and observe what happens. You may notice that pages are faster to load since in some cases your computer has stored the contents of the page and can therefore quickly access it.

8. Explore the site until you are confident that you can recognise links, move between pages and use the Back and Forward buttons.

9. You can jump from one website to another from anywhere, so delete the British Library URL and enter http://www.thebritishmuseum.ac.uk/ in the address bar and press enter.

10. Observe the new website appear. This is the home page of the British Museum website. Explore this site practising linking to new pages, locating links and retracing your path.

11. When you are confident about navigating sites, close the browser by selecting the File menu and the Close option or click on the window close button in the top right-hand corner of the browser. You can exit the browser from any page within a site.

## Searching a website

Many websites are very complex and contain a large volume of material. Locating precise content is quite difficult if you simply follow the links unless the site is small or has limited links. A large, rich site can be difficult to use, so many have a facility to search the site for chosen topics. Figure 54 shows a site search facility or search engine which will allow you to locate any content that matches your search words.

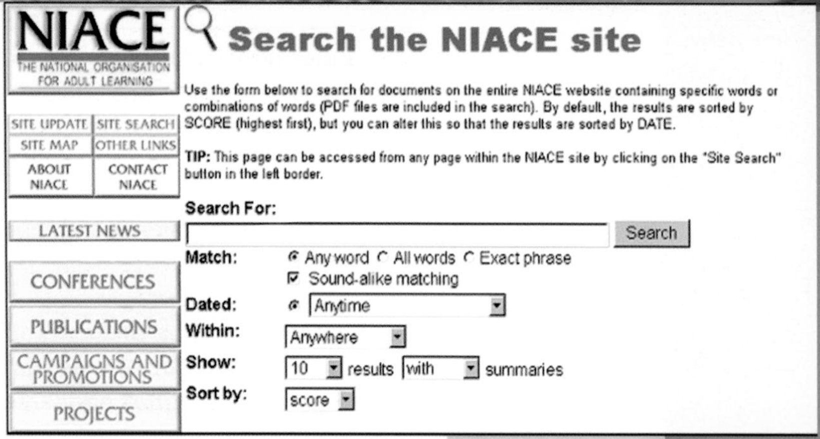

REPRODUCED WITH THE PERMISSION OF ATOMZ.COM

FIGURE 54
**Searching a site**

This search engine works in a similar way to many others in that you enter a word or words and it seeks to match them to content. In this case you are allowed to refine the nature of the match:

**Any words** – any of the words you have entered match any word in the content

**All words –** all the search words appear in the content in any order

**Exact phrase –** the search phrase is matched exactly in the content

**Sound-alike matching –** you can match with any words that sound like your search words

The search engine gives each match a score indicating the closeness of the match. In many cases search engines give you a number of matches which you have review to see if they are correct. It is normal to start with a very wide search and then to refine it so that you do not get too many to review.

# Exercise 18

## Search a single site

**1.** Establish a connection to the Internet – this will depend on your location (i.e. home, work or college).

**2.** Using either the Programs menu or by clicking on the Internet Explorer icon on the desktop, load the browser. The browser may appear filling the entire screen or in a window. If you want to expand the window to fill the whole screen, use the maximise button in the top right-hand corner of the window.

**3.** Enter http://www.niace.org.uk/newsearch.htm in the address bar and press enter – this is the website of the National Institute of Adult Continuing Education (NIACE). This URL will jump you into the page on which the search engine is located.

**4.** Investigate the site search engine by trying a number of different searches.

**5.** Enter 'information and communication technology' with option Any word (click into the radio button alongside the option) and click on the Search button. A list of matches appears with a brief summary describing them to help you identify if it is the correct one. You can display matches without a summary by changing the 'with summary' option (click on the down arrow to select other options).

**6.** This search reported 1329 matches and showed me the top 10 matches. You can change the number displayed by altering the Show option (click on the down arrow to select a new number). The number of matches you will find will be different since websites are always changing and developing.

**7.** If you scroll down to the bottom of the results page you will again find the search engine. Alternatively click on the Back button.

**8.** Search again for 'information and communication technology' with option All words and click on the Search button. In this case, the search engine reports 110 matches and again displays the top ten. Your number will be different because the site will have changed since I searched it.

**9.** Search again for 'information and communication technology' with option Exact phrase and click on the Search button. In this case, the search engine reports 24 matches and again displays the top ten. Your number will be different because the site will have changed since I searched it.

**10.** Even though your number of matches will be different you will have noticed that the more restrictive your search options, the smaller number of matches.

**11.** Explore the search engine using different combinations of options until you are confident you understand how it works.

**12.** You can jump to the content matched by clicking on the link shown with each match (e.g. underlined and coloured words). You will have to do this frequently to check if it is what you are searching for. To return, use the Back button.

**13.** When you are confident about searching, close the browser by selecting the File menu then the Close option or click on the window close button in the top right-hand corner of the browser.

# Searching the World Wide Web

There are millions of websites covering almost every subject. A key issue is simply locating sites that you are interested in. This is similar to the problem of searching an individual site but on a far larger scale. Many organisations provide search engines to help you locate content on the World Wide Web. They have indexed web pages so that you can search them by using key words. This is similar to searching a single website. However, it is relatively easy to find the content on a single site using a site search engine. It is far more difficult on the World Wide Web because it is composed of millions of sites. World Wide Web search engines search for individual web pages rather than entire sites. Figure 55 shows the Altavista search engine.

Search engines are essentially large databases of web pages which have been amassed automatically by the engine. This is carried out by using tools called spiders or robots which follow links between pages and index the pages they find. The index is directly related to the words presented on the web pages. When you enter your keywords for the information, you are searching the database and not the World Wide Web itself.

There are many search engines and although they all work in broadly similar ways, there are differences between them. They differ:

in the range of search options they provide

in how they present or rank the results of a search

There are two different types of search engine:

individual

meta

FIGURE 55
**Altavista Website**

Individual search engine is essentially what we have been describing. A meta engine does not develop its own database but rather searches the databases of several other individual search engines. They are therefore very useful in finding more illusive content.

There is another way of finding content on the World Wide Web. This uses devices called directories. Directories are very different from search engines. While you search an engine using key words that you select as being related to what you are seeking, a directory provides you with categories to choose from. The contents of directories are chosen for you. The staff pick sites that they believe you will be interested in so they are in a sense making recommendations while a search engine leaves the whole choice to you. Directories are very quick to use while a search engine can take time to identify suitable pages. However, the categories available to you in a directory are limited to what has been identified as popular items (e.g. computers, shopping and holidays), while a search engine places no limits on categories you can search for. In many cases you are offered the choice of a search engine and a directory.

There are many different search engines and directories, of which several have United kingdom versions. The list below provides you with a range of examples:

| | |
|---|---|
| AltaVista | http://www.altavista.digital.com/ |
| | http://www.uk.altavista.com/ |
| Bigbook | http://www.bigbook.com |
| Chubba | http://www.chubba.com/ |
| Excite | http://www.excite.com/ |
| Fast | http://www.alltheweb.com |
| Google | http://www.google.com |
| | http://www.google.co.uk |
| HotBot | http://www.hotbot.com/ |
| Infoseek | http://www.infoseek.com/ |
| | http://www.uk.infoseek.com |
| Looksmart | http://www.looksmart.com/ |
| Lycos | http://www-uk.lycos.com/ |
| Magellan | http://www.mckinley.com/ |
| Northern Lights | http://www.nlsearch.com/ |
| Webcrawler | http://www.webcrawler.com/ |
| Yahoo | http://www.yahoo.com |

Search engines can also be used to find individual e-mail addresses. There are several that specialise in locating e-mail addresses.

| | |
|---|---|
| Bigfoot | http://www.bigfoot.com/ |
| Four11 | http://www.Four11.com/ |
| InfoSpace | http://www.www.infospace.com/ |
| Whowhere | http://www.whowhere.com/ |
| Yahoo People | http://people.yahoo.com/ |

Meta search engines include:

| | |
|---|---|
| Dogpile | hhtp://.www.dogpile.com/ |
| Metacrawler | http://www.metacrawler.com |
| Lxquick | http://www.lxquick.com |
| Ask Jeeves | http://www.ask.com |

Searching is simple to do, but can be difficult to do well. Most search engines offer help in a variety of ways. It is useful to investigate these options. Different search engines operate in different ways so that undertaking an identical search using several will produce different results. The next two exercises are based on comparing the same search using two different search engines (i.e.Altavista and Google).

# Exercise 19

## Searching the World Wide Web – Altavista

**1.** Establish a connection to the Internet – this will depend on your location (i.e. home, work or college).

**2.** Load the browser by using either the Programs menu or by double clicking on the Internet Explorer icon on the desktop.

**3.** Enter http://www.uk.altavista.com in the address bar and press enter - this is the website of the Altavista search engine. If you would like to compare this search engine with a directory then visit http://bigbook.com

**4.** Return to the Altavista search engine. We will try to locate a hotel in Edinburgh. So enter the word hotels into the Find This box of the search engine and select the option which restricts the search to the United Kingdom (click on the radio button – a small circle which when you click on it inserts a dot in its centre to show it is active). Click on the Search button.

The result of the search were:
8,105,604 pages which match the word hotels and also offer a number of directories about hotels but none relate to Edinburgh. Your results will be different since the World Wide Web is continuously changing.

**5.** This is not very useful as there are too many matches. Let's refine the search by adding the word Edinburgh. You should enter hotels Edinburgh, select the UK option and click on the Search button.

**6.** In my case the results of this search were: 1,966,900 pages which match the words hotels Edinburgh and also provide a directory (i.e. Edinburgh, Scotland – Hotels & Resorts) which offers 15 entries relating to hotels. Although these are sites selected by the Altavista Editor, they are certainly a way of narrowing the field.

**7.** The number of matches is still too high but the directory will help you to locate a hotel.

**8.** Refine the search by joining the words with a plus sign – hotels+Edinburgh. The engine will now search for pages containing both words. In this case Altavista located 97 web pages which matched. This is now starting to be useful.

**9.** A final search involves enclosing the words in inverted commas. This normally makes the engine search for pages which have the phrase 'hotels Edinburgh' in. Altavista again located 97 pages since this search engine treats inverted commas in the same way as joining the words with a plus.

**10.** You can jump to any matching webpage by clicking on the link (underlined and coloured words) to check if it is what you are looking for. To return to the search engine, use the Back button. Explore the search engine by carrying out a search to find web pages that interest you (e.g. look for pages about a hobby, football team, government or places of interest).

**11.** When you are confident about searching, close the browser by selecting the File menu and the Close option or click on the window close button in the top right-hand corner of the browser.

# Exercise 20

## Searching the World Wide Web - Google

**1.** Establish a connection to the Internet – this will depend on your location (i.e. home, work or college).

**2.** Load the browser by using either the Programs menu or by clicking on the Internet Explorer icon on the desktop.

**3.** Enter http://www.google.com in the address bar and press enter - this is the website of the Google search engine.

**4.** Notice that this search engine offers buttons to link you to the Google Web Directory (i.e. selected sites) and Google Groups.

**5.** We will try to locate a hotel in Edinburgh, so enter the word hotels into the search box. Click the Google Search button.

**6.** The result of the search were:
Google – located 12,000,000 pages with matches to the word hotels. Your results will be different since the World Wide Web is continuously changing.

Again, however, these results are far from useful in finding a hotel in Edinburgh since there are far too many matches. Let's refine the search by adding the word Edinburgh. You should enter hotels Edinburgh and click on the Google Search button.

This search located 135,000 pages which match the words hotels Edinburgh. The difference between Altavista and Google is due to the way that the two search engines work. Altavista will search for pages which have either word while Google looks for pages which have both words and is therefore more effective in narrowing the search.

**7.** A third possible step is to modify the search by joining the words with a plus sign. The engine will search for pages containing both words. Google – located 135,000 pages showing that it treated hotels Edinburgh the same as hotels+Edinburgh

**8.** A final search is to enclose the words in inverted commas. This normally makes the engine search for pages which have the phrase 'hotels Edinburgh' in.

**9.** Goggle located 357 web pages. This difference between the two search engines is again because of the ways that they work. Altavista treats inverted commas in the same way as joining the words with a plus, while Google searches for the phrase "hotels Edinburgh".

**10.** Compare the results of the two searches and consider the effectiveness of different search approaches, search engines and the value of directories. It is important to be aware of how the search engines you use work or you may find using them a frustrating experience.

**11.** Explore the Google search engine by carrying out a search to find webpages that interest you (e.g. look for a pages about a hobby, football team, government or places of interest).

**12.** When you are confident about searching, close the browser by selecting the File menu and the Close option or click on the window close button in the top right-hand corner of the browser.

# Saving information

Browsers provide functions to allow you to save the contents of web pages, save the URL so you can return to the page and to print the page. All these functions require the browser to be accessing the chosen web page.

To print the page, select the File menu then the Print option, which will open the Print dialogue box. Press the OK button in the Print dialogue box and the webpage will now be printed using the printer default settings. Webpages are often longer than an A4 sheet, so printing a webpage can produce several A4 sheets. Figure 56 shows the File menu.

In a similar way, the contents of the web page can be saved by selecting the File menu and the Save or Save As options. This opens the Save dialogue box. In order to save a webpage as a file, you need to identify a folder in

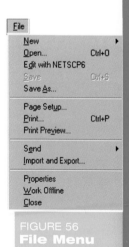

FIGURE 56
**File Menu**

FIGURE 57
**Favorites**

which to save it to. This is done by clicking on the down arrow at the end of the Save in box. This will open a list of the drives and folders. To select one, you need to single click on it. Once you have selected a folder you can name your file by clicking in the File name box and entering the name using the keyboard. The file can now be saved by clicking the Save button. The latest browsers allow you to save both the text and images while the earlier ones only allowed you to save the text and left gaps where the pictures should be.

Once you have found a useful website it is important to be able to find it again. Internet Explorer lets you save the URLs in a special area called Favorites. To store a URL, you need to be accessing the chosen website. You then select the Favorites menu and the Add to Favorites option. Figure 57 shows a list of favorites. To return to a favorite website you simply click on it. You can organise your favorites into folders, grouping related sites together.

Another way of returning to a useful website is to use the browser's history records. Internet Explorer keeps records of sites visited. However, this record system is often set to keep the list of sites visited only for a few times or even a single day so it's main task is to allow you to return to a particular site after a session visiting many different websites. Figure 58 shows the History record open. It is accessed by clicking on the History button on the toolbar.

FIGURE 58
**History**

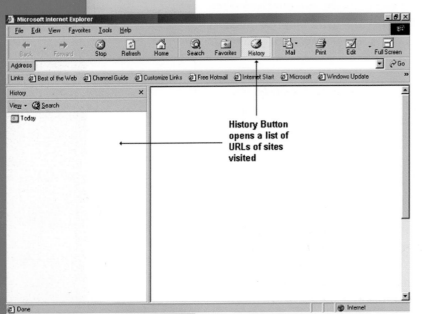

History Button opens a list of URLs of sites visited

## Microsoft Outlook Express (Figure 51)

When you first start to use e-mail it has a magical quality. You connect to the Internet, open your e-mail application (e.g. Microsoft Outlook Express) and your e-mails arrive. What happens is that an e-mail is addressed in the same way as a letter or postcard. This address directs the e-mail to a location on the Internet where it is stored on a computer until you collect it. This is normally the computer of the Internet Service Provider who supplies your access to the Internet. In some cases that may be your employer or college. As soon as you connect to the Internet and open your e-mail application, the mail is automatically sent to you.

An important issue to remember is that computer viruses are often distributed by e-mail. You should always protect your computer system with up-to-date virus protection software.

Microsoft Outlook Express is an e-mail system. You can access it from

Internet Explorer (Figure 50), from the Programs menu or by clicking on the Outlook Express icon on the Windows desktop. This means you can therefore use it independently from Internet Explorer. You do not need to be connected to the Internet in order to use Outlook Express to read old e-mail, to write a new e-mail or reply to one that you have received.

However, to send or receive new e-mails does require a connection to the Internet. Once you are connected then the e-mails you have created can be sent. This is like writing a letter at home and having to walk to the post-box to post it. This process of writing or reading e-mails while not being connected is called 'working off-line'. This is important since it will save you the telephone charges associated with being connected.

Figure 51 shows you the major features of the application (Outlook Express). These are:

**Inbox –** this is the folder in which your e-mail is stored when it is received; this is sometimes called the mailbox

**Outbox –** this is the folder in which your e-mails are stored until they are sent (i.e. after you connect to the Internet)

**Sent Items –** this is the folder in which all your e-mails that have been sent are stored

**Deleted Items –** this is the folder in which e-mails that have been deleted are stored. This is very useful to prevent mistakes from being made

**Drafts –** this is the folder in which e-mails that are only partially written are stored

**Addresses (Toolbar button) –** this provides access to an electronic address book where e-mail addresses can be stored

These functions are all shown on the left-hand side of the application in the small window marked 'Folders' with the exception of Addresses which is a toolbar button. Outlook Express provides you with these features to ensure that e-mails are safeguarded and organised. However, you can also use standard windows file saving methods to save e-mails as files in other folders. This is useful if the e-mail relates to a particular topic and you have already created a folder for other files so that you can keep everything together.

To save an e-mail to an external folder, select the File menu and the Save As option. This will open Save Message As window (Figure 59). Figure 59 shows that the file called Welcome to Outlook Express 5 is being prepared to be saved in the folder My Documents. Inside this folder are four other folders (i.e. Alan, Chris, My Pictures and Peter). If you wanted to save the message into these folders you would need to click on the chosen folder. This would change the Save in box to the name of the chosen one. It is also possible to save the message to an entirely different folder by clicking on the down arrow

Electronic Communication

at the end of Save in box. This will reveal a list of other drives (e.g. floppy disk) and folders (see Figure 59). To select a new folder or drive, you again need to click on your selected location.

The name of the file in which the message will be stored can be changed by clicking in the File name box. Windows provides you with a name based on the contents of the document but it is always best to name your own files to ensure you can remember them.

## Sending messages

To send an e-mail, you must click on the New Mail button on the toolbar of Outlook Express. This will open the New Message window (Figure 60). The layout of the message window guides you through how to write your message. You click into the area where you want to enter text. You need to enter an e-mail address, a subject and the contents of your message. You can also send copies of your message to other people. When you have completed your message, send it by clicking on the Send button. If you are connected to the Internet, the e-mail will be sent immediately. If you are working off-line (i.e. you are not connected to the Internet) then the e-mail is stored in the Outbox and the number stored will be shown in brackets next to the title Outbox. You should see the number increase by one when you click on the Send button. The e-mail will be dispatched as soon as you next connect to the Internet.

E-mail are normally short messages but other computer files such as spreadsheet, word-processor or presentation files can be attached. This allows far more detailed information to be communicated. Sales staff, for example can send their expense claims as a spreadsheet file. Managers can send reports as word-processor files. Attachments are very useful and are easily added using the Attach button (i.e. shown by a paperclip).

E-mail is very useful in business in that your mail carries the sender's details (i.e. in the Sent Items folder). It automatically gets assigned a date and time of creation so that messages can be more easily traced or kept in order. These features allow detailed records to be straightforwardly maintained. Equally important is that any e-mails you receive can be kept.

The address of an e-mail follows a standard convention. They are a combination of the users name with a domain name (often the e-mail's computer host or Internet Service Provider) joined by the @ symbol. Some examples of e-mail addresses are:

FIGURE 59
**Save Message As**

FIGURE 60
**New Message**

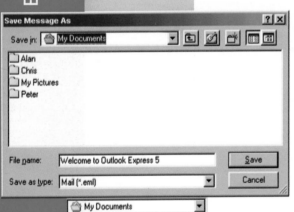

Copies
Message Area
Attachments
E-mail title
Address
Send your e-mail

68

Aaa@acme.co.uk

Bbb@acme.net

Ccc@acme.harry.org.uk

Ddd@acme.com

# Exercise 21

## Send an e-mail

**1.** Load Outlook Express using either the Programs menu or by clicking on the Outlook Express icon on the desktop.

**2.** Open a new message by selecting the File menu, highlight New and click on Mail Message. The New Message window is opened. An alternative approach is to click on the New Mail button on the toolbar.

**3.** If you are studying OCR New CLAIT as part of a class, ask your learning colleagues if you can send them an e-mail or ask a work colleague for her address.

Enter the following text

> To:                    e-mail address of your colleague
>
> Subject   Practice e-mail
>
> This is my first e-mail and I would be grateful if you would reply to it so that I can see what happens.
>
> Name

**4.** Before you send your e-mail check that you have entered the address accurately. It must be 100% correct or it will not be delivered.

**5.** Click on the Send button as soon as you have completed the message. If you are not connected to the Internet you will see the message added to Outbox (number in brackets will increase by one). If you are connected then the message will be sent immediately and a copy placed in the Sent folder. Check this folder and see if your message has been added.

**6.** If you are not connected to the Internet you should then connect and you will see your message sent. It should only take a moment or two.

**7.** Explore Outlook Express by clicking on menus and buttons and investigating the different options (e.g. local folders and addresses). Observe the changes to the display.

**8.** When you are confident that you understand the layout of the application, close Outlook Express selecting the File menu and the Exit option or click on the window close button in the top right-hand corner of the application window.

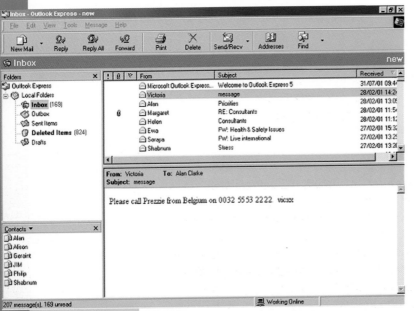

FIGURE 61
**Inbox**

# Receiving e-mails

When you open Outlook Express e-mails that have been sent to you will appear in the inbox. Figure 61 illustrates an open inbox. If you click on the inbox, it will be highlighted and in the box to the right of the folders a list of messages will appear. The list gives you details of who the message is from, its subject and the date and time it was received. This information can be proceeded by a symbol (i.e. a paperclip indicates an attachment and an exclamation mark, an important message). If you single click on a message it will be highlighted and its contents will be revealed in the box below the list. If you double click on the message then a new window will open (Figure 62) showing the message. When you receive an e-mail you have a variety of options. You can:

FIGURE 62
**Message**

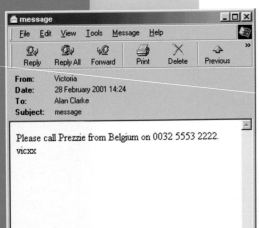

**read then delete the message** (with the e-mail highlighted or the message window open, click on the Delete button on toolbar)

**read, save and delete the message** (with the e-mail highlighted or the message window open select the File menu and the Save As option)

**read and reply to the original e-mail sender** (with the e-mail highlighted or the message window open, click on the Reply button on the toolbar)

**read and reply to everyone who received the original e-mail** (i.e. copies) (with the e-mail highlighted or the message window open click on Reply All button on toolbar)

**read and forward the message to someone else** (with the e-mail highlighted or the message window open, click on the Forward button on the toolbar and enter the e-mail address of the person you want the message copied to)

**read and copy the message to a folder** (with the e-mail highlighted or the message window open, select the Edit menu and the Copy to

Folder option. This allows you to place a copy of the message to one of the existing local folders or to a new local folder. This is useful in that within Outlook Express you begin to create a filing system for your communications)

**print the message** (with the e-mail highlighted or the message window open, select the Edit menu and the Print option)

The process of deleting messages from your inbox once you have acted on them is important since very quickly after starting to use e-mail you are likely to have hundreds and even thousands of old messages. It is vital that these are organised (e.g. saved into folders) or you will rapidly become confused by the mountain of correspondence.

Some of the e-mails you receive will be accompanied by attachments. These are files of information (e.g. word-processor files). Figure 63 illustrates an attachment. To open an attachment double click on it and it will open providing you have the appropriate application available on your computer. A Word file requires Microsoft Word, an Excel file requires Microsoft Excel and so on. If the appropriate application is not present then you will see an error message stating that it cannot identify the application. Once an attachment is open you can save or print it using its application. The appropriate application will be opened automatically by the attachment.

Viruses are frequently transmitted by e-mail attachments. It is therefore important not to open an attachment unless you know who has sent you the message. Equally important is to have up to date virus protection software on your computer. Many virus protection systems allow you to check attachments before opening them. It is good practice to check e-mail attachments even if you know the sender. Some viruses automatically send e-mail messages to spread their effects.

FIGURE 63
**Attachment**

# Exercise 22

## Receiving e-mails

**1.** Load Outlook Express using either the Programs menu or by clicking on the Outlook Express icon on the desktop.

**2.** Single click on the inbox which will be highlighted and a list of e-mails received will be listed. E-mail messages that you have not opened are shown in bold. You will possibly find a reply to your previous e-mail but even if no one has sent you a message, Outlook Express normally shows a welcome e-mail from the Outlook Express team.

**3.** Single click on the Welcome to Outlook Express e-mail, your reply or another message. You will see the content displayed. This is very useful if you are seeking to check your e-mail rapidly.

**4.** Double click on your Welcome to Outlook Express e-mail and you will see the Message window open (Figure 64).

FIGURE 64
**Message Window**

**5.** Click on the Reply button and a new window will appear (Figure 65). This shows the original message but reverses the sender and receiver. In the space above the original message you enter your reply. This enables both the original message and reply to be sent. If this e-mail provokes a response the e-mail will have the original, the reply and the second reply. E-mails contain the whole communication.

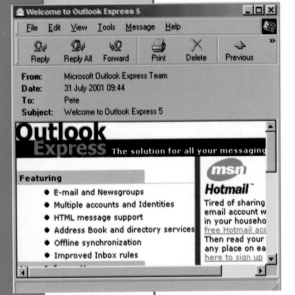

**6.** Enter a reply:

Thank you for your welcome

Name

**7.** Click on the Send button as soon as you have finished. If you are connected to the Internet your message will be sent. If you are working off-line then the message will be stored in the Outbox and you will see the number in the box increase.

**8.** Open the e-mail again and this time, click on Reply All and you will see the same window (Figure 65) open. This is because the original e-mail was sent only to you. If the original message had been copied to other people then your reply would go to everyone. Close the window, select the File menu and the Close option or click on the close button in top right-hand corner of window.

FIGURE 55
**Reply**

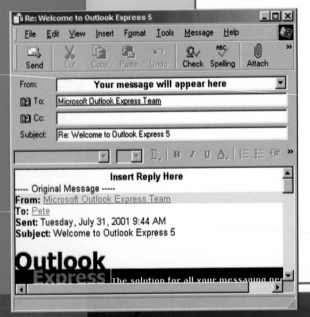

**9.** Open the e-mail again and click on the Forward button. You will see the same window (Figure 65) open again but with a blank To line. This allows you to send your message to another person. You can also add an extra message. To close the window, select the File menu and the Close option or click on close button in the top right-hand corner of the window.

**10.** Compare the Reply, Reply All and Forward functions.

**11.** When you are confident that you understand the three functions, close Outlook Express by selecting the File menu and the Exit option or click on the window close button in the top right-hand corner of the application window.

## Attaching files

Attaching files to an e-mail can be very useful. You initially need to start a new e-mail (click on the New Mail button) which opens the Message (Figure 60) window. To add an attachment click, on the Attach button on the toolbar. This will open the Insert Attachment window (Figure 66).

This window gives you access to all your saved files. To move around the different drives, use the drop down arrow next to the look in box and then click on the selected folder or drive. When you have identified the file, double click on it or single click the file and then click on the Attach button. The attached file will appear on your message (Figure 63).

FIGURE 66
**Insert Attachment**

## Electronic address book

An important function that Outlook Express provides is the storage of e-mail addresses. You can copy addresses from e-mails that are sent to you or enter new addresses manually. Once you have created an entry in the electronic address book, you can send an e-mail directly from the entry.

With the e-mail message window open, you can save the address by selecting the Tools menu and highlight the Add to Address Book option. This reveals a series of options which lets you save the sender's address. You select the option by clicking on it.

# Exercise 23

### Using an address book

**1.** Load Outlook Express using either the Programs menu or by clicking on the Outlook Express icon on the desktop.

**2.** Open a message (e.g. the Welcome to Outlook Express e-mail) and save the sender's address by selecting the Tool menu, highlighting the Add to Address Book option and clicking on Sender.

**3.** Close the message window by clicking on the close button in the top right-hand corner of the window or by selecting the File menu and the Close option.

**4.** Check that your new address has been saved by clicking on the Addresses button on toolbar. The address book will now open revealing a list of all the addresses you have saved (Figure 67).

**5.** If you single click on an address it will be highlighted and by selecting the Action button and the Send Mail option, you can send an e-mail to this address. If you double click on an address you can add more information to your record such as postal address.

**6.** Select an address and send a new e-mail. A New Message window will appear with the address you have selected inserted in the In box.

FIGURE 67
**Address Book**

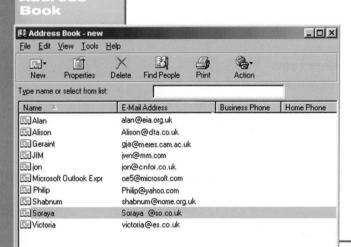

**7.** Close the Message window and the address book by selecting the close button in the top right-hand corner of the window or select the File menu and the Close or Exit options.

**8.** When you are confident about saving addresses, close Outlook Express by selecting the File menu and the Exit option or click on the window close button in the top right-hand corner of the application window.

## Web-based e-mail

Another way of providing yourself with an e-mail account if you have access to the Internet is through web-based e-mail suppliers. Many websites offer users free e-mail accounts. However, to send or receive their messages they must be connected to the World Wide Web. This has the advantage that you can access your messages from any computer connected to the Internet in the world. However, it has the disadvantage that you must be online to read or send messages.

Almost all the web-based services are free but you will find advertising related to both the sites you have to visit and in some cases the e-mails you send. In order to establish an account you normally only have to visit the site, complete some online forms, and choose a user name and password. Once this is done you are ready to send and receive e-mail.

## Company policy and legislation

Although the World Wide Web provides a huge amount of useful information it also contains offensive material, pornography and information which is incorrect. Many employers have established policies about the use of the World Wide Web. It is critical that you are aware of your organisation's policy. Policies frequently forbid the use of the World Wide Web to access offensive material and in many cases it is a serious disciplinary offence to breach the policy. The legal position should also be considered. There have been several prominent court cases about using the World Wide Web to access pornography. It is important to be aware of both the law and access policy. In a similar way, learning centres, colleges and libraries which provide public access to the Internet also place restrictions on the use of the system.

Many organisations have also developed policies regarding the use of e-mail which you should be fully aware of. In simple terms, it is always best to include in an e-mail only material you would write in a letter. You are just as liable for what you write in an e-mail as in a letter.

## Extra Practice

**1.** Send an e-mail to a colleague with one of your files (one that you have created in another unit) attached

**2.** Search the World Wide Web for opportunities to shop for books, compact discs or videos

**3.** Search the World Wide Web for your favourite football, rugby or cricket team

**4.** Many websites provide you with the opportunity to e-mail the developers with your feedback so take advantage of this to practise sending e-mails

**5.** Many television and radio programmes ask listeners and viewers to send them e-mails. This will give you an opportunity to practise your e-mailing

# Summary    Electronic Communication

**1. Load Internet Explorer** Use either the Start button and the Programs menu or double click on the Internet Explorer icon on the Windows desktop.

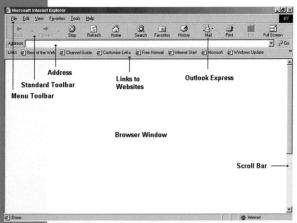

FIGURE 50 **Internet Explorer**

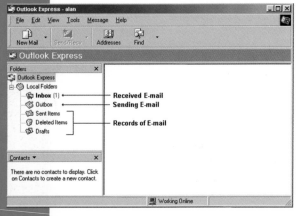

FIGURE 51 **Outlook Express**

**2. Close the Internet Explorer Application** Click on the File menu item and the Close option or click on the close button in the top right-hand corner of the application window (Figure 50).

**3. Load Microsoft Outlook Express** Use either the Start button and the Programs menu or double click on the Outlook Express icon on Windows desktop. A third way is to click on the Mail button within Internet Explorer and select the Read Mail option.

**4. Close Microsoft Outlook Express** Click on the File menu item and the Exit option or click on the close button in the top right-hand corner of the application window (Figure 51).

**5. URL (Uniform Resource Locator)** Website addresses are unique and consist of http (Hypertext Transfer Protocol), www (world Wide Web), the website host, a code to explain the type of organisation and a country code (e.g. http://www.bbc.co.uk).

Perfect accuracy is essential.

**6. Links** Links connect different web pages both within a particular website and to other websites. Links are indicated by underlined words, coloured text, the mouse pointer changing shape (i.e. from an arrow to an hand) and areas being highlighted by the mouse moving across them.

**7. Retracing your route** Internet Explorer provides you with two buttons - Back and Forward. These allow you either to retrace your steps or to return along your route.

**8. Searching** Complex websites often provide a means of searching for distinct pages. In a similar way there are search engines that will locate websites which relate to a users' interest. The search engines tend to operate by matching words which the users enter describing their interest. They match the words in different ways such as:

match with any words entered

match with all words entered in any order

match with the exact phrase entered

FIGURE 62 **Message**

## 9. Saving web addresses

Internet Explorer lets you save URLs (website addresses) so that you can return to the website later. From the chosen website, select the F<u>a</u>vorites menu and the <u>A</u>dd to favorites option to save the URL.

## 10. Saving a web page Select
the <u>F</u>ile menu and the <u>S</u>ave option

## 11. Printing a web page Select
the <u>F</u>ile menu and the <u>P</u>rint option

## 12. Create a new e-mail Select
the New Mail button on the toolbar of Outlook Express and the New Message window (Figure 62) will be revealed. Enter your message and address, then click on the Send button

If you are connected to the Internet, the e-mail will be sent immediately.

If you are working off-line (i.e. you are not connected to the Internet) then the e-mail is stored in the Outbox and the number of messages stored will be shown in brackets next to the title Outbox.

## 13. Read a message E-mails are stored in the inbox. Clicking on the
inbox will reveal a list of messages. If you single click on a message, it will be highlighted and its contents revealed in the box below the list. If you double click on the message, then a new window will open, showing the message.

## 14. Reply, Forward and Copy messages With the
message window open, you can reply to the e-mail, forward its contents to another person or copy the message to a folder.

**Reply -** with the e-mail highlighted or the message window Open, click on the Reply or Reply All buttons on toolbar.

**Forward the message -** with the e-mail highlighted or the message window open, click on the Forward button on the toolbar and enter e-mail address of the person you want the message copied to.

**Copy the message to a folder -** with the e-mail highlighted or the message window open, select the Edit menu and the Copy to Folder option. This allows you to place a copy of the message to one of the existing local folders or to new local folder.

## 15. Attached Files To open an attachment, double click on it and it will open providing you have the appropriate application available on your computer.

To attach a file, start a new e-mail (click on the New Mail button) and click on the Attach button on the toolbar. This will open the Insert Attachment window from where you can select a file.

## 16. Save and recall e-mail addresses With the e-mail message window open, select the Tools menu and highlight the Add to Address Book option. This reveals a series of options which allow you to save the sender's address.

## 17. Send an e-mail using a saved address With the address book open, highlight the chosen address (single click), select the Action button and Send Mail.

## 18. Print an e-mail With the e-mail highlighted or the message window open, select the Edit menu and Print option.

## 19. Company Policies and Legislation It is essential to be aware of both your organisation's policy and the law relating to the use of the Internet.

# Spreadsheets

This chapter will help you to use a spreadsheet to:

identify and use spreadsheet software correctly

use an input device to enter and edit data accurately

insert, replicate and format arithmetical formulae

use common numerical formatting and alignment

manage and print spreadsheet documents

## Assessment

This unit does not assume any previous experience of spredsheets. However, you may find it useful if you have previously undertaken Unit 1 (Using a Computer). After studying Unit 4 your skills and understanding will be assessed during a 2-hour practical assignment. This is set by OCR and marked locally. However, the marking will be externally moderated by OCR. This ensures that the standard is being applied correctly across the many different providers of OCR New CLAIT.

## Spreadsheet Applications

Figure 68 shows Microsoft Excel. It is similar to other Microsoft Office applications in that it comprises a Menu and Toolbars (e.g.Standard Toolbar), work area and a status bar at the bottom of the display. However, there are some differences which are:

1. The work area is divided into a grid of rows and columns to form many individual cells. The cell illustrated in Figure 68 is in row 11 and J column and is know as J11. When you are developing formulae it is important to identify particular cells and this is done by stating the column and row intersection.

2. At the bottom of the work area is an extra bar with tabs indicating Sheet 1, Sheet 2 and Sheet 3. This shows which worksheet is being used and Excel allows you to group sheets together to form a workbook. Figure 68 shows that Sheet 1 is being displayed.

3. Beneath the formatting toolbar is a row called the Formula Bar which shows J11 at the left hand end followed by a greyed out area and an equals sign. The J11 indicates the cell in which the cursor is currently placed and therefore this changes as the cursor moves. After the equals sign, any formulae which are in the current cell are displayed. We will discuss formulae later in this chapter.

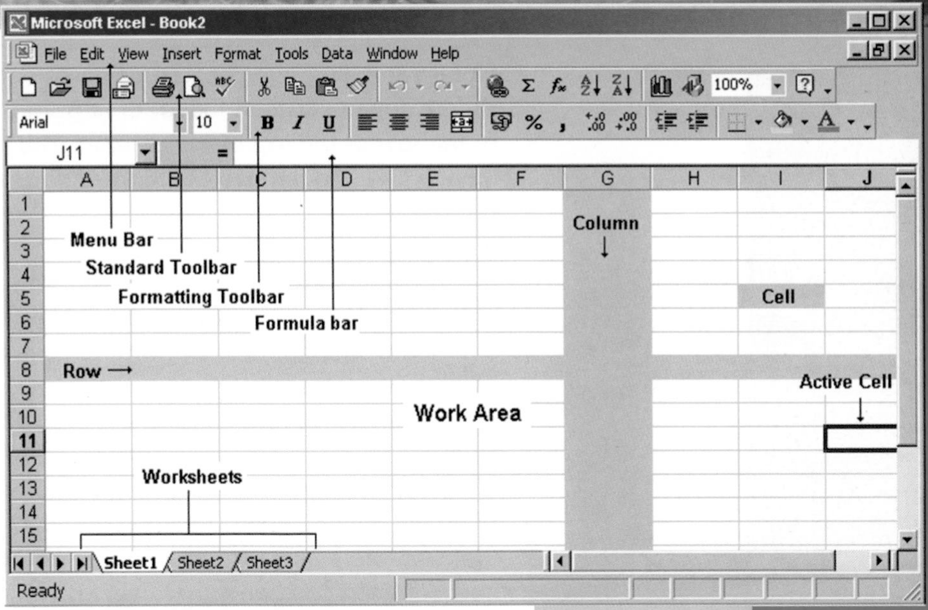

There are several ways of loading an application such as Microsoft Excel. The two most common are those using:

the Start button

the Microsoft Excel Icon on the Windows desktop

In the bottom left-hand corner of the Windows desktop is a button called Start. This allows you to access many applications and standard features of the operating system. If you single click on Start, a menu will pop-up. If you place the mouse pointer over the Programs item it will become highlighted (i.e. the background will change colour) and a new menu will appear alongside. If you click on the item shown as Microsoft Excel then the application will load. In a similar way if you double click on the Excel icon shown on the desktop then Excel will again load.

FIGURE 68
**Microsoft Excel 2000**

The exercises included in the chapter are intended to help you understand how to use spreadsheets. They are simplified representations of the world and are not intended to be tutorials on accountancy but explanations of Excel.

# Exercise 24

## Load and use Microsoft Excel

**1.** Load Microsoft Excel using either the Programs menu or the Excel icon on the desktop.

**2.** Enter the table of information below to form your first spreadsheet. It shows a simple breakdown of the costs of operating the Acme Newsagent.

|  | Costs | Overheads | Total Costs |
|---|---|---|---|
| Newspapers | 12,000 |  |  |
| Groceries | 10,000 |  |  |
| Stationery | 8,000 |  |  |
| Wages | 6,000 |  |  |
| Total |  |  |  |

**3.** To select an individual cell you need to click within it and it will be

FIGURE 69
**Insert Menu**

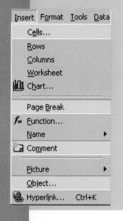

| Insert | Format | Tools | Data |
|---|---|---|---|
| Cells... | | | |
| Rows | | | |
| Columns | | | |
| Worksheet | | | |
| Chart... | | | |
| Page Break | | | |
| Function... | | | |
| Name | | | |
| Comment | | | |
| Picture | | | |
| Object... | | | |
| Hyperlink... | Ctrl+K | | |

|  | G |
|---|---|
| 1 | |
| 2 | |
| 3 | |
| 4 | |
| 5 | |
| 6 | Income |
| 7 | |
| 8 | 21,750 |
| 9 | |
| 10 | 14,600 |
| 11 | |
| 12 | 15,690 |
| 13 | |
| 14 | |
| 15 | |

FIGURE 70
**Extra Column**

highlighted. However, you can also select a whole row or column. To select a row or column click in the letter (e.g. A) or number (e.g. 1) which is at the end of the row or the top of the column. The row or column will then be highlighted . To remove the highlighting you need to click in another part of the sheet.

**4.** Position your pointer in cell C3 and you will see the cell is highlighted by its borders becoming emboldened. Now enter Acme Newsagent. Repeat this entering Newspapers in B8, Groceries in B9, Stationery in B10, Wages in B11, Total in B12, Costs in C6, Overheads in D6 and Total Costs in E6. Now add the numeric cost data to form the column of figures in column C in rows 8, 9, 10 and 11.

**5.** If you make a mistake when entering text or numbers then you can delete the characters using the backspace key. However, if you have moved to a new cell then you can either overwrite your original entry by clicking on the cell with the error and entering the correct text or numbers or edit the text as it appears on the formula bar. If you highlight the cell which contains the error you will see its contents appear on the formula bar and you use your mouse pointer to position your cursor in order to amend the text.

**6.** This table is perhaps a little crowded so you need to separate the rows with a blank row. Excel allows you to insert new rows and columns. To insert a row, click on Groceries to tell Excel where you want to insert the row (it is inserted above the row the cursor is in) and then on the Insert Menu (Figure 69) then on the Rows item. A new row will be inserted between Groceries and Newspapers.

**7.** Now add a row between Groceries and Stationery; and Stationery and Wages and finally, Wages and Total.

**8.** Insert the column of information in Figure 70 Extra Column.

**9.** Enter another heading 'Total Profit' in cell H6.

**10.** Save the spreadsheet you have created on to a floppy disk. This procedure is the same in all Windows applications - you save a spreadsheet, database or graphic image in exactly the same way.

insert a floppy disk into drive A:

click on the File menu item and a menu will open showing a list of options. Select Save and a window will open.

**11.** Click in the box File name and Enter A:\Acme Newsagent. Now click on the Save button on the right of the window. You have now saved the table as a file called Acme Newsagent. You may hear drive A: work during this process.

**12.** It is possible to save the spreadsheet again under a different file name so that you have two identical files but because they have different file names, they are treated as individual files.

**13.** You can close Excel now by either clicking on the File menu item and a menu will appear with a list of options. At the bottom of the list is the option Exit. If you click on Exit then Excel will close. An alternative way is to click on the close button in the top right-hand corner of the application window.

# New

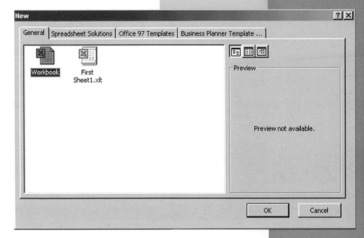

FIGURE 71
**New Window**

On occasions you will want to start a new spreadsheet once you have completed one. This is achieved by selecting the File menu and the New option. This opens the New window (Figure 71) which is divided into a number of sections that you access by clicking on the tabs on the top of the window. These provide access to many standard templates for spreadsheets. For the purpose of this chapter you should select the General tab and the Workbook icon. If you click on the Workbook icon it will be highlighted and can be selected by clicking on the OK button or by double clicking the Workbook icon. A new blank spreadsheet will appear.

# Delete, Clear and Hide

Excel provides you with three useful functions linked to deleting the contents of cells, rows and columns. These are:

Delete (Figure 72)

Clear (Figure 72)

Hide (Figure 79)

FIGURE 72
**Delete and Clear**

The first step in using the functions above is to identify the row, column, cell or area of the spreadsheet by highlighting or placing mouse pointer in the cell or row or column. The Edit menu provides access to Delete and Clear options. If Delete is selected, then a small Delete window appears providing different options for removing the item. Delete permanently removes the item and adjusts the spreadsheet layout.

If Clear is selected, then another menu of options appears (e.g. if All is chosen the contents of the selected area are removed but not the spreadsheet structure/layout).

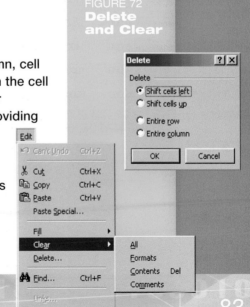

The difference between delete and clear is that delete removes the contents and the spreadsheet structure, while clear simply removes the contents. Clear also provides some extra options such as removing the formatting of an entry while leaving contents behind. You would probably use Clear to amend an area in the heart of a spreadsheet and Delete if you wanted to start again.

The Hide function is accessed by selecting the Format menu, then the options Row, Column or Sheet (Figure 79). Again you identify the area you want to hide by highlighting or placing mouse pointer in the particular row or column. By selecting Hide, that area of the spreadsheet will disappear. It can be returned by selecting the Unhide option. Hide does not delete the items. It only hides them from view, useful if you did not want to disclose confidential information.

# Spreadsheet Formulae

Figure 73 shows a spreadsheet of the costs and income of the Acme Newsagent. This spreadsheet employs a number of formulae to:

add up columns and rows of figures

calculate overheads

calculate the total profit of the business

FIGURE 73
**Acme Newsagent**

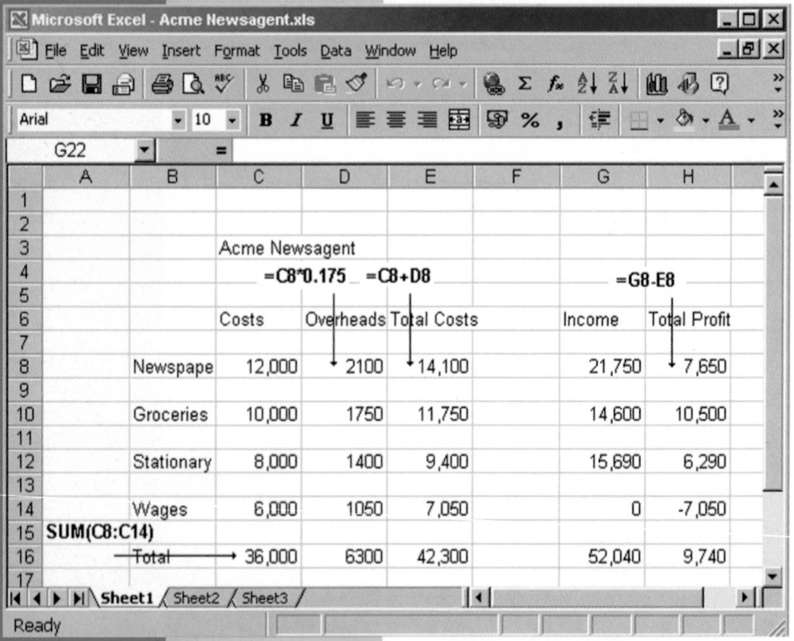

Fomulae are used by spreadsheets to calculate numerical values. They allow you to add up columns of figures to produce a total, subtract the contents of different cells, multiply, divide and undertake more complex calculations. One of the most important features of a spreadsheet is that you can build formulae within the sheet to calculate almost anything.

The mathematical operators used in Excel are:

| | |
|---|---|
| + | add |
| – | subtract |
| * | multiply |
| / | divide |

Brackets are also important in that they tell Excel to calculate anything in the brackets first before going on with the remaining parts of the calculation.

Formulas are based on giving each cell a unique reference (e.g. **A1**, **D12**, **M7** etc.). This is made up of the column letter and the row number.

## Example

**B8**       B Column and 8 Row

In Figure 73 you can see the column letters and row numbers. Cell **C8** (Column C and Row 8) contains the number 12,000. To calculate overheads (i.e. contents of **D8**) of the newspapers this number needs to be multiplied by 0.175 which represents the current rate of overheads (17.5 or 0.175). The formula is **C8**\*0.175 (i.e. contents of cell **C8** multiplied by overhead rate). By using a formula referring to the cell's unique address **C8** then each time the number placed in the cell changes the new value of overheads is automatically calculated.

## Example

**C8** = 12000   **D8** = 2100 (Overheads)
**C8** = 8000   **D8** = 1400 (Overheads)
**C8** = 4000   **D8** = 700 (Overheads)

It is possible to have formula based on the actual number so that our example overhead formula could be 12000 * 0.175. This would give the correct value but each time the cost of newspapers changed you would also need to change the formula.

Figure 73 shows four examples of formulas. These are:

**1. Cell D8**          = **C8**\*0.175
Overheads on groceries are the cost of the groceries (Cell **C10**) multiplied by 0.175 which produces 17.5% of the cost (the current rate of overheads). To avoid confusion with the letter x, spreadsheets use the symbol * as the multiplication sign.

**2. Cell E8**          =**C8**+**D8**
To produce the total cost of newspapers requires the cost of the papers (**C8**) to be added to the Overheads (**D8**)

**3. Cell H8**          =**G8**-**E8**
Total profit is income minus cost, so the profit on newspaper sales is the total income of the newspaper (cell **G8**) less their total cost (cell **E8**).

**4. Cell C16**         =SUM(**C8:C14**)
To total or add up a column or row of figures, the Microsoft Excel spreadsheet provides a standard formula called SUM. This formula means that all the contents of cells between **E8** to **E14** are added together (i.e **E8**+**E9**+**E10**+**E11**+**E12**+**E13**+**E14**)

These four examples show that a spreadsheet is able to add, subtract and multiply the contents of any cell or combination of cells.

It is also possible to divide the contents of any cell. If we want to know what the profit was likely to be in a quarter (three months) we could divide the total profit (cell **H16**) by 4 (**H16/4**). The use of brackets tells Excel to calculate anything inside them first. This is important since it changes the result.

### Example

**C8=5** and **D8=8**      C8+D8/2 = 9 but (**C8+D8**)/2 = 6.5

# Exercise 25

## Formulae

**1.** In the previous exercise you saved a file called Acme Newsagent and we are now going to load this file into Microsoft Excel.

**2.** Using either the <u>P</u>rograms menu or the Excel icon methods, load Microsoft Excel.

**3.** You can load a file by single clicking on the <u>F</u>ile menu item to open up the menu which has an option called <u>O</u>pen. Click on <u>O</u>pen and a window called Open will appear.

**4.** The Look <u>i</u>n box tells you which drive the window is looking at. You need to aim it at drive A: (Floppy (A:) ). You do this by clicking on the small button with the down arrow at the end of the Look <u>i</u>n box. A menu will appear. Click on the Floppy Disk option and the details of Acme Newsagent will appear in the main working area. To open the file, click on the file once to highlight it and then on the open button on the right-hand side of the window. An alternative way is to double click on the Acme Newsagent file. In either case the text of the file should now appear in the working area of Excel

FIGURE 74
**Standard Toolbar – SUM function**

Undo  Redo    SUM    Sort      Magnifier

**5.** The first step is to enter a formula to calculate the Overheads on the Costs. Overheads is 17.5% of the costs so if you multiply costs by 0.175 you will calculate the Overheads. Enter =C8*0.175 into cell D8. To enter the other Overheads amounts you can use a technique called replication. Highlight cell D8 by single clicking on the cell and clicking on the copy icon on the Standard Toolbar or the <u>E</u>dit menu and the <u>C</u>opy option. Now click on the cell you want to copy formulae to (e.g. D10) by highlighting the cell and clicking on paste on the Standard Toolbar or the <u>P</u>aste option in the <u>E</u>dit menu. The formula is copied into the new cell but will change to adapt to its new location so it will now read =C10*0.175. Paste the formula into D12 (=C12*0.175) and D14 (=C14*0.175).

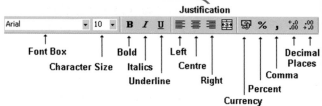

Justification: Font Box, Character Size, Italics, Bold, Underline, Left, Centre, Right, Percent, Currency, Comma, Decimal Places

**FIGURE 75**
**Format Toolbar**

**6.** The second step is to enter the formula to total Costs and Overheads. Excel provides a standard function called Sum, available on the Standard Toolbar (Figure 74). You highlight both cells C8 and D8 by clicking on C8 and holding down the left mouse button then dragging the pointer over D8 and E8 and releasing. The three cells should now be highlighted. By clicking on the Sum icon on the toolbar you will see the formula appear in E8 (=SUM(C8:D8)). Repeat this action for rows 10,12 and 14. This will produce formulae in E10 (=SUM(C10:D10)), E12 (=SUM(C12:D12)) and E14 (=SUM(C14:D14)).

**FIGURE 76**
**Format Cells Menu**

**7.** Now enter the formula to calculate Total profits. This is equal to Income minus Total Costs. In cell H8 enter =G8-E8 and then replicate the formula in H10, H12 and H14.

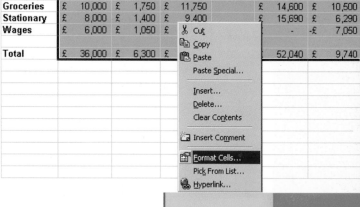

| | Costs | Overheads | Total Costs | | Income | Total Profit |
|---|---|---|---|---|---|---|
| Newspapers | £ 12,000 | £ 2,100 | £ 14,100 | | £ 21,750 | £ 7,650 |
| Groceries | £ 10,000 | £ 1,750 | £ 11,750 | | £ 14,600 | £ 10,500 |
| Stationary | £ 8,000 | £ 1,400 | £ 9,400 | | £ 15,690 | £ 6,290 |
| Wages | £ 6,000 | £ 1,050 | £ | | - | -£ 7,050 |
| Total | £ 36,000 | £ 6,300 | £ | | 52,040 | £ 9,740 |

(Menu: Cut, Copy, Paste, Paste Special..., Insert..., Delete..., Clear Contents, Insert Comment, Format Cells..., Pick From List..., Hyperlink...)

**8.** Now total each column using the Sum function (i.e. highlight C8 to C16 and click on the Sum function to enter the formula in cell C16 =SUM(C8:C14)).

**9.** Save the new file on your floppy disk as file A:/Acme Newsagent Formula. Select the File menu and the Save As option which will reveal the Save As window and you can save the file under a new name. If you select the Save option you will overwrite your original file. The Save As function allows you to save files under different names.

**10.** Close Microsoft Excel by selecting the File menu and the Exit option or click on the close button in the top right-hand corner of the application window.

**FIGURE 77**
**Format Cells Window**

## Presentation

Microsoft Excel provides the normal presentation functions that are available in many Microsoft Office applications. You can therefore change or select:

font (Figure 75)

character size (Figure 75)

embolden, italics and underline text (Figure 75)

justify text (Left, right and centre text – Figure 75)

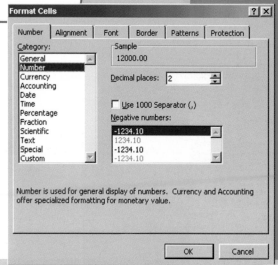

Format Cells dialog box — Number tab selected. Category: General, Number, Currency, Accounting, Date, Time, Percentage, Fraction, Scientific, Text, Special, Custom. Sample: 12000.00. Decimal places: 2. Use 1000 Separator (,). Negative numbers: -1234.10, 1234.10, -1234.10, -1234.10. Number is used for general display of numbers. Currency and Accounting offer specialized formatting for monetary value. OK / Cancel.

change the format of numerical data (Figure 75)

change the width and depth of row (Format menu – Figure 79)

These presentation functions work in a similar way to other Microsoft Office products. You can either select the option (e.g. font) before you enter text or numbers or change the option later. You change the formatting by highlighting the area that needs to be changed (e.g. cell, row or column) and then select the desired option.

Spreadsheets have extra formatting functions to allow numerical information to be presented in a variety of ways. These include (Figure 75):

**Currency** – to display numerical information with a £ sign in a currency format

**Percent –** to display data in percentage style

**Comma –** formats numbers with commas in appropriate places

**Decimal places –** increase and decrease the number of decimal points shown

An alternative approach to changing the formatting is to use a pop-up menu that appears if you right click on the item or highlighted area you want to change. This opens a menu
(Figure 76) with the option Format Cells which, if selected opens a window of format options (Figure 77). This allows you, among other functions, to change the format of numbers (i.e. decimal points, currency etc.) by selecting the Number tab or under the Font tab to select fonts, character size, embolden, italicise and underline. By selecting Format Cells, a window of options will appear.

FIGURE 77
**Format Cells Window**

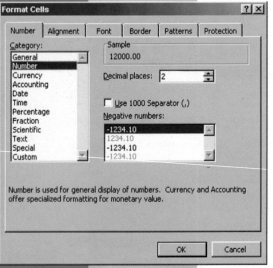

## Calculation

When you change some of the data in a spreadsheet it will recalculate other values that are dependent upon the item. This may be carried out automatically so it can be confusing if you are unaware that it has happened.

The calculation takes account of the true value of the item not simply what is displayed. If the display has removed or limited the number of decimal places then the values displayed will reflect the formatting. However, the calculation will be based on actual value with all decimal places. The example below shows that this can be confusing faced with a spreadsheet calculation that adds 20 to 34 to produce 55. This looks wrong if you have forgotten that actual values are 20.2 and 34.4 and that by selecting no decimal places you round up the result (i.e. 54.6 becomes 55 when rounded up).

Example

Actual Value

20.2 plus 34.4 = 54.6

Excel Spreadsheet format without any decimal places

20 plus 34 = 55 (the decimal value is rounded up to the next whole number)

# Exercise 26

## Formatting

**1.** In the previous exercise you saved a file called Acme Newsagent Formula and we are now going to load this file into Microsoft Excel.

**2.** Using either the Programs menu or the Excel icon methods load Microsoft Excel.

**3.** You can load a file by single clicking on the File menu item to open up the menu which has an option called Open. Click on Open and a window called Open will appear.
**4.** The Look in box tells you what drive the window is looking at. You need to aim it at drive A: (Floppy (A:) ). You do this by clicking on the small button with the down arrow at the end of the Look in box and a menu will appear. Click on the Floppy Disk option and the details of Acme Newsagent Formula will appear in the main working area. To open the file, click on the file once to highlight it and then on the open button on the right-hand side of the window. An alternative way is to double click on the Acme Newsagent Formula file. In either case the text of the file should now appear in the working area of Excel.

FIGURE 79
**Format Menu – Change Width of Column**

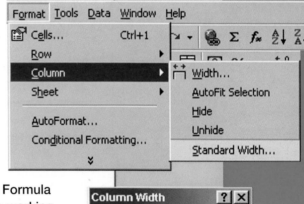

**5.** The title of the spreadsheet is not prominent. Enhance Acme Newsagents by selecting a new font and a new character size. Highlight the title then click on the arrow button on the font box (Format toolbar) and a list of fonts will appear. You select one by single clicking on the item. Explore the fonts until you find one that you like. Now select the character size by using the down arrow next to the size box (the title must still be highlighted). Another list will appear from which you can choose a size. Pick a size that emphasises the importance of the title.

**6.** The headings of the rows and columns need to be emboldened. Highlight the row and column and click on the Bold icon on toolbar. Now centre the row headings by highlighting them and selecting the centre justification icon.

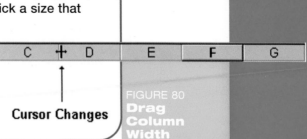

**Cursor Changes**

FIGURE 80
**Drag Column Width**

**7.** Some of the headings are too wide for their columns. The columns can be adjusted by placing the mouse pointer over the row or column headings edge on the line that divides the row or column. The mouse pointer will change shape (Figure 80) and if you hold down the left mouse button you can drag the column wider or narrower. The same is true of adjusting the height of the rows. An alternative approach is to use the Format menu (Figure 79). Select Row or Column and Height or Width respectively.

**8.** Adjust the column widths so that the headings fit their columns better (e.g. Newspapers, Total Costs and Total Profit).

**9.** It is important in a spreadsheet to be able to format the numerical data. In Acme Newsagents we are dealing with money so the data should be formatted as currency. This is achieved by highlighting the data and clicking on the Currency icon on the toolbar. Observe the change – a pounds (£) sign will be added and two decimal points added to show pence.

**10.** This spreadsheet does not have data which include pence so we could remove the decimal points. Highlight the numerical data and click on the decrease decimal point icon (Format Toolbar – Figure 75). Click twice on the icon to remove the two points. Experiment with adding decimal points using the Increase Decimal icon, but finish with a display without decimal points (i.e. no pence).

**11.** Save the new file on your floppy disk as file A:/Acme Newsagent Presentation. Select the File menu and the Save As option which will reveal the Save As window and you can save the file under a new name. If you select the Save option you will overwrite your original file. The Save As function allows you to save files under different names.

**12.** Close Microsoft Excel by selecting the File menu and the Exit option or click on the close button in the top right-hand corner of the application window.

## Printing

It is important to be able to print out a sheet or workbook. Microsoft Excel offers a range of functions linked to printing. These include previewing your sheet as a printed document without wasting any paper. Within the File Menu, Print Preview opens up the window showing in Figure 81. This lets you check if the printed sheet is presented in the way that you want it to be. When you have completed the preview, click on the Close button to return to Excel. If you want to print the spreadsheet immediately there is a Print button to link you to the Print window (Figure 82).

The default is to print in portrait mode, that is, with the narrow edge of the paper at the top so that when you preview your sheet you may discover that

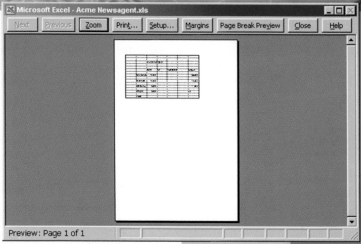

it flows over two pages. If you would prefer it to be presented on a single page, you need to change the default to landscape (i.e. the long edge across the top). This can be carried out from the Print Preview window by selecting the Setup button which opens the Page Setup window. Select Landscape by clicking in the radio button near the Landscape label and then clicking on the OK button to confirm the change. When you print now it will be in landscape mode.

When you are ready to print then click on the File menu and the Print option. The window shown in Figure 82 appears. You are presented with a number of options which people initially often find puzzling.

**FIGURE 81**
**Print Preview**

1. You must first select the printer on which your document is to be printed. This is shown in the Printer area at the top of the window in the box entitled Name. Microsoft Windows operating system allows you to link many different printers to a single stand-alone computer whilst a computer network may provide access to many printers. The list of printers is shown when you click on the down arrow next to the Name box. Select your printer by clicking on it. The printer shown is the default printer and you should normally use that one.

2. You need to decide how much of the document you want to print
(Print range). The choices are:

All – whole document

Pages – you enter the page range you want to print
(e.g. 23-34)

The default setting is All.

**FIGURE 82**
**Printing**

**FIGURE 83**
**Printing Gridlines**

3. You can select what to print (Print what). The choices are:

Selection (an area of the sheet)

Active sheet(s) (whole sheet)

Entire workbook (multiple related sheets)

The default is Active sheet(s).

4. You can select how many copies to print (Copies).

When you ready click on OK button to start the printer. If you change none of the settings, the default ones will be used.

When printing a spreadsheet. It is important to decide whether you want to include the gridlines or not. This has to be set in the Page Setup option of the File menu within the Sheet tab (Figure 83). The box next to the Gridlines item must be clicked in, which will put a tick in the box. Gridlines will be inserted in the spreadsheet printout.

Another important option is to print the sheet showing the formulae. This can be achieved by selecting the Tools menu and the Options item. This opens the Options window. Click on the View tab (Figure 84) and look for the Windows option section and the Formulas box. You need to click in this box. A tick will appear and then you can click on the OK button to confirm the change. When you are looking at the Options window notice that there is an option for Gridlines. This is an alternative way of selecting printing with gridlines and should be used if you want to select both gridlines and formulae. To return to printing with the actual numbers you will have to repeat this operation and click once more in the Formulas box. This will remove the tick. Confirm the change by clicking on the OK button.

When you choose to print the formulae, your spreadsheet format will change to accommodate their different lengths. It will change back when you de-select this option.

As part of your assessment you will need to be able to print a spreadsheet showing the formulae.

FIGURE 84
**Options**

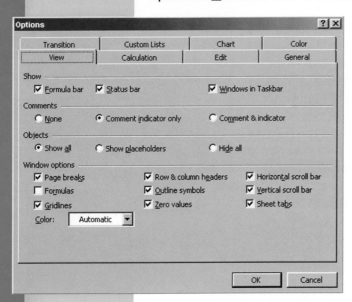

# Exercise 27

## More Practice 1

**1.** Load Microsoft Excel using either the Programs menu or the Excel icon on the desktop.

**2.** Enter the table of information below to form a spreadsheet with 2 decimal places. It shows a production plan of an engineering company called Tames Engineering.

| | Volume | Cost | Price | Potential Profit |
|---|---|---|---|---|
| Nuts | 6,000,000 | 0.03 | 0.04 | (Price minus Cost) x Volume |
| Bolts | 2,300,000 | 0.07 | 0.09 | (Price minus Cost) x Volume |
| Bar | 560,000 | 3.45 | 4.95 | (Price minus Cost) x Volume |
| Sheet | 76,000 | 12.87 | 15.32 | (Price minus Cost) x Volume |
| Plate | 17,000 | 36.80 | 39.50 | (Price minus Cost) x Volume |

Total

**3.** Insert formulae to calculate potential profit, total Volume and Potential Profit columns (remember to replicate your formulae). You need to check if your formulae are correct. Once they are, you can change your numerical data many times with the confidence that the calculations will be accurate. When you have inserted all the formulae calculate the total potential profit.

**4.** Improve the appearance of the sheet by:

**Adding a title –** Tame Engineering in Tahoma, size 14 and bold

**Centring all the column heading** and changing their font size to 14 and making them bold

**Changing the column widths** of Volume and Potential Profits so that they fit

**Embolden all the row headings** and change their fonts to 14 and make them bold

**5.** Change the format of Columns Cost, Price and Potential Profit to currency.

**6.** Reduce decimal places in Potential Profit column to nil.

**7.** Print your spreadsheet, showing gridlines and both formula and actual values.

**8.** Investigate the effect on Potential Profit if you reduce prices to: 0.035, 0.08, 4.70, 14.85 and 38.50 respectively. This is a key advantage of spreadsheets in that it allows you to model what will happen if you made changes to increase output, increased prices or if costs changed.

**9.** Print your spreadsheet showing gridlines and actual values.

**10.** Investigate what happens to the spreadsheet if you set the cost column to show only one decimal place. What you should observe is that the cost of nuts appears to be 0.0 while the profit remains the same. This is because the formula operate on the real value not on what is presented. Change the cost column back to two decimal places.

**11.** Figure 85 shows the layout of the Tames Engineering

FIGURE 85
**Tames Engineering**

| | | Volume | Cost | Price | Potential Profit |
|---|---|---|---|---|---|
| Tames Engineering | | | | | |
| **Nuts** | | 6,000,000 | £ 0.03 | £ 0.04 | £ 30,000 |
| **Bolts** | | 2,300,000 | £ 0.07 | £ 0.08 | £ 23,000 |
| **Bar** | | 560,000 | £ 3.45 | £ 4.70 | £ 700,000 |
| **Sheet** | | 76,000 | £ 12.87 | £ 14.85 | £ 150,480 |
| **Plate** | | 17,000 | £ 36.80 | £ 38.50 | £ 28,900 |
| **Total** | | 8,953,000 | | | £ 932,380 |

**12.** Save the spreadsheet you have created on to a floppy disk. This procedure is the same in all Windows applications. You save a spreadsheet, database or graphic image in exactly the same way.

insert a floppy disk into drive A:

click on the File menu item and a menu will open showing a list of options. Select Save and a window will open.

**13.** Click in the box File name and Enter A:\Tames Engineering. Now click on Save button on the right of the window. You have now saved your spreadsheet as a file called Tames Engineering. You may hear drive A: work during this process.

**14.** You can close Excel now by clicking on the File menu item and a menu will appear with a list of options. At the bottom of the list is the option Exit. If you click on Exit then Excel will close. An alternative way is to click on the close button in the top right-hand corner of the application window.

# Exercise 28

## More Practice 2

**1.** Load Microsoft Excel using either the Programs menu or the Excel icon on the desktop.

**2.** Enter the table of information below to form a spreadsheet with 2 decimal places. It shows the sales forecast of a printer, Jones Printing.

|  | April | May | June | Total | Price | Cash Flow |
|---|---|---|---|---|---|---|
| Books | 6,000 | 7,500 | 5,600 | | 1.84 | (Total multiplied by Price ) |
| Journals | 11,000 | 9,890 | 7,600 | | 0.37 | (Total multiplied by Price ) |
| Stationery | 4,300 | 7,600 | 5,500 | | 0.11 | (Total multiplied by Price ) |
| Catologues | 5,600 | 2,300 | 4,500 | | 0.45 | (Total multiplied by Price ) |
| Total | | | | | | |

FIGURE 86A
**Jones Printing**

### Jones Printing

|  | April | May | June | Total | Price | Cash Flow |
|---|---|---|---|---|---|---|
| **Books** | 6,000 | 7,500 | 6,000 | 19,500 | £ 1.84 | £ 35,880.00 |
| **Journals** | 11,000 | 9,890 | 8,000 | 28,890 | £ 0.37 | £ 10,689.30 |
| **Stationery** | 4,300 | 7,600 | 6,000 | 17,900 | £ 0.11 | £ 1,969.00 |
| **Catalogues** | 5,600 | 2,300 | 5,000 | 12,900 | £ 0.45 | £ 5,805.00 |
| **Total** | 26,900 | 27,290 | 25,000 | 79,190 | | £ 54,343.30 |

**3.** Insert formulae in Total (April+May+June) and Cash Flow (Total multiplied by Price) rows as well as totals for April, May, June, Total and Cash Flow columns (remember to replicate your formulae). You need to check that your formula are correct. Once they are, you can change your numerical data many times with the confidence that the calculations will be accurate.

**4.** Improve the appearance of the sheet by:

**Adding a title –** Jones Printing in Arial, size 16 and bold

**Changing all the column heading** to Centred Times New Roman. Change their font size to 14 and make them bold

**Emboldening all the row headings** and change their fonts to Times New Roman, character size14

**Changing the column width of Cash Flow** and the row headings so that they fit

**5.** Change the format of Columns Price and Cash Flow to currency.

**6.** Print your spreadsheet showing gridlines and both formulae and actual values.

**7.** Investigate the effect on Cash Flow of increasing volumes during June to 6,000, 8,000, 6,000 and 5,000 respectively. This is a key advantage of spreadsheets in that they allow you to model what would happen if you make changes.

FIGURE 85B
**Jones Printing – Grids and Formulas**

| Jones Printing | | | | | | |
|---|---|---|---|---|---|---|
| | **April** | **May** | **June** | **Total** | **Price** | **Cash Flow** |
| **Books** | 6000 | 7500 | 5600 | =SUM(C8:E8) | 1.84 | =F8*G8 |
| **Journals** | 11000 | 9890 | 7600 | =SUM(C9:E9) | 0.37 | =F9*G9 |
| **Stationery** | 4300 | 7600 | 5500 | =SUM(C10:E10) | 0.11 | =F10*G10 |
| **Catalogues** | 5600 | 2300 | 4500 | =SUM(C11:E11) | 0.45 | =F11*G11 |
| **Total** | =SUM(C8:C12) | =SUM(D8:D12) | =SUM(E8:E12) | =SUM(F8:F12) | | =SUM(H8:H12) |

**8.** Print your spreadsheet showing gridlines and actual values.

**9.** Figure 86A shows the layout of Jones Printing, while Figure 86B shows the layout with formulas.

**10.** Save the spreadsheet you have created on to a floppy disk. This procedure is the same in all Windows applications. You save a spreadsheet, database or graphic image in exactly the same way.

**insert a floppy** disk into drive A:

**click on the File menu** item and a menu will open showing a list of options. Select Save and a window will open.

**11.** Click in the box File name and Enter A:\Jones Printing. Now click on the Save button on the right of the window. You have now saved your spreadsheet as a file called Jones Printing. You may hear drive A: work during this process.

**12.** You can close Excel now by clicking on File menu item and a menu will appear with a list of options. At the bottom of the list is the option Exit. If you click on Exit then Excel will close. An alternative way is to click on the close button in the top right-hand corner of the application window.

# Summary

**1. Load Microsoft Excel** Load Microsoft Excel by selecting the Start button, highlighting the Programs menu and clicking on the Microsoft Excel item or click on the Excel icon on the desktop

**2. Close spreadsheet** Select the File menu item and the Exit option or click on the close button in the top right-hand corner of the application window

**3. New** Select the File menu and the New option. This opens a New window. Select General tab, the Workbook icon and the OK button

**4. Enter text or numerical data** Click on the chosen cell and enter text or numbers from the keyboard

**5. Delete, Close and Hide** Select the Edit menu and either the Delete or Clear options. Each will provide you with a range of choices

Select the Format menu, one of the options Row, Column or Sheet and the Hide option. The Unhide option is also available.

**6. Cell references** Each cell has a unique reference which is made up of the column letters and row number (e.g. A7, P16 and F12).

**7. Enter formulae** Fomulas are used to calculate numerical values (e.g. total columns of figures).

Formulae start with = sign (e.g. = F5-F9)

Mathematical Operators
+    add
-    subtract
*    multiply
/    divide

Standard formula (SUM) adds together the contents of a highlighted row or column of numbers (e.g. C3:C6 =C3+C4+C5+C6)

Brackets – operations inside brackets are carried out first

**8. Change Presentation** Highlight the item and select the font, character size, embolden, italics, underline text and justify text icons from the Format Toolbar

Numerical formatting is again based on highlighting the item or area and then selecting the icon from the Format Toolbar:

**Currency** – to display numerical information with a £ sign in a currency format
**Per cent** – to display data in percentage style

**Comma** – formats numbers with commas in appropriate places

**Decimal points** – Increase and decrease the number of decimal points shown

## Change the width and depth of row

Place the mouse pointer over the row or column heading edge until the pointer changes shape. Hold down the left mouse button and drag the edge to widen or narrow the row or column

## Alternative

Right click on the chosen item or highlighted area to reveal a pop-up menu. Select the Format Cells option to open a Format Cells window

## 9. Preview printing Select the File Menu and the Print Preview option

## 10. Printing **Either** Select the Print button within Print Preview window
**Or** Select the File menu, the Print option and the OK button

## 11. Print Gridlines and Formulae **Either** Select the File menu, the Page Setup option, the Sheet tab, click in the Gridlines box and the OK button **Or** Select the Tools menu, the Options item, the View tab, click in the Gridlines box and the OK button

Formulae Select the Tools menu, the Options item, the View tab, click in the Formulas box and the OK button

# Databases

This chapter will help you to use a database to:

identify and use database software correctly

use an input device to enter and edit data accurately

create simple queries/searches on one or two criteria

present selected data sorted alphabetically and numerically

manage and print database files

## Assessment

This unit does not assume any previous experience of databases. However, you may find it useful if you have previously undertaken Unit 1 (Using a Computer). After studying Unit 5 your skills and understanding are assessed during a 2-hour practical assignment. This is set by OCR and marked locally. However, the marking will be externally moderated by OCR. This ensures that the standard is being applied correctly across the many different providers of OCR New CLAIT.

## New CLAIT Syllabus

New CLAIT does not require you to create a database table only to add and edit its contents and query them. This chapter offers you the opportunity to create small straightforward databases and then to practice adding and editing their contents. This is useful if you are planning to extend your studies to CLAIT Plus, which does require students to develop a database, or if you are studying on your own without any access to a database to practice with.

FIGURE 87
**Microsoft Access**

If you do not want to create a database (i.e. undertake the extra tasks) then the databases are available from the supporting website (www.hodderclait.co.uk) and you are free to download them. We suggest that you download and save them onto a floppy disk.

Exercises which are not part of the New CLAIT requirements are marked as OPTIONAL.

## Database applications

Microsoft Access is a database creation application. You can use it to design your own databases. These can be for your own personal use (e.g. records of your video collection) or for

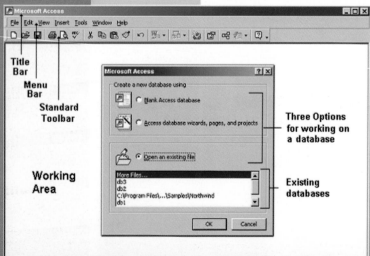

Title Bar
Menu Bar
Standard Toolbar
Working Area

Three Options for working on a database

Existing databases

a multi-national enterprise (e.g. customer information). In this chapter you will learn how to create a table of information in which information can be entered, stored and presented. A database can have one or many tables depending on the complexity of the system. In our exercises, we will concentrate on a single table which is the basic building block of more extensive databases.

Figure 87 shows the opening display of Microsoft Access. This consists of two windows. The overlayed window offers you the options to:

start creating a new blank database

access a Wizard

open an existing database

The application window resembles other Office applications in that it is divided into:

menu and toolbars at the top of the display

a working area in which to develop the database

status bar at the bottom of the window

# Spreadsheets versus databases

Both spreadsheets and databases create tables of information and so appear to be very similar. However, there are considerable differences between them. A database can be designed so that:

**Data** can be continuously changed in an efficient and effective way without the operator needing to know about the structure of the database

**Information** held in the database can be presented in many different ways to meet a wide range of needs

**Information** held in a database can be searched to locate any combination of data that it contains and the results of the search can be presented in a wide variety of ways

Microsoft Access provides:

**Forms** – these offer different ways of entering, editing and viewing information

**Queries** – these allow you to answer any questions you may have about the information contained in the database

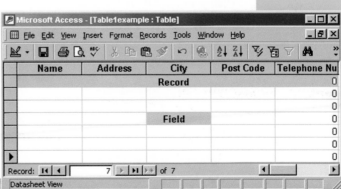
FIGURE 88
**Table**

**Reports** – these allow you to present information combining data from several tables

## Tables

The key feature of a database is a table. Figure 88 shows an Access table. Tables are groups of records. A record is a group of related fields, a field being a single item of the record, e.g. name, address, city, post code and telephone number.

In Access there are many different types of field. These include: text, number, yes/no (i.e. can only contain a yes or a no), memo (i.e. a longer piece of text), date/time, currency (i.e. money), autonumber (i.e. automatically numbers the records in a table) and hyperlink (i.e. links to a website). The number fields can be used as part of your calculations.

When you are creating a database table, you need to define the type of each field within the records. In Figure 88 name, address, city and post code are all text fields whereas telephone number is a number field.

## Creating a new database - optional

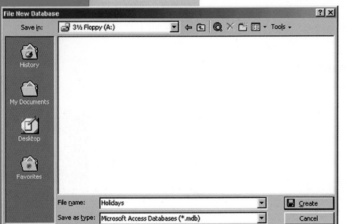

FIGURE 89
**File New
Database**

The first step in creating a database is to consider the information you may want it to contain. The example below shows the information that you might want to include in a staff holiday record table.

### Example

**Name** - individual's name (i.e. text field)
**Team** - which team the individual works in (i.e. text field)
**Staff Number** - pay number (i.e. number field)
**Holiday** - number of days holiday entitlement (i.e. number field)
**Taken** - number of days taken (i.e. number field)

| Name | Team | Staff Number | Holiday | Taken |
|------|------|--------------|---------|-------|
| Singh | Personnel | 23 | 25 | 12 |
| Brown | Computers | 35 | 30 | 15 |
| Jones | Production | 41 | 25 | 10 |
| Carr | Sales | 44 | 35 | 25 |
| Patel | Computers | 17 | 25 | 18 |
| Scott | Personnel | 14 | 30 | 20 |
| Jenks | Production | 51 | 30 | 14 |

This table of information consists of seven records with each record composed of five fields.

## Optional
# Exercise 29

## Creating a database table

**1.** Load Microsoft Access by selecting Start, highlighting the Programs menu and clicking on the Microsoft Access item or click on the Access icon on the desktop.

**2.** Microsoft Access application will load (Figure 87). Select Blank Access database by clicking in the radio button. The File New Database window opens to enable you to save your new database.

You need to select a drive or folder in which to store your new database as a file. If you click on the arrow button next to the Save in box you can select floppy disk.

Next you need to give the file a name. Insert the name Holidays in the File Name box and click on the Create button (Figure 89). You will have saved your blank database as a file called Holidays on your floppy disk. The Holidays Database window is now shown (Figure 90).

**3.** The Holidays Database window shows three options with the Tables object on the left-hand side selected:

create a table in Design view

create a table by using wizard

create a table by entering data

Double click on Create a table in Design view and the table window opens (Figure 91)

**4.** You need to insert your field names and their types. If you enter name in Field Name box and click in the corresponding Data Type box, a small down arrow will appear revealing a list of types. Select text and click in the next Field Name box then enter Team. Complete the table, as shown in Figure 91.

**5.** When you enter a type, you should observe that in field size a value (e.g. 50) will appear with a text type and Long Integer with a number type. The value 50 indicates the number of characters that the field

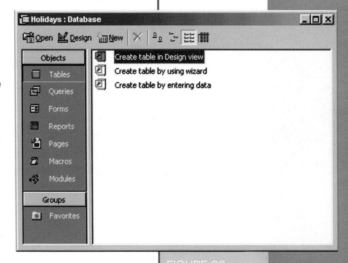

FIGURE 90
**Holidays Database Window**

FIGURE 91
**Table Window**

can store while a Long Integer is a whole number (i.e. no decimal places). If you wanted to show real numbers (i.e. with decimal places) then you would need to click in the Long Integer box to produce a down arrow which if clicked, gives you other options. In this case all our numbers are whole.

**6.** You need to save your table. If you select the File menu and the Save As option, the Save As window appears. Enter Records and click on the OK button.

**7.** A warning message will now appear asking you if you need a primary key. In this case you do not need to define one so click on the No button. A primary key is a unique number which allows different tables to relate to each other. The table window reappears and you should close it by clicking on the close button in the top right hand corner of the table window. You can now see the Holidays Database window (Figure 92) but with an extra item now added – Records.

**8.** Double click on Records allows you to begin entering the data. We will return to this table to enter the data later. Close the window by clicking on the close button in the top right hand corner of the Holidays Database window.

**9.** Close Access by clicking on close button in top right-hand corner of the main application window or select the File and the Exit option. Unless you wish to immediately carry on with the next exercise.

# Exercise 30

The database Holidays is available on the supporting website (www.hodderclait.co.uk) if you would like to undertake this exercise without completing Exercise 29 (i.e. creating a database table)

## Entering data

FIGURE 92
**Records Table**

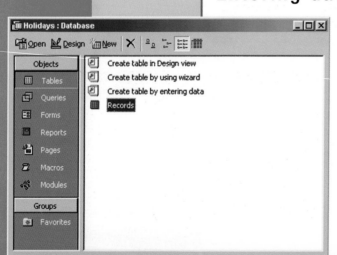

**1.** Insert your floppy disk into your drive. Load Microsoft Access by selecting Start, highlighting the Programs menu and clicking on the Microsoft Access item or click on the Access icon on the desktop.

**2.** Microsoft Access application will load (Figure 87). At the bottom of the overlaid window is a list of the databases available and you should see A:\ Holidays in the list (this assumes you have saved the file on a floppy disk). Double click this item and the Holidays Database window will be displayed (Figure 92).

**3.** Double click on Records and a blank table will

**Records : Table**

| Name | | Team | Staff Number | Holiday | | Taken |
|------|---|------|--------------|---------|---|-------|
| Singh | | Personnel | 23 | 25 | | 12 |
| Brown | | Computers | 35 | 30 | | 15 |
| Jones | **Arrow** | Production | 41 | 25 | **Cross** | 10 |
| Carr | | Sales | 44 | 35 | **Arrows** | 25 |
| Patel | | Computers | 17 | 25 | | 18 |
| Scott | | Personnel | 14 | 30 | | 20 |
| Jenks | | Production | 51 | 30 | | 14 |
| * | | | 0 | 0 | | 0 |

appear (Figure 93). Complete the records, moving between the fields by clicking in each box. Alternatively use the arrow keys, tab key or press the enter key to move between fields.

**4.** When you have completed the table check each entry against the original data. It is vital that database information is correct since you will use this data later and often base decisions on it. If you find an error, click into the field box to move the cursor into the box, and delete the mistake and insert the correct entry.

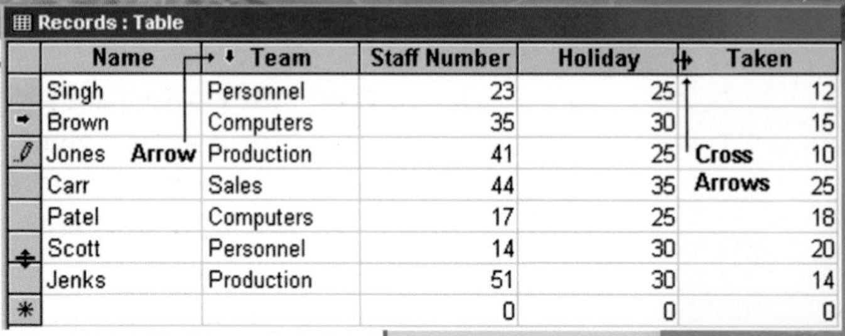

**5.** If you move your mouse pointer across the table row or column heading you will see it change shape into an arrow (pointing to the right in the row heading and down in the column heading). If the pointer goes over the edge of the heading it changes into cross arrows. By holding down the left mouse button you can drag the columns wider or row higher (Figure 93) when the arrows pointer is shaped as cross arrows.

The down or right pointing single arrow will select (highlight) the row or column if clicked.

**6.** You now need to save the completed table. This is straightforward since it is saved automatically by closing the window. Click on the close button in the top right-hand corner of the window.

**7.** Close Access by selecting the File menu and the Exit option.

FIGURE 93
**Change Row and Columns**

FIGURE 94
**Amending Tables**

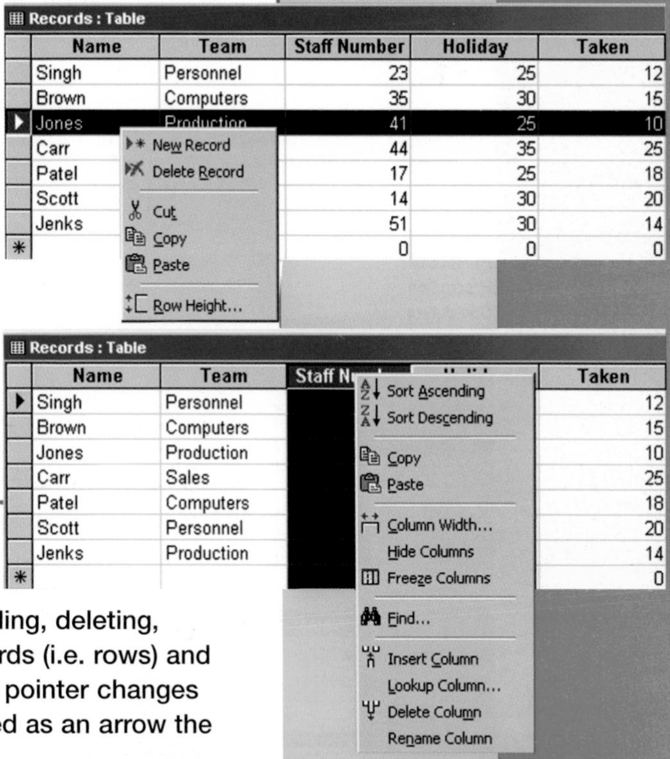

**Records : Table**

| Name | Team | Staff Number | Holiday | Taken |
|------|------|--------------|---------|-------|
| Singh | Personnel | 23 | 25 | 12 |
| Brown | Computers | 35 | 30 | 15 |
| Jones | Production | 41 | 25 | 10 |
| Carr | 44 | 35 | | 25 |
| Patel | 17 | 25 | | 18 |
| Scott | 14 | 30 | | 20 |
| Jenks | 51 | 30 | | 14 |
| * | 0 | 0 | | 0 |

(context menu)
- New Record
- Delete Record
- Cut
- Copy
- Paste
- Row Height...

**Records : Table**

| Name | Team | Staff N | | | Taken |
|------|------|---------|---|---|-------|
| Singh | Personnel | | | | 12 |
| Brown | Computers | | | | 15 |
| Jones | Production | | | | 10 |
| Carr | Sales | | | | 25 |
| Patel | Computers | | | | 18 |
| Scott | Personnel | | | | 20 |
| Jenks | Production | | | | 14 |
| * | | | | | 0 |

(context menu)
- Sort Ascending
- Sort Descending
- Copy
- Paste
- Column Width...
- Hide Columns
- Freeze Columns
- Find...
- Insert Column
- Lookup Column...
- Delete Column
- Rename Column

## Editing data

Microsoft Access has several tools to assist you with adding, deleting, amending and inserting records. You can insert new records (i.e. rows) and fields (i.e. columns). Figure 93 shows you how the mouse pointer changes shape into a arrow. If you left click with the pointer shaped as an arrow the row or column is highlighted. By then clicking the right mouse button, a menu appears. Figure 94 illustrates the menus for both the rows and columns. For OCR New CLAIT requires that you are able to delete a record (i.e. a row or a column).

To alter a single field you need to click into the field and delete the entry before entering the new content. If you have a large database and a number of changes to make then it is more efficient to use the Search and Replace functions in Access rather than change each one

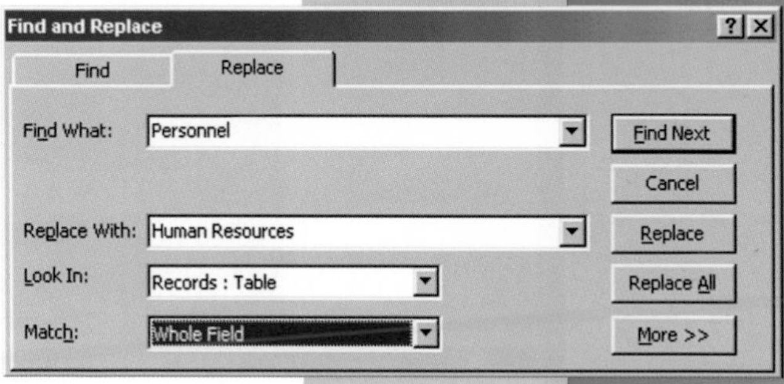

**Find and Replace** [?] [X]

| Find | Replace |
|------|---------|

Find What: Personnel
Replace With: Human Resources
Look In: Records : Table
Match: Whole Field

- Find Next
- Cancel
- Replace
- Replace All
- More >>

FIGURE 95
**Find and Replace**

separately. In the example we have been working on you might want to change a team's name (e.g. from Personnel to Human Resources). You could do this by going through all the records and manually changing them one by one. This is both time consuming and also likely to produce errors. The more efficient way is to use Search and Replace tool that is available on the Edit menu under the Replace option. If you select this option the Find and Replace window is revealed as shown in Figure 95.

# Exercise 31

## Editing data

**1.** Insert your floppy disk into your drive. Load Microsoft Access by selecting Start, highlighting the Programs menu and clicking on the Microsoft Access item or click on the Access icon on the desktop.

FIGURE 96
**Amended Table**

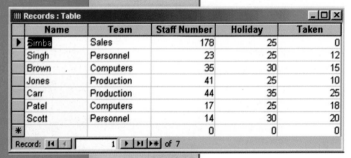

**2.** Microsoft Access application will load (Figure 87). At the bottom of the overlaid window is a list of the databases available and you should see A:\ Holidays in the list. Double click this item and the Holidays Database window will be displayed (Figure 92).

**3.** Double click on Records and the Holiday table will appear.

**4.** The records need to be amended.

FIGURE 97
**Print Preview Window**

Carr has been transferred to Production so change the team field by clicking in the field. Delete Sales using the delete keys and enter Production.

Printer

Jenks has left the company so the record needs to be deleted. Position the mouse pointer over the row heading and when the pointer has changed into an arrow, click on the right mouse button. The menu (Figure 94) will appear. By clicking on Delete Record you will remove the Jenks record. You may see a message appear asking if you are certain that you want to delete a record. Click on Yes to remove the record.

A new person has joined the company so you need to insert a record for Simba. The record is:

Simba, Sales, 178, 25, 0

If you click in the bottom empty line of the table in the Name field you can begin to enter the new record. You move between fields by clicking or pressing the tab or enter keys.

**5.** When you have finished entering the new record and amending the others, carefully check the table. It is vital that databases contain no errors or all the information you extract from it will be flawed. Figure 96 shows you the final table.

**6.** You now need to save your changes. Close the table by clicking on the close button in the top right hand corner of the table window. Your changes will be saved automatically.

**7.** Close Access by selecting the File menu and the Exit option.

# Printing

An important aspect of all computer applications is the ability to print information. Access provides you with the functionality to print a table. This is available from the File menu and the Print option, which reveals the Print window and you can print using the default settings by clicking on the OK button.

Print Preview allows you to check the appearance of the printed document before you print it. Figure 97 shows the Print Preview Window of the Holiday table. If you are content with the appearance you can print it immediately by clicking on the printer icon and then on the OK button on the Print window which will then appear.

# Sorting, querying and searching

With a database, you can store a large amount of information and access it in anyway that you need to. Microsoft Access provides you with functions that allow you to sort, query (i.e. question) and search the information.

Sorting lets you reorder the information and present it in a new sequence. You can sort the records into alphabetical, numerical or date order. This is useful if you wanted a list of the holidays information presented in the order of Staff Number, alphabetically by the name of the employee or date of starting work. You can sort both ascending or descending.

## Example

A, B, C and D – ascending or D, C, B and A - descending
**or**
1, 2, 3 and 4 – ascending or 4, 3, 2 and 1 – descending

Searching is the term used for finding a particular piece of information within the database. By selecting the Edit menu and the Find Option, you reveal the Find and Replace window which enables you to search the table for a particular field of information. This would be useful if you wanted to find those employees who had not taken any holiday, those who had 25 days holiday entitlement or, indeed, any other item of information.

By using the Access functions, you can sort or search the database at any time but in each case you need to enter your requirements. These are useful for individual questions that you are unlikely to want to repeat. However, Access also provides a way of saving useful searches or sorts by using a Query.

# Exercise 32

## Simple sorting (alphabetically and numerically)

**1.** Insert your floppy disk into your drive. Load Microsoft Access by selecting Start, highlighting the Programs menu and clicking on the Microsoft Access item or click on the Access icon on the desktop.

**2.** Microsoft Access application will load (Figure 87). At the bottom of the overlaid window is a list of the databases available and you should see A:\ Holidays in the list. Double click this item and the Holidays Database window will be displayed (Figure 92).

**3.** Double click on Records and the Holiday table will appear.

FIGURE 98
**Simple Sorting**

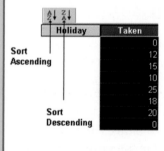

FIGURE 99
**Ascend and Descend**

**4.** Highlight the Taken column by placing your mouse pointer over the column heading until the mouse pointer has changed to an arrow. Click on the left mouse button and the column will be highlighted.

**5.** With the column highlighted, you can sort the information using the Ascending and Descending icons on the toolbar (Figure 98).

**6.** Explore sorting this table using these icons and print each option (e.g. numercial ascending and descending). Select the Edit Menu, the Print option and the OK button. Figure 99 shows both options.

**7.** Experiment with alphabetical sorting using the Name column and again print each option.

**8.** Compare your printouts.

**9.** Close the table by clicking on the close button

| Name | Team | Staff Number | Holiday | Taken |
|---|---|---|---|---|
| Carr | Production | 44 | 35 | 25 |
| Scott | Personnel | 14 | 30 | 20 |
| Patel | Computers | 17 | 25 | 18 |
| Brown | Computers | 35 | 30 | 15 |
| Singh | Personnel | 23 | 25 | 12 |
| Jones | Production | 41 | 25 | 10 |
| Simba | Sales | 178 | 25 | 0 |
| * | | 0 | 0 | 0 |

| Name | Team | Staff Number | Holiday | Taken |
|---|---|---|---|---|
| Simba | Sales | 178 | 25 | 0 |
| Jones | Production | 41 | 25 | 10 |
| Singh | Personnel | 23 | 25 | 12 |
| Brown | Computers | 35 | 30 | 15 |
| Patel | Computers | 17 | 25 | 18 |
| Scott | Personnel | 14 | 30 | 20 |
| Carr | Production | 44 | 35 | 25 |
| * | | 0 | 0 | 0 |

in the top right hand corner of the table window. You will be asked if you want to save the changes you have made (i.e. save the new format of your table). In this case click on the No button so that the original layout of the table is preserved.

**10.** Close Access by selecting the File menu and the Exit option unless you wish to continue with the next exercise in which case close the records window in the work area and go to paragraph 3 of the next exercise.

## Creating a Query

# Exercise 33

## Create a query

**1.** Insert your floppy disk into your drive. Load Microsoft Access by selecting Start, highlighting the Programs menu and clicking on the Microsoft Access item or click on the Access icon on the desktop.

**2.** Microsoft Access application will load (Figure 87). At the bottom of the overlaid window is a list of the databases available and you should see A:\ Holidays in the list. Double click this item and the Holidays Database window will be displayed (Figure 92).

FIGURE 100
**Queries Button**

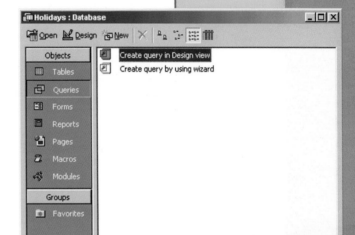

**3.** Select the Queries button in the list of Objects on the left hand side of the window. Figure 100 shows the new view. Double click on the Create query in Design View. A new window will open with an overlaid window called Show Table. Click on the Add button on Show Table and Figure 101 will appear.

FIGURE 101
**Design View**

**4.** Click on the Close button on Show Table window to remove it.

**5.** In the Query window, a small box (Records) will have been added which shows the fields that make up the Holidays table. The cursor will be flashing in the first Field box and a small down arrow will be shown at the end of the same box. Click on the down arrow and a list of the Record fields will appear. Select Name by clicking on it. Name will appear in the first box.

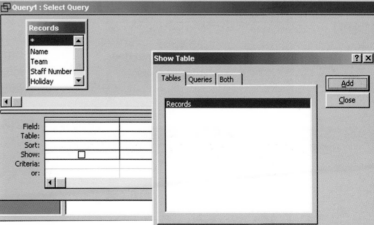

Move to the next box and repeat the operation selecting Team this time and so on, until all the fields have been chosen.

**6.** In the Table row you will see the name of the Holidays table records appear.

**7.** The third row is called Sort. If you click in any of the boxes you will see a down arrow appear which if you click on it reveals a list showing Ascending, Descending or Not Sorted. This enables you to sort the table in this query in any way you choose. Lets repeat one of the earlier sorts. Select the Taken field sort box and select Ascending. The query will sort the table of information into the order of days of holiday taken, from lowest to highest.

**8.** We can now save this query by selecting the File menu and the Save As option. The Save As window will appear and you need to enter Holidays Taken in the box entitled Save Query then click on the OK button.

FIGURE 103
**Holidays
Database**

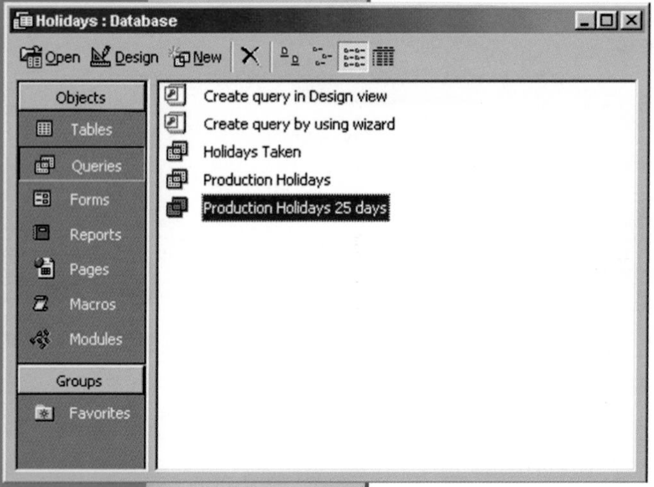

**9.** We could now close the query window by clicking on the Close button but instead we are going to create another query. First remove the sort from Taken by clicking on the down arrow in the Taken Sort field and select not sorted.

**10.** In the Show field you will have noticed that there is a tick in each field. This indicates that when the query is run, the contents of this field will be shown. If you click on the tick, it will disappear and then that field will not be shown. The tick is replaced by clicking again in the tick box.

**11.** The query you are going to create will show the holiday records of all people working in the Production team.

**12.** In the Criteria field on Team enter Production. When you click away from this field, you will see Production enclosed in inverted commas (e.g. "Production".  If you make a mistake when entering production then the query will not find any information since it cannot match the fields – your entry must be perfect.

FIGURE 103
**Results
of the
Queries**

**Production Holidays 25 days : Select Query**

| Name | Team | Staff Number | Holiday | Taken |
|------|------|--------------|---------|-------|
| ▶ Jones | Production | 41 | 25 | 10 |
| * | | 0 | 0 | 0 |

**Production Holidays : Select Query**

| Name | Team | Holiday | Taken |
|------|------|---------|-------|
| ▶ Jones | Production | 25 | 10 |
| Carr | Production | 35 | 25 |
| * | | 0 | 0 |

**Holidays Taken : Select Query**

| Name | Team | Staff Number | Holiday | Taken |
|------|------|--------------|---------|-------|
| ▶ Simba | Sales | 178 | 25 | 0 |
| Jones | Production | 41 | 25 | 10 |
| Singh | Personnel | 23 | 25 | 12 |
| Brown | Computers | 35 | 30 | 15 |
| Patel | Computers | 17 | 25 | 18 |
| Scott | Personnel | 14 | 30 | 20 |
| Carr | Production | 44 | 35 | 25 |
| * | | 0 | 0 | 0 |

**13.** Save this query by selecting the File menu and the Save As option. Then enter Production Holidays as the name of the query and click the OK button.

**14.** Again, you could close this window but we will extend this query by adding a second criterion. In the criteria field on Holiday enter 25. In this case the number is not enclosed in inverted commas. Your query will show all the Production employees who have 25 days holiday entitlement.

**15.** Save this query by selecting the <u>F</u>ile menu and the Save <u>A</u>s option and entering Production Holidays 25 days as the name of the query. Then click on the OK button.

**16.** Close the window by selecting the Close button in the top right hand corner of the window. You will now see Figure 102 which shows the three saved queries. To run a query double click it. Try the three queries to see if they are producing the results you desire. The results of the query are removed by clicking on the close button.

**17.** If you find that the query is producing the wrong outcomes you can amend the query by single clicking the query to highlight it and then on the Design button. This will open the query to allow you to make the required changes.

**18.** When each query is run, print the results by selecting the <u>F</u>ile menu, the <u>P</u>rint option and the OK button.

**19.** Compare each printout and think about the queries you have created. Figure 103 shows the results of the three queries.

**20.** Close the Database window by selecting the Close button and then Access by selecting the <u>F</u>ile menu and the E<u>x</u>it option.

## Search criteria

In the last exercise we used a numerical criteria. It is possible to qualify the numerical criteria using the following symbols:

>     greater than
<     less than
>=   greater than or equal to
<=   less than or equal to
<>   not equal to

These symbols are available on the keyboard.

>     greater than(hold the shift key down and then full stop key)
<     less than (hold the shift key down and then the comma key)
>=   greater than or equal to (hold the shift key down and then the full stop key, release the keys and press the equal key)

Databases

<= less than or equal to (hold the shift key down and then the comma key, release the keys and press the equal key)

<> not equal to (hold the shift key down, press the comma key and then the full stop key)

In your exercise you used the criteria of selecting records for Production employees with 25 days holiday entitlement. With these symbols you could vary these criteria to select employees with less than 25 (i.e. <25), more than 25 (i.e. >25), greater than or equal to 25 (i.e. >=25), less than or equal to 25 (i.e. <=25) and not equal to 25 (i.e. <>25).

# Exercise 34

## Numerical criteria

**1.** Insert your floppy disk into your drive. Load Microsoft Access by selecting Start, highlighting the Programs menu and clicking on the Microsoft Access item or click on the Access icon on the desktop.

**2.** Microsoft Access application will load (Figure 87). At the bottom of the overlaid window is a list of the databases available and you should see A:\ Holidays in the list. Double click this item and the Holidays Database window will be displayed.

**3.** Select the Queries button in the list of Objects on the left hand side of the window. Double click on the Create query in Design View. A new window will open with an overlaid window called Show Table. Click on the Add button on Show Table and Figure 101 will appear.

**4.** Click on the Close button on Show Table window to remove it.

**5.** In the Query window a small box (Records) will have been added which shows the fields that make up the Holidays table. The cursor will be flashing in the first Field box and a small down arrow will be shown at the end of the same box. Click on the down arrow and a list of the Holiday fields will appear. Select Name by clicking on it. Name will appear in the first box. Move to the next box and repeat the operation selecting Team this time and so on until all the fields have been chosen.

**6.** You are going to create a query which will identify the holidays for staff with Staff Numbers less than 40 who have taken more than 5 days holiday.

**7.** Click in the Staff Number criteria field and enter <40 and then click in the Taken criteria field and enter >5

**8.** Save this query by selecting the File menu and the Save As option then enter Staff Numbers as the name of the query and click the OK button.

**9.** Close the window by clicking on the Close button in the top right-hand corner of the window.

**10.** Run the new query and check the results that it produces. Amend if necessary.

**11.** Print the results of your query (select the File menu, the Print option and the OK button).

**12.** Close the Database window by selecting the Close button and then Access by selecting the File menu and the Exit option.

## Optional
# Exercise 35

## More Practice 1 Creating a table

1. Load Microsoft Access by selecting Start, highlighting the Programs menu and clicking on the Microsoft Access item or click on the Access icon on the desktop.

2. Microsoft Access application will load (Figure 87). Select Blank Access database by clicking on the radio button. The File New Database is opened which will let you save your new database.

You need to select a drive or folder in which to store your new database as a file. If you click on the arrow button next to the Save in box you can select floppy disk.

Next we need to give the file a name. Insert the name Customer Accounts in the File name box and click on the Create button. You will have saved your blank database as a file called Customer Accounts on your floppy disk.

**3.** The Customer Accounts Database window shows three options with the Table object on the left-hand side selected:

create table in Design view

create table by using wizard

create table by entering data

Double click on Create table in Design view and the table window opens.

FIGURE 104
**Customer Accounts Table**

FIGURE 104 Customer Accounts Table

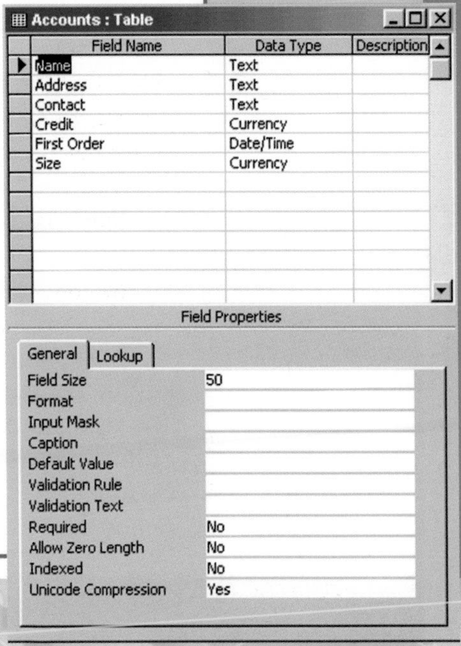

**4.** You are going to create the table below:

Customer Accounts

| | |
|---|---|
| Name | - company name (i.e. text field) |
| Address | - address of the company (i.e. text field) |
| Contact | - name of company customer contact (i.e. text field) |
| Credit | - upper limit of order (i.e. number field) |
| First Order | - date of the first order |
| Size | - value of last order (i.e. number field) |

| Name | Address | Contact | Credit | First Order | Size |
|---|---|---|---|---|---|
| Deans | London | Anne | 2500 | 01/10/90 | 500 |
| Big Shop | Birmingham | Keith | 1500 | 13/02/92 | 750 |
| Mint | Sheffield | Jane | 1000 | 26/06/96 | 250 |
| Gordons | London | Stephanie | 3000 | 19/08/95 | 250 |
| Youngs | Manchester | David | 2000 | 30/04/94 | 900 |
| Palmers | Sheffield | Peter | 3000 | 07/11/96 | 750 |

This table of information consists of six records with each record comprising six fields.

You need to insert your field names and their types. If you enter Name in the Field Name box and click in the corresponding Data Type box, a small down arrow will appear revealing a list of types. Select text then click in the next Field Name box and enter Address. Complete the table Contact, Credit, First Order and Size. Both Credit and Size are currency type. First Order is type Date/Time.

**5.** When you enter a type you should observe that in field size a value (e.g. 50) will appear with a text type and Long Integer with a number type. The value 50 indicates the number of characters that the field can store while a Long Integer is a whole number (i.e. no decimal places). Figure 104 shows the result.

FIGURE 105
**Customer
Accounts**

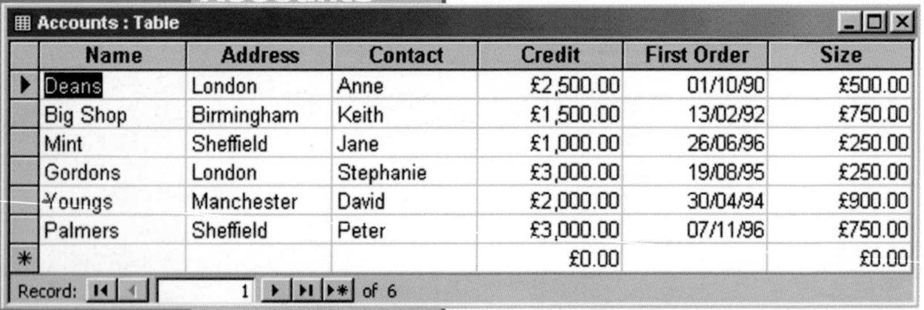

| Accounts : Table | | | | | | |
|---|---|---|---|---|---|
| **Name** | **Address** | **Contact** | **Credit** | **First Order** | **Size** |
| ▶ Deans | London | Anne | £2,500.00 | 01/10/90 | £500.00 |
| Big Shop | Birmingham | Keith | £1,500.00 | 13/02/92 | £750.00 |
| Mint | Sheffield | Jane | £1,000.00 | 26/06/96 | £250.00 |
| Gordons | London | Stephanie | £3,000.00 | 19/08/95 | £250.00 |
| Youngs | Manchester | David | £2,000.00 | 30/04/94 | £900.00 |
| Palmers | Sheffield | Peter | £3,000.00 | 07/11/96 | £750.00 |
| * | | | £0.00 | | £0.00 |

Record: |◄ ◄ | 1 | ► ►| ►* | of 6

**6.** Save your table by selecting the File menu and Save As option. The Save As window appears, enter Accounts and click on the OK button.

**7.** A warning message will now appear asking you if you need a primary key. In this case you do not need to define one, so click on the No button. The table window reappears and you should close it by clicking on the close button in the top right-hand corner of the table window. You can now see the Customer Accounts Database window but with an extra item added – Accounts.

8. Close the window and the Customer Accounts window will be revealed. You can now enter the data by double clicking on Accounts. Enter the text to produce Figure 105.

9. When you have completed the table check each entry against the original data. If you find an error click into the field box to move the cursor into the box. Delete the mistake and insert the correct entry.

10. Explore sorting the information using the Ascending and Descending icons on the toolbar. Sort the Name, Credit and First Order Fields. This will show you how to sort alphabetically, numerically and by date.
11. Close the window. The completed table will be saved automatically.

12. Click on the close button in the top right-hand corner of the window.

13. Close Access by selecting the File menu and the Exit option.

# Exercise 36

The database Customer Accounts is available on the supporting website (www.hodderclait.co.uk) if you would like to undertake this exercise without creating the database in Exercise 35.

## More Practice 2    Queries

1. Insert your floppy disk into your drive. Load Microsoft Access by selecting Start, highlighting the Programs menu and clicking on the Microsoft Access item or click on the Access icon on the desktop.

2. Microsoft Access application will load (Figure 87). At the bottom of the overlaid window is a list of the databases available and you should see A:\ Customer Accounts in the list. Double click this item and the Customer Accounts Database window will be displayed.

3. Select the Queries button in the list of Objects on the left hand side of the window. Double click on Create query in Design View. A new window will

FIGURE 106
**Location and Credit Query**

open with an overlaid window called Show Table. Click on the Add button on Show Table and then on the Close button.

**4.** In the Query window a small box (Accounts) will have been added which shows the fields that make up the Customer Accounts table. The cursor will be flashing in the first Field box and a small down arrow will be shown at the end of the same box. Click on the down arrow and a list of the Customer Account fields will appear. Select Name by clicking on it. Name will appear in the first box. Move to the next box and repeat the operation selecting Address this time and so on until all the fields have been chosen.

**5.** You are going to create a query based on two criteria. These are:

Selecting Customers in London who have a Credit limit greater than or equal to £2500

**6.** Click in the criteria box of Address and enter London

**7.** Click in the criteria box of Credit and enter >=2500

**8.** Save this query by selecting the File menu and the Save As option then enter Location and Credit as the name of the query and click on the OK button.

**9.** Close the window by selecting the Close button in the top right hand corner of the window. You will now see the Customer Accounts window that shows the query. Double click on the query to see if it produces the desired results (Figure 106). The results of the query are removed by clicking on the Close button.

**10.** If you find that the query is producing the wrong outcomes then you can amend it by single clicking the query to highlight it and then on the Design

FIGURE 107
**Date
Query**

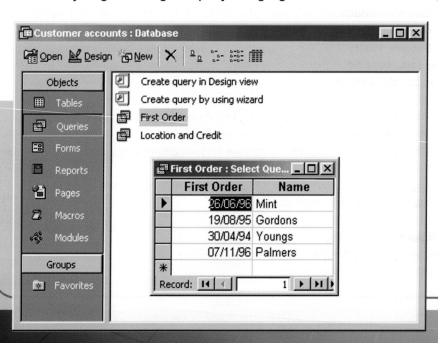

button. This will open the query to allow you to make the required changes.

**11.** When the query is run print the results by selecting the File menu, the Print option and the OK button.

**12.** You are now going to design a query to identify all customers who have placed an order on or after 30/04/94. The Customer Accounts Database window should be displayed.

**13.** Select the Queries button in the list of Objects on the left-hand side of the window. Double click on Create query in Design View. A new window will open with an overlaid window called Show Table. Click on the Add button on Show Table and then on the Close button.

**14.** In the Query window a small box (Accounts) will have been added which shows the fields that make up the Customer Accounts table. The cursor will be flashing in the first Field box and a small down arrow will be shown at the end of the same box. Click on the down arrow and a list of the Customer Account fields will appear. Select First Order by clicking on it. First Order will appear in the first box. Move to the next box and repeat the operation selecting Name this time. You simply want to identify the names of the cutomers.

**15.** You are going to create a query based on one criteria. This is:

Selecting Customers who have placed orders on or after the 30/04/94

**16.** Click in the criteria box of First Name and enter >=30/04/94

**17.** Save this query by selecting the File menu and the Save As option then enter First Order as the name of the query and click on the OK button.

**18.** Close the window by selecting the close button in the top right-hand corner of the window. You will now see the Customer Accounts window that shows the new query. Double click on the query First order to see if it produces the desired results (Figure 107). The results of the query are removed by clicking on the close button.

**19.** If you find that the query is producing the wrong outcomes then you can amend it by single clicking the query to highlight it and then on the Design button. This will open the query to allow you to make the required changes.

**20.** When the query is run print the results by selecting the File menu, the Print option and the OK button.

**21.** Close the Database window by selecting the close button and then Access by selecting the File menu and the Exit option.

## OPTIONAL

The database Postcards is available on the supporting website (www.hodderclait.co.uk) if you would like to undertake the adding, editing and query tasks

## Another example

Create the following database
Postcard Collecting

**Category -** different groups of cards
**Type -** specific types of cards
**Date -** date first cards published
**Condition -** physical condition of card
**Price -** price paid for card
**Value -** current market price
**Location -** album card stored in

Category Fields are Glamour, Message, Liverpool and Modern

| Type | Date | Condition | Price | Value | Location |
|------|------|-----------|-------|-------|----------|
| **Glamour** | | | | | |
| Barribal | 12/03/88 | Mint | £8 | £10 | A |
| Nanni | 23/01/79 | Good | £4 | £5 | B |
| Others | 01/12/92 | Poor | £1 | £1 | B |
| | | | | | |
| **Message** | | | | | |
| Davies | 24/08/94 | Very Good | £1.50 | £1.50 | C |
| Other | 13/06/93 | Good | £0.75 | £1 | C |
| | | | | | |
| **Liverpool** | | | | | |
| Tunnel | 07/09/92 | Good | £2 | £1.50 | D |
| Centre | 17/11/93 | Poor | £3 | £2 | A |
| Suburbs | 03/04/91 | Poor | £5 | £6 | B |
| Other | 29/01/90 | Poor | £2 | £1 | C |
| | | | | | |
| **Modern** | | | | | |
| Political | 22/07/91 | Mint | £0.75 | £0.25 | D |
| Royalty | 11/05/90 | Mint | £0.50 | £0.50 | E |
| Cricket | 20/12/90 | Very Good | £1 | £1.25 | F |
| Football | 14/02/89 | Very Good | £0.60 | £1 | G |

The table is shown in Figure 107.

FIGURE 107
**Postcard
Table**

| Category | Type | Date | Condition | Price | Value | Location |
|---|---|---|---|---|---|---|
| Glamour | Barribal | 12/03/88 | Mint | £8.00 | £10.00 | A |
| Glamour | Nanni | 23/01/79 | Good | £4.00 | £5.00 | B |
| Glamour | Other | 01/12/92 | Poor | £1.00 | £1.00 | B |
| Message | Davies | 24/08/94 | Very Good | £1.50 | £1.50 | C |
| Message | Other | 13/06/93 | Good | £0.75 | £1.00 | C |
| Liverpool | Tunnel | 07/09/92 | Good | £2.00 | £1.50 | D |
| Liverpool | Centre | 17/11/93 | Poor | £3.00 | £2.00 | A |
| Liverpool | Suburbs | 03/04/91 | Poor | £5.00 | £6.00 | B |
| Liverpool | Other | 29/01/90 | Poor | £2.00 | £1.00 | C |
| Modern | Political | 22/07/91 | Mint | £0.75 | £0.25 | D |
| Modern | Royalty | 11/05/90 | Mint | £0.50 | £0.50 | E |
| Modern | Cricket | 20/12/90 | Very Good | £1.00 | £1.25 | F |
| Modern | Football | 14/02/89 | Very Good | £0.60 | £1.00 | G |
| * | | | | £0.00 | £0.00 | |

Record: 1 of 13

Amend your table to:

1. Change the condition of Liverpool Centre to Good from Poor
2. Delete the Modern Cricket record
3. Insert Message American, 11/05/91, Very Good, £1, £1.50, C

Create the following Queries

1. Query to sort the records by ascending value
2. Query to find records with a price less than £2
3. Query to find all the records in album A with a value greater than £5

Print each query result

Save all the queries.

**1. Load Microsoft Access** Use either the Start button and the Programs menu or double click on the Access icon on Windows desktop

**2. Close** Click on File menu item and Exit option or click on the close button in the top right hand corner of the application or other window.

**3. Create a database - optional** Load Microsoft Access, select Blank Access database by clicking on the radio button. The File New Database is opened to enable you to save your new database.

Select a drive or folder in which to store your new database as a file. If you click on the arrow button next to the Save in box you can select floppy disk.

Give the file a name. Insert the name in the File name box and click on the Create button. Your database is now saved.

The Database window is now revealed with three options with the Table object on the left-hand side selected:

create a table in Design view

create a table by using wizard

create a table by entering data

Double click on Create table in Design view and the table window opens

Insert your field names and their types.

Save your table by selecting the File menu and Save As option.

**4. Enter Data** Load Access. Double click on the database of your choice in the list at the bottom of the overlay window. The database window will appear.

Double click on table of your choice and the blank table will appear. Complete the records, moving between the fields by clicking in each box. Alternatively use the arrow keys, tab key or press the enter key to move between fields.

Check each entry against the original data.

To amend a single field, click on the field, delete its incorrect content and then re-enter the data

**5. Deleting a record** Highlight the record by positioning the mouse pointer over the row heading until the pointer changes shape. Click the left mouse button. Right click with the pointer in the highlighted row, the menu will appear and you select Delete Record.

**6. Add a record** Click on the blank row at the bottom of table and insert data, moving between fields using tab or enter keys or by clicking in the next field.

**7. Creating a Query** Select the Queries button in the list of Objects on the left hand side of the database window. Double click on the Create query in Design View option. A new window will open with an overlaid window called Show Table. Click on the Add button on Show Table and then on the Close button.

In the Query window a small box will be shown which shows the fields that make up the table. The cursor will be flashing in the first Field box and a small down arrow will be shown at the end of the same box. Click on the down arrow and a list of the table fields will appear. Select the field which will then appear in the box. Move across the boxes, entering the chosen fields.

Enter criteria in appropriate box

Sort data by clicking in the sort box. Select the down arrow and choose Ascending, Descending or not sorted.

**8. Save Query** Save the query by selecting the File menu and the Save As option and entering the name of the query then clicking the OK button.

**9. Printing** Select the File menu and the Print option. This reveals the Print window and you can print using the default settings by clicking on the OK button.
**or**
Select the File menu and Print Preview to check the appearance of the printed document before you print it. Click on the printer icon and then on the OK button in the Print window.

# Desktop Publishing

This chapter will help you to use desktop publishing to:

identify and use appropriate software correctly

set up a standard page layout and text properties

import and place text and image files

manipulate text and images to balance a page

manage publications and print composite proofs

## Assessment

This unit does not assume any previous experience of desktop publishing, but you may find it useful if you have previously undertaken Unit 1 (Using a Computer) and Unit 2 (Word processing). After studying Unit 6 your skills and understanding are assessed during a 2-hour practical assignment. This is set by OCR and marked locally. However, the marking will be externally moderated by OCR. This ensures that the standard is being applied correctly across the many different providers of OCR New CLAIT.

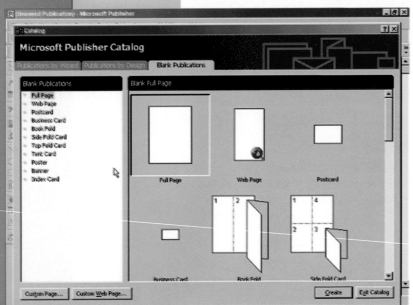

FIGURE 108
**Microsoft Publisher Catalog**

## Microsoft Publisher

Microsoft Publisher is a desktop publishing application with which you create new publications. These can be for your own personal use (e.g. a village newsletter) or for your business (e.g. an advertising leaflet). In this chapter you will learn how to create a publication using images and text. Many people find it difficult to understand the difference between word processing and desktop publishing (DTP). Word processing is about producing a document while a desktop publisher provides tools to control the precise presentation of text and images. DTP is more a tool for laying out text and pictures. It gives you control over the flow of text and the positioning and size of images.

Figure 108 shows the opening display of Microsoft Publisher Catalog. This consists of three tabs: Publications by Wizard, Publications by Design and

Blank Publications. The catalog provides you with a choice of type of publication such as web pages, postcards, book pages, poster and index cards. It also lets you open an existing publication. The Wizard and Design tabs provide you with the means of rapidly producing a publication based on a set of standard designs while the Blank Publications tab assumes you want to start with scratch. Once you have chosen your option you click on the Create button to reveal the main Publisher window (Figure 109).

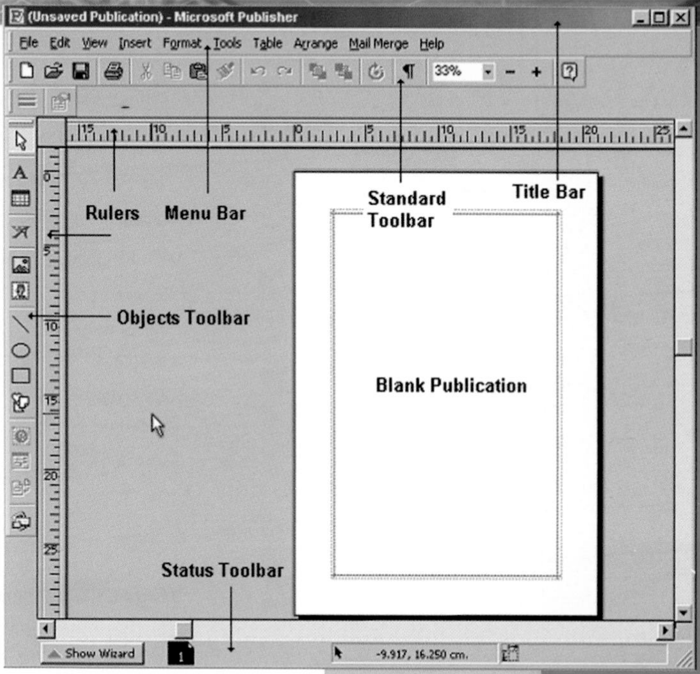

Figure 109 shows the Publisher window consisting of a working area in which the publication appears. In this case you are observing a blank full page publication. At the bottom of the screen on the status line is a button called Show Wizard which will reveal the help (i.e. Quick Publication Wizard) that Publisher provides you when you are designing a publication. It offers a choice of designs, colours, layouts and information on how to include your own personal data in the publication.

FIGURE 109
**Microsoft Publisher**

The application provides access to a range of tools through menus and toolbars. To the left of the window is the objects toolbar which offers a range of tools (e.g. create WordArt, draw rectangles and access clip art). At the top of the window are a series of toolbars which allow you to print, save and format your publication. The menu toolbar provides alternative routes to the same functions and other tools such as the selection of page sizes, margins and to check your spelling.

# Exercise 37

## Exploring Microsoft Publisher

**1.** Load Publisher by selecting the Start button, highlighting the Programs option and clicking on the Microsoft Publisher item or click on the Publisher icon on the desktop. Observe that the publisher catalog opens as shown in Figure 108

**2.** Explore the three tabs by clicking on each in turn and look at the different options. In the publications by Design notice that you are provided within many master sets of designs. These are outline publications which provide with particular design styles (e.g. boarders, lines and bars) around which to develop your content. If you have limited design skills these masters help you to produce a quality publication quickly. Blank Publications locate the Full Page, Poster and Postcard options. They are selected by clicking on

FIGURE 110
**Objects Toolbar**

- Pointer Tool
- Text Frame Tool
- Table Frame Tool
- WordArt Frame Tool
- Picture Frame Tool
- Clip Gallery Tool
- Line Tool
- Oval Tool
- Rectangle Tool
- Custom Shapes

- Design Gallery Object

them. Click on the Full Page option and you will see it enclosed in an indented square.

**3.** When you are ready and with Full Page selected, click on the Create button in the bottom right hand corner and the Publisher application will appear (Figure 109) either with or without the Wizard showing as in Figure 109. In the former, the button below the wizard will read Hide Wizard.

**4.** The blank full page will occupy the centre of the work area. If you look at the standard toolbar you will see towards the right side of the bar a percentage (e.g. 33%). This tells you the relative size of the document. The working area is enclosed in a ruler. If you move the mouse pointer you will see that on the both the top and left-hand ruler a faint line moves with respect to the mouse. This gives you guidance as the position you are working on the document.

**5,** On the left hand edge are a series of tools (Figure 110).

**6.** Explore the menus – what functions do each contain? Try to locate Page Setup which is on the File menu, Layout Guides (Arrange menu), Copy (Edit menu) and Picture (Insert menu).

**7.** Click on the Show Wizard button to reveal the Quick Publication Wizard panel (Figure 111). Click on each of the five options (i.e. Introduction, Design, Color Scheme, Layout and Personal Information). This will reveal a series of options or information. Consider each option and the sub-options linked to them.

**8.** When you are confident that you are familiar with the application's display, close Publisher by clicking on the close button in the top right-hand corner of the window or by selecting the File menu and the Exit option.

FIGURE 111
**Quick Publication Wizard**

Quick Publication Wizard

- Introduction
- Design
- Color Scheme
- Layout
- Personal Information

Introduction

Use the options above to change your answers to the wizard's layout questions.

As you edit your publication, you'll want to explore Publisher's menus and commands to see what additional formatting options are available to you.

▼ Hide Wizard

## Designing

Publisher provides you with the tools to produce professional publications but it leaves the design to you. The critical factors in designing a publication are:

**Modest use of variables** – few things are worse than over use of the desktop publishing features (e.g. too many colours, fonts (sometimes called a typeface) character sizes etc). A useful rule is to use a feature for a distinct reason (e.g. using a different character size for each heading – main heading size 36, sub-headings 20 and ordinary text size 12)

**Consistency –** in a way the design is a form of code that tells your readers how to understand the document so it is important that you follow a consistent design plan (e.g. address is always in bottom right hand corner of a page)

**Attractive –** ideally you want your publications to be read and initially they need to be visually attractive so that people will consider reading them. The use (not overuse) of pictures, colour and different fonts can provide an interesting publication. It is important for a document to be visually balanced

**Appropriate –** consider who your readers are and design for them

**Readability –** a good publication is one which is easy to read. Readability is a combination of many factors but some simple tips are to provide plenty of white space (e.g. overcrowding text makes it difficult to read so do not reduce line spacing unless you have no other choice), pictures relating to the text increase the readers' interest and short sections are often easier to understand than long ones)

## Standard Page Setup

The first task in designing a publication is to set the page size, orientation and margins.

To set the page size and orientation select the File menu then the Page Setup option. This will reveal the Page Setup window (Figure 112) which provides you with options to choose the publication layout, paper size and orientation (i.e. either portrait or landscape). When you select a layout, you are able to see your choice in the Preview area. Layouts are chosen by clicking on the radio buttons. Click on the OK button to confirm your selections.

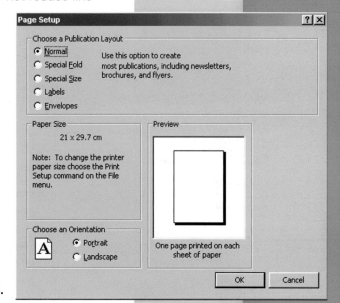

FIGURE 112
**Page Setup**

To set the margins, select the Arrange menu then the Layout Guides to reveal the Layout Guides window (Figure 113). This allows you to preview your choices. You can change each margin left, right, top and bottom by clicking on the up and down arrows.

## Frames

Every item (e.g. images and text) that makes up a desktop publication is an individual object. Each object is enclosed in a frame which is invisible when printed unless you chose to create a border around it. Frames can be resized and moved using your mouse. They can be placed on top of each other so that a series of layers are created. Figure 114 shows a highlighted frame. The small black squares which form part of the enclosure and allow you to resize the frame are called handles.

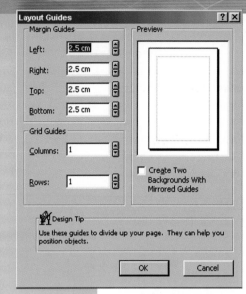

PAGE 113
**Layout**

FIGURE 114
**Frames**

# Template

A template is a simple but useful idea that can save you a great deal of time and trouble. It is essentially a basic model of the publication which you use over and over again. Normally you will define the layout and format of the publication and then use this foundation to create new versions of the publication. This is useful if you are regularly publishing a document such as a monthly newsletter which you would like to have a standard appearance but with a variable content.

You create a template in the same way that you produce any other publication except that you save the layout and format before adding the detail content. When you next want to create a similar publication you load the template and immediately begin to add the detail. In this way you save time and also produce a consistent document. A company may create templates for all their standard documents such as sales leaflets, technical data sheets and briefing sheets. This allows them to present a desired image to their customers to align with wider marketing activities.

# Master Page

The master page concept is similar to that of a template. You create a standard page which is reused throughout a multiple page publication. This again provides a standard and consistent appearance to a document. There are no particular rules for layout of a master page since it depends on what you are designing. A textbook is going to need a different master to a sales brochure.

A master page allows you to increase your productivity while maintaining a high standard of presentation since you have spent your time producing a good master page. In addition readers like a consistent presentation since it aids readability and helps them locate information.

# Exercise 38

## Page Setup

**1.** Load Publisher by selecting the Start button, highlighting the Programs option and clicking on the Microsoft Publisher item or by clicking on the Publisher icon on the desktop.

**2.** Click on the Blank Publications Tab, select the Full Page option and click on the Create button.

**3.** The Publisher application will appear (Figure 109). A blank full page will occupy the centre of the work area.

**4.** Select the File menu, then the Page Setup option to reveal the Page Setup window. Explore the different layouts by considering their appearance in the Preview window before selecting the Normal option. Options are chosen by clicking on the radio button (i.e. small circle - selected when a dot appears in its centre). Change the page orientation to landscape and observe its appearance in the preview window. When you are ready, click on the OK button to confirm the changes.

**5.** Select the Arrange menu then the Layout Guides to reveal the Layout Guides window. Explore changing the margins by observing the selections in the Preview area. When you are confident that you understand the choices set the right and left margins to 4 cms and the top and bottom to 3 cms. Click on the OK button to confirm your selections. You can also change the size of the margins by simply clicking in the numbers box and entering your sizes from the keyboard.

**6.** You have now created a basic layout for a publication which might be useful as a newsletter or a handout in a presentation. This is a good time to save your outline publication. You could consider it as a master document or template. Publisher provides several master documents for you to choose from but you can also create your own. A master is simply a framework which serves a particular purpose that you can use over and over again to produce a particular type of publication. If you regularly produce a newsletter, it aids productivity and ensures they all follow a consistent design.

**7.** Insert a floppy disk into the computer's drive.To save your outline publication select the File menu then the Save option to reveal the Save As window. You need to choose the location in which to store your publication by clicking on the down arrow at the end of the Save in box. This will reveal a list. Click on the floppy disk option. You will then see this appear in the box. Now click in the File name box and enter from the keyboard the name 'Landscape Columns' then click on the Save button. You will hear the drive working and the publication will be saved on the floppy disk as a file called Landscape Columns.

**8.** It is good practice to save your work early and to update your saved file at regular intervals. This safeguards you against any problems with the application or computer. You will always have most of your work saved so that you can start again later without having to repeat all of it.

**9.** You have now established a basic layout. The next step is to consider where to place your text. Select theText frame tool on the Objects toolbar

(Figure 110). The mouse pointer will change to a crosshair that allows you to accurately position your text. We are going to establish a text frame or area that will cover the top half of the page. You do this by positioning your pointer in the top left-hand corner of the column and then holding the mouse button down. Move the pointer down to form a rectangle at the top of the column. Your rectangle will be framed as shown in Figure 115. You can drag the rectangle to adjust the frame to your needs. Use the layout guides to help position the text frame.

**10.** If you move your mouse pointer across the frame it will change to explain its purpose:

resize – double headed arrow whenever you place the pointer on one of the small black squares (called handles) at the corners or middle of the lines. This allows you to change the size of the text frame

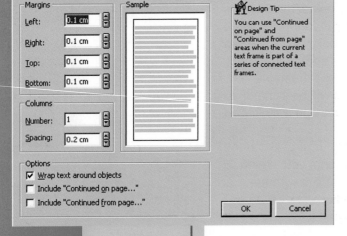

FIGURE 115
**Text Frame**

move – a small vehicle whenever you place your pointer near the rectangle lines away from the handles. This lets you move the whole frame.

**11.** Experiment with changing the size of the rectangle and moving it. When you have finished place the frame to cover the top half of the page. If you click away from the frame the heavy lines and handles will disappear (i.e. it is no longer highlighted) to show you it is fixed. However, if you need to manipulate it, highlight it again by clicking on the rectangle. If you make a mistake and need to delete the frame, you must highlight it then press the delete key or select the Edit menu, then the Delete Object option.

**12.** Publisher provides you with tools to manipulate the text frame precisely. With the text frame highlighted, select the Format menu, then the Text Frame Properties option to reveal the Text Frame Properties window (Figure 116).

**13.** With the Text Frame Properties window you can divide your text frame into columns, set the spacing between them and set the four margins for the text frame. These may seem peripheral matters but desktop publishing is about providing you with the tools to produce accurate and detailed publications. Desktop publishing (Microsoft Publisher) lets you produce publications equivalent to those of professional printers.

FIGURE 116
**Text Frame Properties**

**14.** Set all the margins of your text frame to 0.5 cms and create three columns with a spacing of 0.3cm.

FIGURE 117
**Format Toolbar**

**15.** You will notice that within your text box the cursor is flashing. This is the place where any text you enter will appear. Enter the heading Guinea pigs. You may see a message appear to tell you the text is too small to be visible and offering you the option of zooming in on the text. The zoom option is available on the Edit menu or in the toolbar box.

**16.** You can resize the text by highlighting it (click on the start of the text and holding the left mouse button down, move the pointer to the end of the text). Now select the character size icon on the format toolbar. The small down arrow button to the right of the character size box will reveal a list of sizes. In a similar way, the down arrow next to the font box will list fonts that you can select (Figure 117). Fonts are also called typefaces.

For this publication you are creating the initial heading so it is important to select a font and character size that is eye catching. The list of fonts includes two types called serif and sans serif. These are different groups of fonts. A serif type font has small flags on the ends of the characters (e.g. ALGERIAN) while a sans serif type font does not. You might say that serif fonts have more fancy characters or that sans serif fonts have plain characters. You need to experiment with your choice of fonts to find the ones that you like.

## Example

Serif Font Character     Sans Serif Character

# F T             **F T**

**17.** Select a character size of 20 by clicking on that number in the list and then select Aardvark (or one of your own choice) font. Observe how your title now appears. You are going to create a heading that will fit the first column of the publication. While you are selecting your font scroll down the list and you should notice many with similar names. These are likely to belong to the same family of fonts. Fonts are divided into families which vary in size from a single item to ones with many elements.

**18.** Save your publication by selecting the File menu and the Save option. The Save As window will not appear since the system assumes you are updating your previously saved file Landscape Column. If you wanted to create a new saved file then you would need to select the Save As option. This will reveal the Save As window and you can enter a new file name.

**19.** Close the application by clicking on the close button in the top right-hand corner of the window or by selecting File and then the Exit option.

# Editing fonts

An alternative way to manipulate the fonts and character sizes is available from the Format menu (Figure 118). Select the Font option revealing the Font window. The Text frame and the selected words need to be highlighted for these options to be available. The Font window provides you with an alternative way of changing your fonts and character size. You can also embolden, underline and display your text in italics style from this window, although these options are, of course, also available on the format toolbar.

**FIGURE 118**
**Font Option**

# Justification

You can also justify your words using the icons on the format toolbar. These allow you to justify your text in four ways (Figure 119). These are:

**left –** the left text edge is parallel with the margin and the right is ragged

**right –** the right text edge is parallel with the margin and the left is ragged

**centred –** text is aligned down the centre of the page with both edges ragged

**double –** both left and right text edges are parallel with the Margins (it is called Justify on the Format Toolbar)

**FIGURE 119    Justification Options**

| Left | Right | Centred | Double | | | | |
|------|-------|---------|--------|---|---|---|---|
| AAAAA | AAAAA | AAAAA | A | A | A | A | A |
| AAA | AAA | AAA | A | | A | | A |
| AAAA | AAAA | AAAA | A | A | A | | A |
| AA | AA | AA | A | | | | A |
| AAAA | AAAA | AAAA | A | A | A | | A |

Highlight the text and select the respective icons from the toolbar.

# Inserting text and pictures

Although you can enter text into your publication from the keyboard, desktop publishing is primarily designed to allow you to manipulate objects to produce high quality presentations of information. One such object is text which is best prepared using a word processor. This can either be in the form of text copied from other Office applications and pasted into the publication or by importing text files.

To insert text files you select the Insert menu and the Text File option. This opens the Insert Text window which allows you to choose the file you want to insert. In a similar way you can insert pictures by copying them from other Office applications, inserting image files or choosing images from clip art collections. Figure 120 shows the menu options.

When you first select these options you may be presented with a message that indicates that the functions need to be installed from the Microsoft Office master disks. If this happens, seek help unless you are confident that you can install the functions. They convert files to a format that Publisher can accept. Clip Art collections provided by Microsoft Office are often not installed on the computer and need to have the CD-ROMs which hold them inserted in the correct drive so that they can be accessed.

FIGURE 120
**Importing Text and Pictures**

## Lines and borders

All Publisher objects are enclosed in frames which are invisible when printed unless they are turned into borders. Publisher provides you with the functions to enclose frames with lines of different thicknesses or more artistic surrounds. These are available by selecting the

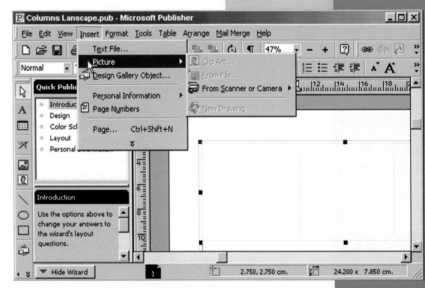

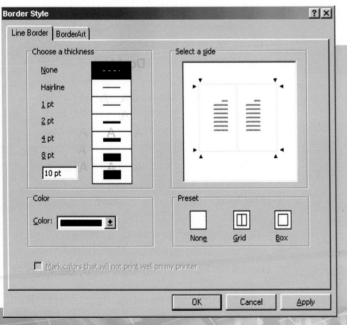

FIGURE 122
**Border Style**

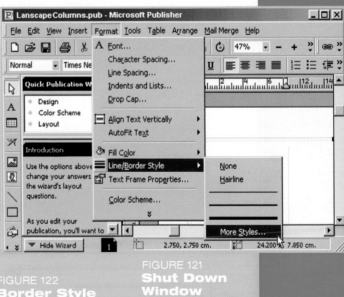

FIGURE 121
**Shut Down Window**

Format menu, then highlighting Line/Border Style (Figure 121) to reveal the Border Style window (Figure 122).

With the Border Style window you can experiment with different line styles including artistic choices available by clicking on the Border/Art tab. These appear in the preview area which also allows you to use lines on particular sides of the frame. You do this by selecting the line style and then clicking on the side or sides in the Select a side area. In a similar way you can change column boundaries.

# Exercise 39

## Importing text and pictures

**1.** Load Publisher by selecting the Start button, highlighting the Programs option and clicking on the Microsoft Publisher item or by clicking on the Publisher icon on the desktop.

**2.** Close the Microsoft Publisher Catalog by clicking on the close button in the top right hand corner of the window.

**3.** The Publisher application will appear. If you have only recently completed the previous exercise (i.e. in this session) then if you select the File menu, you will see the Landscape Columns file at the bottom of the menu. This can be loaded by clicking on it.

If you completed the exercise some time ago then you will need to load it from your floppy disk. Insert the disk into the drive and select the File menu then the Open option to reveal the Open Publication window (Figure 123). Select the floppy disk in the Look in box by clicking on the down arrow button to reveal list of options. This will reveal the files on your floppy disk.

FIGURE 123
**Open Publications**

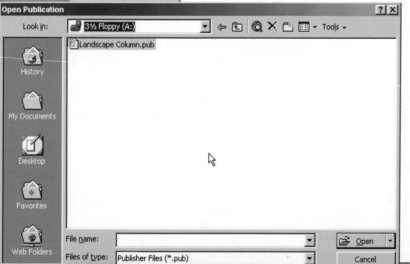

Double click on the Landscape Columns publication to load the file or single click on it and then on the Open button.

**4.** The publication will appear in the work area. If you click within the text frame you will see the location of the flashing cursor. Move the cursor to one line below the heading (Guinea Pigs) by pressing the Enter key from the end of the heading.

**5.** In the word processing unit you undertook an exercise and created some text about guinea pigs. We are now going to import this text file into the publication. Highlight the text frame, select the Insert menu and the Text File option to reveal the Insert Text window (Figure 124). Insert your floppy disk containing the Guinea Pig file or if you do not have the file, then select any other text file containing a short passage since this is a practice publication.

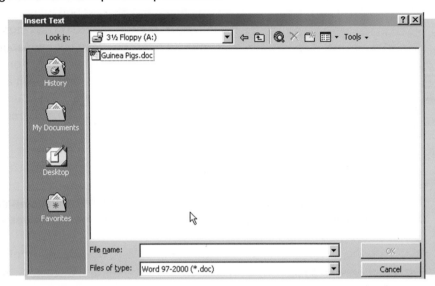

FIGURE 124
**Insert Text
window**

**6.** Select the floppy disk in the Look in box by clicking on the down arrow button to reveal a list of options. This will reveal the files on your floppy disk. Double click on the Guinea Pigs file to load it or single click on it and then on the Open button.

**7.** The text file will load into your publication starting at the cursor and flowing across the three columns. If it overflows the columns you will see a message appear asking if you want the automatic flow of text to be undertaken. Click on Yes to accept the automatic flow. Another message will appear asking if you want Publisher to create a new page. Again click on Yes and a final message telling you a new page has been created will appear. Click on OK to remove it and observe your publication.

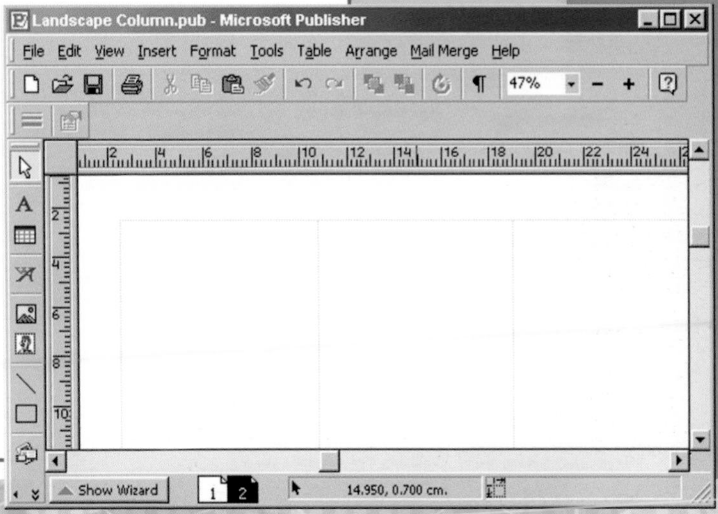

You should see a new page with three columns and below the work area you will see two number 1 and 2 with 2 highlighted indicating that it is page two you are considering. If you click on 1 then the first or original page will appear. Figures 125 and 126 shows the two pages.

FIGURE 125
**Import Text
- New Page**

**8.** The next step is to insert a picture into your publication. Select the Picture Frame Tool from the Objects toolbar and draw a picture frame below the text box occupying about an eighth of the page. With the picture frame highlighted, select the Insert menu, highlight the Picture and

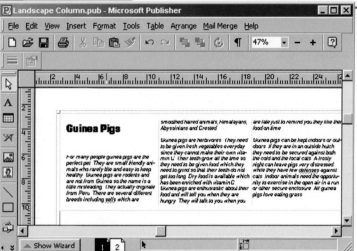

FIGURE 126
**Import Text
– Original
page**

FIGURE 127
**Publication**

FIGURE 128
**Revised
Publication**

click on <u>C</u>lip Art. This will reveal the Insert Clip Art window showing the various categories of images available. Click on a category (e.g. Animals) to reveal a range of images. Explore the pictures and choose one by clicking on it to open a short menu. By placing your mouse over the menu a small label will appear to tell you what the options are. The Insert Clip is the first option and the one you should select. The picture will now appear inside the picture frame.

**9.** You can move the picture or resize it using the mouse pointer in the same way as with the text frame. Experiment with moving the image, including placing the picture inside the text frame. You will see the text move to make room for the image. This shows that you can stack frames on top of each other.

**10.** With the image inside it, resize the text frame to occupy the whole page and observe what happens.

**11.** The publication should now look similar to Figure 127.

**12.** You can change the justification and alignment of the text using the Format toolbar. Centre the heading text (Guinea Pigs) by highlighting the words and using the centre icon on the toolbar. Change the imported text to Aardvark (or a font of your choice), character size 12 and double justify the text by again highlighting the text using functions on the toolbar. Your publication should look similar to Figure 128 if you have used the guinea pig text.

**13.** By selecting the F<u>o</u>rmat menu, highlighting Line/<u>B</u>order style and clicking on More <u>S</u>tyles, you will reveal the Border Style window. Explore the options to provide a border for your publication with a faint line dividing the columns and a heavier border around the whole page.

**14.** Save your publication by selecting the <u>F</u>ile menu and the <u>S</u>ave option. The Save As window will not appear since the system assumes you are updating your previously saved file Landscape Column. If you wanted to create a new saved file then you would need to select the Save <u>A</u>s option.

This will reveal the Save As window and you can enter a new file name.

**15.** Close the application by clicking on the close button in the top right-hand corner of the window or by selecting File and then the Exit option.

# Spacing

It is important that the appearance of the text serves the purpose you intend. Often you have only a limited amount of space in which to fit a range of information (i.e. text and pictures). This requires you to balance the content of your publication and is especially true when you have a publication divided into columns. Publisher provides functions with which you can adjust the spacing of your text. These are available in the Format menu within the Character Spacing, the Line Spacing and the Indents and Lists options when the text frame is highlighted.

The Character Spacing (Figure 129) allows you to shrink or stretch the characters. You need to highlight the text you want to work on and then increase or decrease the scaling using the up and down arrows. You can see the effects in the sample area at the bottom of the window.

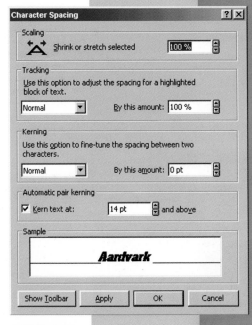

FIGURE 129
**Character Spacing**

The Line Spacing (Figure 130) window provides the means of setting the space between lines of text, before and after paragraphs. These are very useful to finely adjust the presentation between columns or over a page. The changes can be seen in the sample area to help you judge its effects.

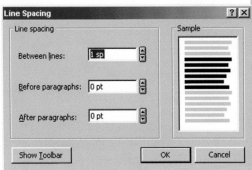

FIGURE 130
**Line Spacing**

Using the Indents and Lists (Figure 131) windows provides you with the means to indent your paragraphs. You can indent the left and right edges of the text or the first line of your paragraph. The sample area allows you to see the effects of your changes. By setting an indent you will provide a standard look to your publication. It is normal to standardise publication (e.g. the first line of each paragraph is indented in the same way).

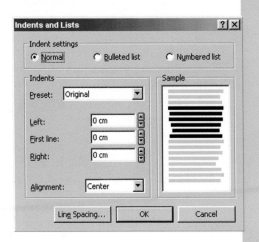

FIGURE 131
**Indents and Lists**

FIGURE 132
**Balanced Publication**

**Guinea Pigs**

For many people guinea pigs are the perfect pet. They are small friendly animals who rarely bite and easy to keep healthy. Guinea pigs are rodents and are not from Guinea so the name is a little misleading. They actually originate from Peru. There are several different breeds including selfs which are smoothed haired animals, Himalayans, Abyssinians and Crested.

Guinea pigs are herbivores. They

need to be given fresh vegetables everyday since they cannot make their own vitamin C. Their teeth grow all the time so they need to be given food which they

need to grind so that their teeth do not get too long. Dry food is available which has been enriched with vitamin C. Guinea

pigs are enthusiastic about their feed and will tell you when they are hungry. They will talk to you when you are late just to remind you they like their feed on time.

Guinea pigs can be kept indoors or outdoors. If they are in an outside hutch they need to be secured against both the cold and the local cats. A frosty night can leave pigs very distressed while they have few defences against cats. Indoor animals need the opportunity to exercise in the open air in a run or other secure enclosure. All guinea pigs love eating grass.

FIGURE 133
**Printing**

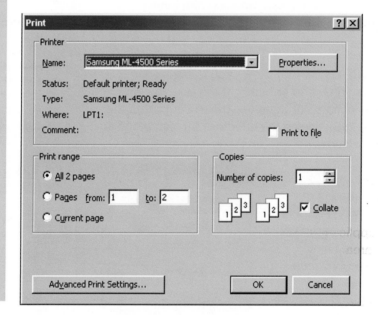

You can also access the Line Spacing window through the button at the bottom of the Indents and Lists window.

Having the ability to change the character size and font of the text with line spacing means you can carefully adjust the balance of each page. It requires some experimentation to gain the best results. Figure 132 shows the Guinea Pigs publication adjusted to fill the whole page. It is not ideal but is a reasonable result.

# Printing

A key factor in desktop publishing is the printing of your publication. You can do this with your own local printer or you can save the publication as a file on a disk to take it an external printer.

Before printing your publication it is important to use Publisher's functions to check your work. A spell checker is available by selecting the Tools menu, highlighting Spelling and clicking on Check Spelling. This will identify spelling mistakes. However, there are other possible errrors within a publication such as the insertion of a blank frame. These can be identified using the Design Checker which is opened by selecting the Tools menu and the Design Checker option. This will open a window which allows you to specify what parts (e.g. pages) of the publication you want to check. A final and probably the best check is simply to read and review the publication yourself.

To print your publication you select the File menu, then the Print option (Figure 133) and click on the OK button. The publication will print your publication using the printer's standard default settings.

# Exercise 40

## More Practice 1

**1.** Load Publisher by selecting the Start button, highlighting the Programs option and clicking on the Microsoft Publisher item or by clicking on the Publisher icon on the desktop. Observe the publisher catalog open.

**2.** Click on the Blank Publications Tab, select the Poster option and click on the Create button.

**3.** The Publisher application will appear. The blank poster will occupy the centre of the work area.
**4.** Your task is to create a poster for an open garden event in a village.

**5.** Using the Page Setup in the File menu, set the layout to Normal and orientation to Portrait.

**6.** Using the Layout Guides in the Arrange menu, set the margins to 2.5cms.

**7.** Create a text frame to cover the top quarter of the poster and Enter Open Gardens as a heading using a character size of 48 and a font called Scribe (or a font of your choice). Centre the heading and embolden the heading.

**8.** Create a picture frame and insert it into the middle of the poster and using the Insert menu option Pictures. Select and insert a relevant item of clip art.

**9.** Finally insert a second text frame at the bottom of the poster.

**10.** Enter the address from where tickets can be obtained for the show

using Scribe and a character size of 20 (e.g Tickets are available at the Post Office). Present the text effectively.

**11.** Now enclose your three frames in suitable borders using the Format menu and the Line/Border and More Styles options. Remember that the border tool operates on a frame.

**12.** Save your poster by selecting the File menu and the Save option.

**13.** Print your poster by selecting the File menu, Print option and OK button.

**14.** Close the application by clicking on the close button in the top right-hand corner of the window or by selecting File and then the Exit option.

# Exercise 41

## More Practice 2

**1.** Load Publisher by selecting the Start button, highlighting the Programs option and clicking on the Microsoft Publisher item or by clicking on the Publisher icon on the desktop. You should observe the publisher catalog open.

**2.** Click on the Blank Publications Tab, select the Blank Full page option and click on the Create button.

**3.** The Publisher application will appear. The blank full page will occupy the centre of the work area.
**4.** Your task is to create a newsletter for a community group.

**5.** Using the Page Setup in the File menu, set the layout to Normal and the orientation to Portrait.

**6.** Using the Layout Guides in the Arrange menu, set the margins to 1.5 cms.

**7.** Create a text frame to cover the whole page. Using the Text Frame Properties window within the Format menu (remember the text frame must be highlighted), divide the page into three columns with a spacing of 0.4 cm.

**8.** Create a second text frame across the top of the page (over the first text frame) in which to place your heading. Enter the heading Community Newsletter in Ariel Black with a character size of 36.

**9.** Create a picture frame and centre it below the heading, covering the three columns. Insert an appropriate clip art picture using Insert menu and <u>P</u>icture option.

**10.** Create another text frame in the bottom right-hand corner of the page in the third (right-hand) columns. This is going to the the Community group's address for correspondence. So enter the address below:

Community Group
Green Community Centre
New Walk
New Town

**11.** Use the <u>L</u>ine Spacing option on the F<u>o</u>rmat menu to set the line spacing to 2.

**12.** Save your newsletter by selecting the <u>F</u>ile menu and the <u>S</u>ave option. You have effectively created a master document for future editions. You can add the remaining text depending on the news when the newsletter is issued. Save the file as Newsletter.

**13.** Import a text file into the newsletter. You can choose any file but ideally it should be only a short piece of text. Use the <u>I</u>nsert menu and the T<u>e</u>xt File option.

**14.** Observe how the text flows around your image frame and down the columns.

**15.** Using the Indents and Lists window indent the paragraphs by 1 cm (remember to hightlight all the text you want included) and then set the line spacing between lines to 1.5, and 1 before and after each paragraph.

**16.** Change the text font to Arial (or a font of your choice) and character size to 12 (or a size of your choice). Set the justification to double (remember to hightlight all the text you want included). Try to produce a balanced newsletter.

**17.** Surround the whole newsletter with an appropriate border and with faint lines separating the columns. Enclose the address and heading frames in separate borders.

**18.** Save the newsletter under a new file name by selecting the <u>F</u>ile menu and the Save <u>A</u>s option. Use the name New Newsletter.

**19.** Print your revised newsletter by selecting the <u>F</u>ile menu, <u>P</u>rint option and OK button.

**20.** Close the application by clicking on the close button in the top right-hand corner of the window or by selecting <u>F</u>ile and then the E<u>x</u>it option.

## Wizard

Publisher, like many Office applications, provides you with the means to create a publication quickly using a variety of standard templates. This exercise is included because it is a practical way of rapidly producing acceptable publications which you may find useful.

# Exercise 42

## Using the wizard to create a newsletter

**1.** Load Publisher by selecting Start button, highlighting Programs and clicking on Microsoft Publisher option or clicking on Publisher icon on the desktop.

**2.** Click on the Publications by Wizard Tab, select the Newsletters option from the left hand list and Bars Newsletter from the templates on the right. Click on the Start Wizard button.

**3.** The Publisher application opens with the chosen newsletter at the centre of the work area. A message may appear telling you that publisher will enter your personal details automatically into the newsletter. Click on the OK button if this happens and a window will open for you to select your personal information. Just press the Update button.

**4.** On the left of the newsletter display is the wizard window. When you are ready, click on the Next button. This will reveal the colour schemes available to you. Select one you like and click on the Next button. You will be presented with the decision about how many columns you want. Make a decision and click the Next button. This process continues asking you about placeholders for customers' addresses, one or two-sided printing and including personal information. If you make a mistake you can go back using the Back button. When you are ready, complete the process by clicking on the Finish button.

**5.** You have created a template for your publication. If you click on the newsletter you can see the different frames and these allow you to enter text, import pictures etc. You can also use the wizard features in the left-hand lists.

**6.** Explore the different options until you are sure that you understand how the wizard works.

**7.** Close the application by clicking on the close button in the top right-hand corner of the window or by selecting File and then the Exit option.

# Summary Desktop Publishing

**1. Load Microsoft Publisher** Use either the Start button and the Programs menu or double click on the Publisher icon on the Windows desktop.

Select the tab option of your choice and click on the Create button.

**2. Close** Click on the File menu item and the Exit option or click on the close button in the top right-hand corner of the application window

**3. Save a file on a floppy disk** Insert a floppy disk into drive A: and click on the File Menu and Save. Select floppy disk and enter the file name.

Having saved a file once, you can update it by clicking on the File Menu and Save without the Save As window appearing again. It simply overwrites the original file.

**4. Set Page Size** Select the File menu then the Page Setup option. This will reveal the Page Setup window.

**5. Set Guides** Select the Arrange menu then the Layout Guides to reveal the Layout Guides window.

**6. Insert a Text Frame** Select theText Frame tool on the Objects toolbar. The mouse pointer will change to a crosshair to allow you to position your text accurately.

Position the top left hand corner of where you would like to locate the frame and then, holding the mouse button down, move the pointer down to form a rectangle.

**7. Move and Resize a Frame** Position the mouse pointer over a handle and the pointer will change shape (double arrow). By holding down the mouse button, you can change the shape of the frame. Position your mouse pointer over the frame lines away from the handles and the pointer will change shape (small vehicle). By holding down the mouse button, you can move the frame.

**8. Change Fonts and Character Size** Highlight the text. Select the small down arrow button to the right of the character size box to reveal a list of sizes. Click on the size of your choice. Select the small down arrow button to the right of the font box to reveal a list of fonts. Click on the font of your choice.

Desktop Publishing

**9. Serif and Sans Serif fonts** The list of fonts includes fonts that are of type serif and sans serif. A serif font has small flags on the ends of the characters (i.e. they are more fancy) while a sans serif does not (i.e. they are more plain).

**10. Justification** Highlight the text and select the respective icons from the format toolbar.

**11. Inserting Text and Pictures** Select the Insert menu and the Text File option. This opens The Insert Text window which allows you to choose the file you want to insert. Select the Insert menu, highlight Picture to reveal four options Clip Art, From File, From Scanner or Camera and New Drawing. Alternatively, text and pictures can be copied and pasted from other Office applications.

**12. Lines and Borders** Select the Format menu, highlight Line/Border Style to reveal the Border Style window.

**13. Character and Line Spacing** Select the Format menu and either the Character Spacing or the Line Spacing options with the text frame highlighted. This will reveal either the Character Spacing or Line Spacing windows.

**14. Indent Paragraphs** Select the Format menu and the Indents and Lists option with the text frame highlighted. This will reveal the Indents and Lists window.

**15. Checking** Select the Tools menu, highlight the Spelling option and click on Check Spelling.

Select the Tools menu and the Design Checker option. This will open a window which allows you to specify what parts (e.g. pages) of the publication you want to check.

**16. Printing** Select the File menu, then the Print option and click on the OK button.

# chapter 7

# Graphs and Charts

This chapter will help you to:

identify and use appropriate software correctly

produce pie charts, line graphs and bar/column charts

select and present single and comparative sets of data

set numerical parameters and format data

manage and print graphs and chart documents

## Assessment

This unit does not assume any previous experience of graphs and charts but you may find it useful if you have previously undertaken Unit 1 (Using a Computer), Unit 4 (Spreadsheets) and Unit 5 (Databases). After studying unit 7, your skills and understanding are assessed using a 2-hour practical assignment. This is set by OCR and marked locally. However, the marking will be externally moderated by OCR. This ensures that the standard is being applied correctly across the many different providers of OCR New CLAIT.

## Graphs and chart applications

When you are presenting people with numerical information, it is sometimes difficult even for highly numerate people to understand the relationship between the different elements. However, if you can convert the information into visual images then it is far easier to see the trends and relationships. There are several forms of visual representations such as pie charts, line graphs and bar or column charts. Microsoft Excel has many functions to turn numerical information into graphs and charts. There are other applications which allow you to model live data. That is, systems which take data as it is created (e.g. output from a process plant) and show it in the form of a chart or a graph. However, these charts and graphs continuously change because the data they are modelling is altering all the time. This type of continuous output is often printed on a special printer called a plotter. Excel graphs and charts are in comparison static representations of data.

However, if the spreadsheet information changes then you can produce new graphs and charts. This would allow you to monitor the information visually. This would be useful if you were producing a monthly spreadsheet of sales figures, salary costs or staff absences.

Spreadsheets allow you to create models of information so that you can see the consequences of changes (e.g. price rises, decreased costs, changes in interest rates and pay increases). These changes can also be converted into graphs and charts to help you analyse the changes and their effect on other factors. A visual presentation of data (i.e. a graph or chart) may allow you to identify effects which are not easy to see in a table of numbers.

Figure 134 shows the costs of running the Acme Newsagent.
The numbers are very important but for many people their relationship may not be obvious.

| Acme Newsagent | |
| --- | --- |
| | Costs |
| Newspape | 12,000 |
| Groceries | 10,000 |
| Stationary | 8,000 |
| Wages | 6,000 |

**FIGURE 134
Numerical Data**

# Pie charts

A Pie chart is used to represent numbers as slices of a circle so that the size of each slice is proportional to the whole. In Figure 135, the pie chart shows the Acme Newsagent's costs and it is easy to see that the cost of newspapers represent the biggest cost while wages are only about half that amount.

# Line graphs

A line graph helps you to compare two different factors. The graph in Figure 136 compares the costs of the different items for the Acme Newsagent.

# Column charts

A column chart represents numbers as columns of different length. Figure 137 shows the column chart for the Acme Newsagent's costs.

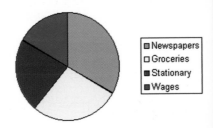

- Newspapers
- Groceries
- Stationary
- Wages

**FIGURE 135
Pie Chart**

# Bar chart

A bar chart is similar to a column chart except that the data is represented as bars rather than columns. Figure 138 shows a bar chart of the Acme Newsagent's costs.

# Comparison

Figures 135, 136, 137 and 138 show the same numerical information (as Figure134) in the form of pie, line, column and bar charts. You should review and compare the different visual presentations. How effective do you feel the displays are in showing the information? The line graph is ineffective in that it is essentially just four isolated items of data. A line drawn between them would not show anything since the numerical data would not follow the line. Line graphs are more useful when they show change over time or where you can plot several pieces of data to produce a range of lines (e.g. plotting the

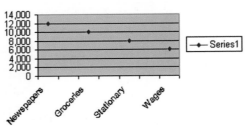

— Series1

**FIGURE 136
Line Graph**

FIGURE 137
**Column Chart**

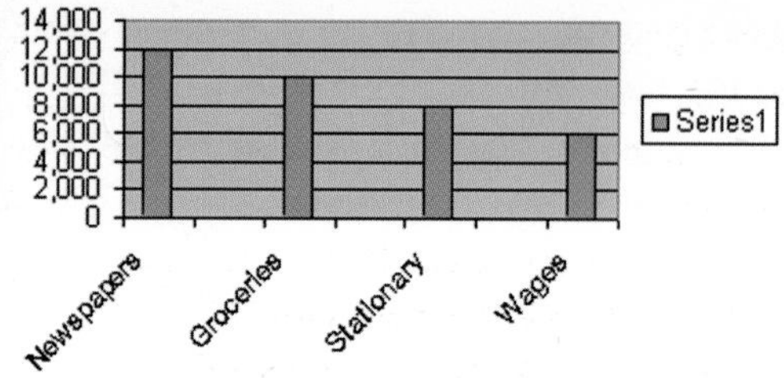

FIGURE 138
**Bar Chart**

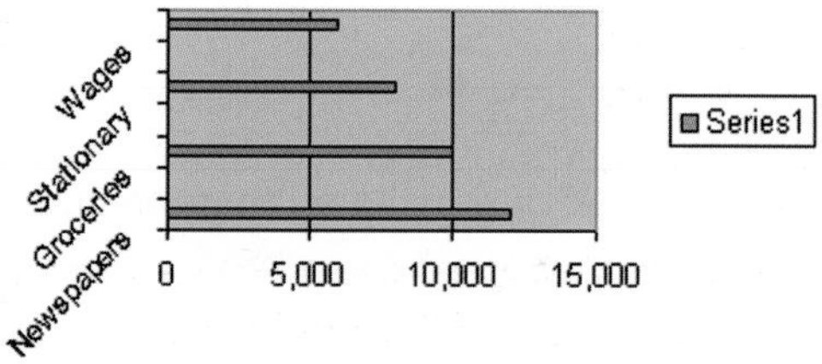

operating costs of several different cars over several years). This allows you to compare different information.

# Microsoft Excel

Unit 4 covers the use of spreadsheets and this chapter is based on Microsoft Excel. This application contains a range of functions to present numerical information in the form of graphs and charts. These functions will be used in this unit. Other applications have similar functionality.

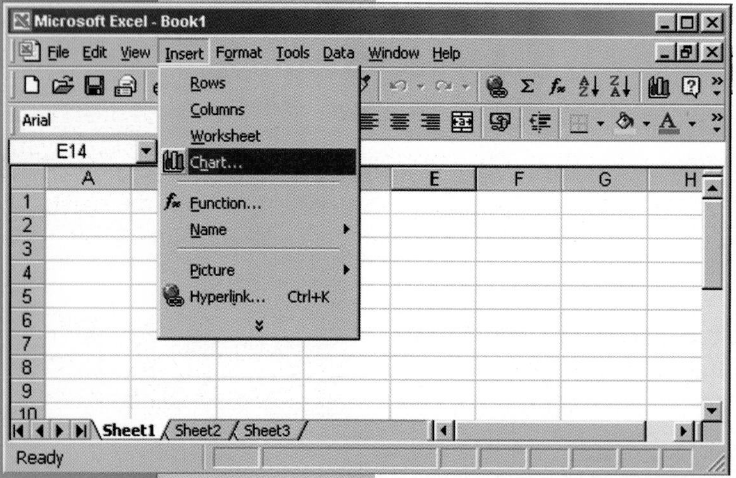

The first step is to insert data into the spreadsheet in the normal way. The data is highlighted, the Insert menu is selected and then Chart (Figure 139). This opens up the Chart Wizard (Figure 140). On the left-hand edge is a list of

FIGURE 139
**Insert Menu**

Chart types from which you need to choose the type of chart or graph you wish to use. This is done by clicking once on the one you select. On the right-hand side of the window the charts will change to show you examples of your chosen chart. Again you need to select the example you want to use. This is achieved by a single click. A description of the chart is given below the examples. If you want to see what your actual chart will look like then you click on the Press and Hold to View sample button holding the left mouse button down. If you release the mouse button then the chart will disappear.

FIGURE 140
**Chart Wizard**

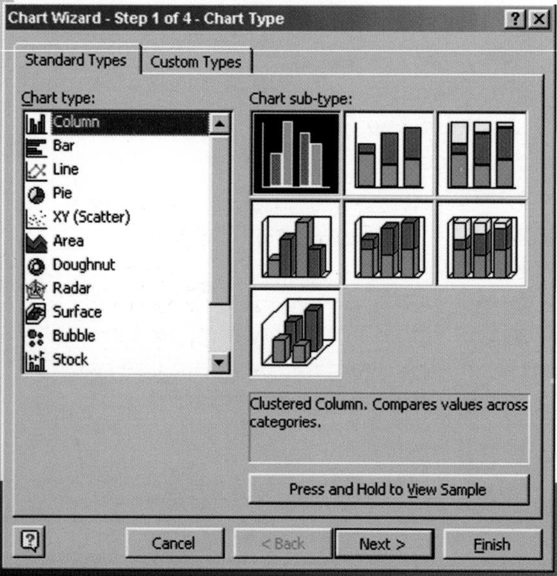

At the top of the Chart Wizard window you will see that it states that it is step 1 of 4. Figure 140 shows step 1 of the process. You move between the steps by clicking on the next button. The second step is shown in Figure 141 which illustrates a pie chart. The data range is shown in this display - =Sheet1!$B$8:$C$14. This may look confusing but if you ignore the $ signs it reads

B8:C14, that, is the data is drawn from sheet 1 and the area B8 to C14.

It is vital to check that the Wizard has used the correct data range. It does not always get the range right and therefore your chart will be wrong. You should check the data range is correct each time you create a graph or chart. Each exercise will ask you to check your data range.

FIGURE 141
**Chart
Wizard
Step 2**

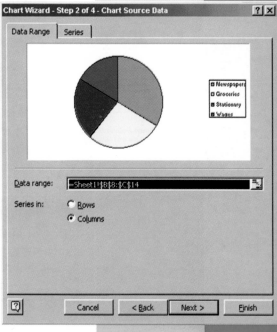

If the next button is clicked again then the display will change to step 3 (Figure 142). This dialogue box allows you to label your chart. You can enter an overall title for the chart or graph, label the axes of the graphs and add a legend. The options available in step 3 will depend on the chart or graph you have selected. For example, a pie chart does not have axes so there is no point in providing options to label them. Figure 144 shows a chart with the different labels identified. The legend is essentially an explanation of the colour coding of the chart. In this example it is not particularly important since there is only a single set of information. However, in a pie chart (Figure 141) we are comparing four items so the legend is important to identify which colour represents each one.

If the next button is clicked again then the display will change to step 4 (Figure 143). This window determines whether the chart is placed on a new sheet or as an additional object in an existing sheet (e.g. a chart placed alongside the data). A chart placed on a separate sheet allows you more freedom to present your chart or graph in the way you want. While placing a chart alongside its related data does help to illustrate their inter-relationship. The exercises will ask you to create your graphs or charts on a separate sheet. However you may wish to experiment with the other option. Once you have made this decision you can complete the process by clicking on the Finish button. At each step you can return to the previous step by clicking on the Back button. This allows you to correct errors.

FIGURE 142
**Chart
Wizard
Step 3**

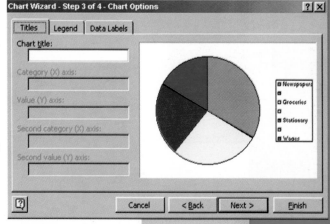

## Changing a chart or graph

Once you have finished a chart or graph you can move it around the display, adjust its size and change the layout. This is done by single clicking on the chart. The chart's surrounding rectangle (enclosure) changes to show small black squares in each corner and the middle of the lines (Figure 144). These are called handles. If the pointer is clicked within the chart's enclosure and the mouse button held down and dragged then the whole chart can be moved to new locations. If the same approach is

FIGURE 143
**Chart
Wizard
Step 4**

FIGURE 144
**Titles and legends**

FIGURE 145
**Mouse Pointers**

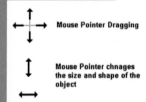

← → Mouse Pointer Dragging

↕ Mouse Pointer chnages the size and shape of the object

← →

FIGURE 146
**Format Chart Area**

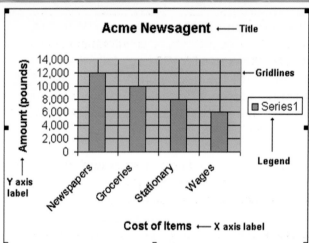

used with individual objects within the chart (e.g. legend in Figure 144) it too will be enclosed in a rectangle and can be dragged to a new position within the chart's overall enclosure.

Figure 145 shows the different shapes of the mouse pointer when dragging the chart enclosure to new positions and when the mouse is being used to change the shape and size of the chart. If you place the mouse over the small black squares (handles) either in the middle of the lines or on the corners then they change shape to double-headed arrows and by holding down the mouse pointer you can drag the side or corner of the enclosure to expand the chart or push the line in to reduce the chart's size.

Once you have created a chart you can still make changes and amend it by right clicking on the enclosure. This reveals a menu of options shown in Figure 146. This is the Format Chart Area menu which allows you to access the options available during the Chart Wizard process and make any changes.

# Exercise 43

## Column chart

**1.** Load Microsoft Excel using either the Programs menu or the Excel icon on the desktop.

**2.** Enter the table of information below to form your first spreadsheet. It shows a simple breakdown of the sales of motor cars over a six month period.

| January | 35,000 |
|---|---|
| February | 47,500 |
| March | 21,000 |
| April | 32,900 |
| May | 16,000 |
| June | 34,780 |

Start your sheet in cell A1 (i.e. January) with the sales information in B1 (i.e. 35,000) so that the table covers the area A1 to B6.

**3.** Highlight the whole table entered (i.e. A1 to B6) by clicking once in A1 and holding down the mouse button, dragging the pointer to B6. The whole table will be highlighted and you can then release the button.

**4.** Select the Chart Wizard (i.e. Insert menu and Chart option). Explore the options of Column, Bar, Line and Pie charts by clicking on each in turn and then considering the different options and their descriptions.

**5.** Finally select Column Chart type and the default sub-type which is in the top left-hand corner. Using the Press and Hold to View sample button review the chart (remember that you must hold down the left mouse button to see the chart. If you release it the image will disappear).

**6.** Select the Next button to move to Step 2 and review the data range to ensure it is correct. Click on the Next button again to move to Step 3.

**7.** In Step 3 select the Title tab and enter:

Chart title – Car Sales
Category (X) axis – Months
Value (Y) axis – Income (pounds)

**8.** In Step 3 select the Legend tab and remove the tick from the radio button Show legend. In this case there is no need for a legend since there is only one set of data.

FIGURE 147
**Car Sales Chart**

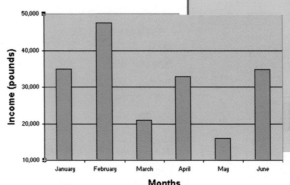

**9.** Select the Next button to move to Step 4.
Select As new sheet and enter Car Sales Column Chart. When you are ready click on the Finish button. The chart will appear on a separate sheet to the data it relates to (Figure 147).

**10.** Save the spreadsheet you have created on to a floppy disk. This procedure is the same in all Windows applications so you can save a spreadsheet, database or graphic image in exactly the same way.

insert      a floppy disk into drive A:
click on    File menu item and a menu will open showing a list of options.
            Select Save and a window will open.

**11.** Click in the box File name and Enter A:\Charts Cars. Now click on the Save button on the right of the window. You have now saved your chart as a file called Charts Cars. You may hear drive A: work during this process.

**12.** You can now close Excel. Either click on the File menu item and a menu will appear with a list of options. At the bottom of the list is the option Exit. If you click on Exit then Excel will close. An alternative way is to click on the close button in the top right-hand corner of the application window.

# Exercise 44

## Line chart/graph

**1.** Load Microsoft Excel using either the Programs menu or the Excel icon on the desktop.

**2.** Enter the table of information below to form another spreadsheet. It shows a breakdown of the travel expenses claimed by an employee of a large company.

| | Mileage | Subsistence | Other |
|---|---|---|---|
| April | 230 | 85 | 56 |
| May | 450 | 120 | 32 |
| June | 80 | 16 | 6 |
| July | 167 | 45 | 14 |
| August | 144 | 23 | 7 |

Start your sheet in cell D8 (i.e. April) with final item of Other in G12 (i.e. 7) so that the table covers the area D8 to G12.

**3.** Highlight the months and mileage part of the table entered (i.e. D8 to E12) by clicking once in D8 and holding down mouse button, dragging the pointer to E12.

| | Mileage |
|---|---|
| April | 230 |
| May | 450 |
| June | 80 |
| July | 167 |
| August | 44 |

**4.** Select the Chart Wizard (i.e. Insert menu and Chart option). Explore the options of Column, Bar, Line and Pie charts by clicking on each in turn and then considering the different options and their descriptions.

**5.** Finally select Line Chart/Graphs type and the default example. Using the Press and Hold to View sample button review the chart (remember that you must hold down the left mouse button to see the chart. If you release it the image will disappear).

**6.** Select the Next button to move to Step 2 and review the data range to ensure it is correct. Then click on the Next button again to move to Step 3.

**7.** In Step 3 select the Title tab and enter:

Chart title – Expenses
Category (X) axis – Months
Value (Y) axis – Claim (pounds)

**8.** In Step 3 select Legend and remove the tick from radio button Show legend. In this case there is no need for a legend since there is only one set of data.

**9.** In Step 3 select gridlines and tick box Category (X) axis Major gridlines. Watch the addition of gridlines.

**10.** Select the Next button to move to Step 4. Select As new sheet and enter Expenses Line Graph. When you are ready click on Finish button. The chart will appear on a separate sheet to the data it relates to (Figure 148).

**11.** Save the spreadsheet you have created on to a floppy disk. This procedure is the same in all Windows applications so you can save a spreadsheet, database or graphic image in exactly the same way.

insert a floppy disk into drive A:
click on File menu item and a menu will open showing a list of options. Select Save and a window will open

**12.** Click in the box File name and Enter A:\Expenses Chart. Now click on Save button on the right of the window. You have now saved your graph as a file called Expenses Chart. You may hear drive A: work during this process.

**13.** You can now close Excel. Either click on the File menu item and a menu will appear with a list of options. At the bottom of the list is the option Exit. If you click on Exit then Excel will close. An alternative way is to click on the close button in the top right-hand corner of the application window.

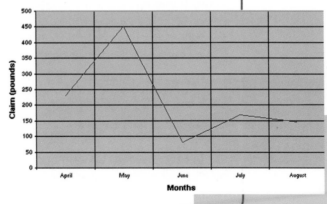

FIGURE 148
**Expenses Chart**

# Exercise 45

## Pie chart

**1.** Load Microsoft Excel using either the Programs menu or the Excel icon on the desktop.

**2.** Enter the table of information below to form your third spreadsheet. It shows the number of books borrowed by type from a small branch library.

Library Books

| | |
|---|---|
| Romance | 126 |
| Historica | I34 |
| Crime | 87 |
| Contemporary | 12 |
| Factual | 95 |

Start your sheet in cell B4 (i.e. Romance) with the final item of expenditure in C8 (i.e. 95) so that the table covers the area B4 to C8.

**3.** Highlight the library data (i.e. B4 to C8) by clicking once in B8 and holding down the mouse button, dragging the pointer to C8 (i.e. do not highlight the title Library Books).

**4.** Select the Chart Wizard (i.e. Insert menu and Chart option). Explore the options of Column, Bar, Line and Pie charts by clicking on each in turn and then considering the different options and their descriptions.

**5.** Finally select Pie Chart type and the default example which is in the top left-hand corner. Using the Press and Hold to View sample button review the chart (remember that you must hold down the left mouse button to see the chart. If you release it the image will disappear).

**6.** Select the Next button to move to Step 2 and review data range to ensure it is correct and then click on the Next button again to move to Step 3.

**7.** In Step 3 select the Title tab and enter:

Chart title – Library Books

**8.** In Step 3 select Legend and change the placement of legend to the left by clicking on the appropriate radio buttons.

**9.** In Step 3 select Data Labels and select Show label by clicking on the radio button. This will label each sector of the Pie chart.

**10.** Select the Next button to move to Step 4. Select As new sheet. The chart will appear on a seperate sheet (Figure 149). This chart has a legend which is appropriate since it is important to know what each colour relates to. In this pie chart we have also added data labels. These can take a variety of forms such as value, per cent, label and label and per cent.

**11.** Save the spreadsheet you have created on to a floppy disk. This procedure is the same in all Windows applications so you can save a spreadsheet, database or graphic image in exactly the same way.

insert     a floppy disk into drive A:
click on    the File menu item and a menu will open showing a list of
           options. Select Save and a window will open.

**12.** Click in the box File name and Enter A:\Library books. Now click on the Save button on the right of the window. You have now saved your chart as a file called Library books. You may hear drive A: work during this process.

**13.** You can close Excel. Either click on the File menu item and a menu will appear with a list of options. At the bottom of the list is the option Exit. If you click on Exit then Excel will close. An alternative way is to click on the close button in the top right-hand corner of the application window

**Library Books**

 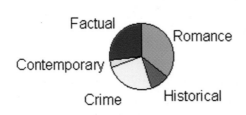

FIGURE 149
**Library
Books**

## Comparative charts and graphs

Displaying a single set of data can be important but charts and graphs are very useful in comparing several sets of information. In Exercise 44 you created a line graph (Figure 148) showing the relationship between months and mileage claimed. The spreadsheet (e.g. Expenses Chart) included data on subsistence and other claims. It is possible to produce a chart comparing these different elements.

# Exercise 46

## Comparison

**1.** Load Microsoft Excel using either the Programs menu or the Excel icon on the desktop.

**2.** Load 'Expenses Chart' by single clicking on File menu item to show the menu which has an option called Open. Click on Open and a window called Open will appear.

The Look in box tells you which drive the window is looking at. You need to aim it at drive A: (Floppy (A:) ). You do this by clicking on the small button with the down arrow at the end of the Look in box. A menu will appear. Click on the Floppy Disk option and the details of Expenses Chart will appear in the main working area. To open the file, click on it once to highlight it and then on the open button on the right hand side of the window. An alternative way is to double click on the Expenses Chart file. In either case the spreadsheet and chart will appear in the working area of Excel.

**3.** The spreadsheet is on sheet1 so click on tab to locate it. Highlight the whole table of data (i.e. D6 to G12). This includes the row and column headings.

**4.** Select the Chart Wizard (i.e. Insert menu and Chart option). Select Bar Chart type and the default example which is in the top left hand corner. Using the Press and Hold to View sample button review the chart (remember that you must hold down the left mouse button to see the chart. If you release it the image will disappear).

**5.** Select the Next button to move to Step 2 and review data range to ensure it is correct. Then click on the Next button again to move to Step 3.

**6.** In Step 3 select the Title tab and enter:

Chart title – Comparing Expenses
Category (X) axis – Months
Value (Y) axis - Amount (pounds)

**7.** In Step 3 select Legend and explore the placement of the legend (top, bottom and right) by clicking on the appropriate radio buttons.

**8.** Select the Next button to move to Step 4. Select As new sheet and enter Comparing Expenses. When you are ready click on Finish button. The chart will appear on a separate sheet to the data it relates to (Figure 150A). The three coloured bars represent the different parts of the expenses claim.

**9.** Now repeat the process but select a line graph instead of a bar chart. Call the new graph Comparing Expences2. Figure 150B shows the line graph. Compare the bar chart with it and decide which you feel provides the more useful image. You could try to identify which one helps you compare the three sets of data.

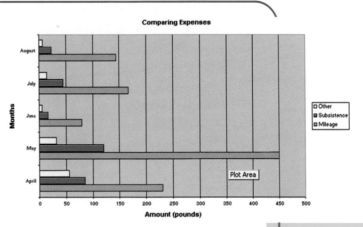

**10.** Save the spreadsheet you have created on to a floppy disk. This procedure is the same in all Windows applications so you can save a spreadsheet, database or graphic image in exactly the same way.

insert    a floppy disk into drive A:

click on    the File menu item and a menu will open showing a list of options. Select Save and a window will open.

**11.** Click in the box File name and Enter A:\Comparing Expenses. Now click on Save button on the right of the window. You have now saved your chart as a file called Comparing Expenses. You may hear drive A: work during this process.

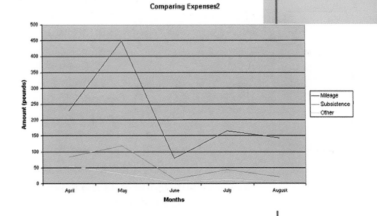

**12.** You can close Excel now. Either click on the File menu item and a menu will appear with a list of options. At the bottom of the list is the option Exit. If you click on Exit then Excel will close. An alternative way is to click on the close button in the top right-hand corner of the application window.

# Set axes and upper and lower limits

With any chart and graph it is important to be able to set the axes since these provide you with the scale against which to judge the display. Microsoft Excel provides the functions to edit the scale. If you click on the corner of your axes then a handle will appear (Figure 151). Double clicking on the value axis (notice a small label appears to help you identify the axis) will open up the

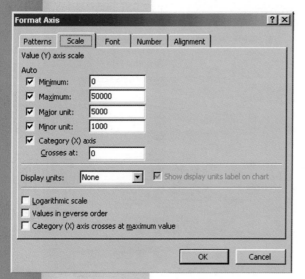

FIGURE 151
**Change
Axes**

**Car Sales**

FIGURE 152
**Format
Axis**

Handle

Format Axis dialogue box (Figure 152).

To change the scale you enter new values in the boxes within the Scales tab. Change Minimum to 10,000, leave Maximum unchanged, Major unit to 10,000 and Minor unit unchanged. This will change the chart to Figure 153.

## Printing a chart

Charts are visual representations of data so it is appropriate to print them in order that they can be distributed. Colour is also employed to distinguish between the different components; it is useful to provide coloured printouts whenever possible. If you do not have access to a colour printer then it is important to check that the colours you are using are clear when reproduced using different shades of grey. You can do this by using the Print Preview option in the File menu. If your computer is connected to a colour printer the preview will be in colour but if your printer is black and while only, then the preview will use different shades of grey.

FIGURE 153
**Changing
Axes**

To print a chart you need to select the File menu and then the Print option. Figure 154 shows the Print dialogue box. The dialogue box is divided into different areas. Printer showing the printer that your computer is connected to, Print Range which allows you to select All or page range, Copies allows you to print multiple copies of the chart and Print what allows you to select which sheet to print of the spreadsheet. The Preview button allows you a final check to see if your chart is correct.

## More examples

It is most important to practise creating charts and graphs. The following examples are provided to help you refine your skills. In each case, create the sheet and produce an appropriate chart or graph. Explore editing the

**Car Sales**

chart by moving it, altering its shape and changing the axes scales. Finally print the chart.

## Example 1

**Population**

| | |
|---|---|
| Town A | 23,000 |
| Town B | 46,000 |
| Town C | 106,000 |
| Town D | 213,000 |
| Town E | 11,000 |

## Example 2

**Household Expendiure**

Family 1 9,700
Family 2 11,870
Family 3 29,450
Family 4 17,600
Family 5 5,600
Family 6 31,700
Family 7 12,150

FIGURE 154
**Print**

## Example 3

**Comparisons**

Internet users

| | | 1997 | 1998 | 1999 | 2000 | 2001 |
|---|---|---|---|---|---|---|
| Education | 1.2 | 1.4 | 1.9 | 2.7 | 3.5 | |
| Business | | 2.1 | 3.15 | 4.65 | 7.2 | 11.7 |
| Home | | 0.2 | 0.3 | 0.45 | 0.7 | 1.35 |

## Example 4

Opinion polls by age

| | 18 to 25 | 26 to 35 | 36 to 50 | 51 to 65 | over 65 |
|---|---|---|---|---|---|
| Albright | 11 | 23 | 35 | 6 | 7 |
| Brown | 17 | 45 | 12 | 3 | 1 |
| Poule | 4 | 15 | 22 | 32 | 21 |
| Singh | 27 | 39 | 31 | 24 | 16 |
| Watson | 3 | 11 | 17 | 9 | 3 |

## Example 5

Operating costs of different cars

| | January | Febuary | March | April | May | June |
|---|---|---|---|---|---|---|
| Model A | 88 | 93 | 90 | 89 | 92 | 96 |
| Model B | 102 | 108 | 101 | 99 | 105 | 111 |
| Model C | 65 | 71 | 70 | 64 | 67 | 64 |

## 1. Load Microsoft Excel
Use either the Start button and the Programs menu or double click on the Excel icon on Windows desktop

## 2. Chart Wizard
Insert data into the spreadsheet. Highlight data and select the Insert menu and the Chart option (Figure 139). This opens up the Chart Wizard (Figure 140).

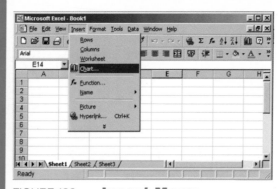

FIGURE 139    **Insert Menu**

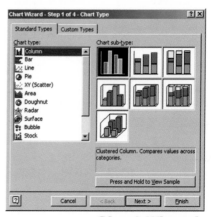

FIGURE 140    **Chart Wizard**

## 3. Column, Bar, Line and Pie charts
At the left-hand edge of Chart Wixard is a list of Chart types. Click once on the type of chart. On the right-hand side of the window are displayed examples of your chart. Select the example with a single click and a description of the chart is given below the examples.

FIGURE 141
**Chart
Wizard
Step 2**

## 4. Preview Charts
Click on the Press and Hold to View sample button holding the left mouse button down. If you release the mouse button then the chart will disappear.

## 5. Data range
The second step of Chart Wizard (Figure 141) shows the data range in the form of   =Sheet1!$B$8:$C$14 – by removing the $ signs, the data range is sheet 1 B8:C14

It is crucial to check that the chart or graph is based on the correct data range

## 6. Titles, legends and labels
Step 3 of Chart Wizard (Figure 142). This dialogue box changes depending on the type of chart being developed.

## 7. Correct Errors
Use the Back button to move back through the Chart Wizard steps.

**8. New Sheet** The fourth step of the Chart Wizard provides you with the options to present your graph or chart on a new sheet or as an additional object in an existing sheet (e.g. the one containing the data it relates to).

**9. Change display** Single clicking on the chart will reveal handles which allow you to move and change the size of the chart using the mouse.

**10. Edit Chart** Right click on the chart enclosure. Format Chart Area menu will appear allowing you to access the options available during the Chart Wizard process and also make any changes.

**11. Alter Axes** Double clicking on the value axis (notice a small label appears to help you identify the axis) will open up Format Axis dialogue box. The Scale tab allows you to change the scale of the chart axes.

**12. Save a file to a floppy disk** Insert a floppy disk into drive A: then click on the File Menu and Save. Select drive (floppy Disk A:) and enter the file name.

Having saved a file once, you can update it by clicking on the File Menu and Save without the Save As window appearing again. It simply overwrites the original file.

**13. Printing** Select the File menu, the Print preview and the Close button to preview the chart before printing.

Select the File menu, the Print option and the OK button to print.

# chapter 8

# Computer Art

This chapter will help you to use a drawing package to:

identify and use appropriate software correctly

import, crop and resize images

enter, amend and resize text

manipulate and format page items

manage and print artwork

## Assessment

This unit does not assume any previous experience of Computer Art. However, you may find it useful if you have previously undertaken Unit 1 (Using a Computer). After studying Unit 8 your skills and understanding are assessed during a 2-hour practical assignment. This is set by OCR and marked locally. However, the marking will be externally moderated by OCR. This ensures that the standard is being applied correctly across the many different providers of OCR New CLAIT.

## Drawing applications

There are many computer applications concerned with the production and manipulation of images. You can capture them using digital cameras and scanners, purchase collections known as clipart or simply create your own from scratch. Almost anyone can draw pictures using a computer drawing package. Computer pictures are called graphics. Windows has a drawing application built into it called Paint (Figure 156). This provides you with tools to draw lines, curves, circles and rectangles as well as to add colour to your images and change the orientation of the image. Microsoft Word has built-in drawing tools (select View menu, highlight the Toolbars option and click on Drawing).

There are two types of graphic images:

bitmaps
vectors

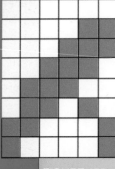

FIGURE 155
**Bitmap**

A bitmap image is composed of many dots called pixels. Figure 155 shows a magnified view of an image illustrating the individual pixels. The more pixels in a given amount of space (e.g. a square inch) the clearer the image or the higher the resolution of the picture (e.g. 72 pixels per inch). Each pixel is associated with the number of colours that can be displayed. An 8 bit image can use 256 colours while a 24 bit image can use 16.7 million colours. Bitmaps can probably show more detail than a vector image since every pixel of the image is employed.

Vector images are defined by mathematical formulae rather than pixels. This defines the start and finish of the line and allows it to be easily changed. Vector images can be resized and still stay in perfect proportion. Although you can change a bitmap image it will often distort if the change is too radical. This chapter is based on CorelDRAW 10, a professional vector drawing package with many useful tools for working with bitmaps and vectors.

## File formats

Graphics created by a painting or drawing package are stored on the computer as files. There are a variety of file formats that are used to represent graphics. The main ones are:

**JPEG –** Joint Photographic Expert Group is a bitmap format which is used extensively on the World Wide Web. Files which are in JPEG format are shown with an extension .jpeg or jpg

**GIF –** Graphics Interchange Format is a bitmap format and is also used extensively on the World Wide Web. Files which are in GIF format are shown by the extension .gif

**TIFF –** Tagged Image File Format is a bitmap format widely used in the graphics industry. Files which are in this format are shown by the extension .tif

**Windows bitmap** is the standard format for graphics in the Windows operating system. Files which are in this format are shown by the extension .bmp

**The Windows vector graphics** standard format is called Windows Metafile. Files in this format are shown by the extension .wmf

**Encapsulated Postscript** is a vector file format which is shown by the extension .eps

There are many other graphic file formats which have been designed for specific tasks. It is possible to convert from one to another but in some case this will effect the quality of the image.

## CorelDRAW

Figure 157 shows the CorelDRAW Application. When it is loaded, an image overlays the application offering you a variety of choices in the form of six icons. These are:

FIGURE 156
**Windows
Paint**

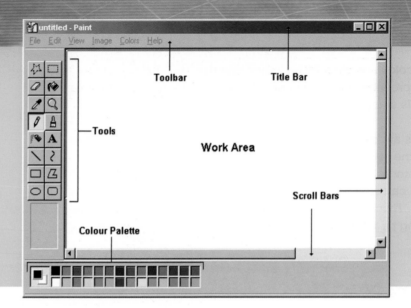

New Graphic – to start a new image
**Open Last Edited –** to allow you to continue working on the
last image
**Open Graphic –** to open an existing image
**Template –** to open a standard template
**CorelTutor –** to access a tutorial on how to use CorelDRAW
**What's New? –** provides you with an overview of CorelDRAW

You should select the New Graphic icon (Figure 157) and the overlay window
will open. This is the main application display. The centre of the display
shows the document area in which you can create a new graphic image. On
the left is the Toolbox containing many of the drawing tools, on the right is the
colour palette which allows you to select drawing and painting colours and on
the top are the menu and toolbars. The nearest toolbar to the work area
shows the size of the document that you are creating. In Figure 158 it shows
an A4 page. The toolbars in CorelDRAW change according to the action you
are undertaking. This can be initially confusing.

# Exercise 47

## Explore CorelDRAW

**1.** CorelDRAW is opened by either selecting the Start button, highlighting
Programs and clicking on CorelDRAW item or by double clicking on the
CorelDRAW icon on the Windows desktop.

**2.** Select the New Graphics icon.

**3.** Explore the different menus and toolbars.

**4** Explore the use of the drawing tools. Change the size of the drawing document using the down arrow on the toolbar near to A4 box (left hand side of the toolbar).

**5.** Select the File menu and locate the Import, Print and Save options.

**6.** Move your mouse pointer across the document and observe the rulers. You should see that the pointer's position is mirrored on each ruler. This is intended to help you position items on the page.

**7.** Locate the colour palette on the right-hand side of window.

**8.** Continue to explore until you are comfortable with finding your way around the application

**9.** Close the application by either selecting the File menu and the Exit option or clicking on the close button in the top right-hand corner of the window.

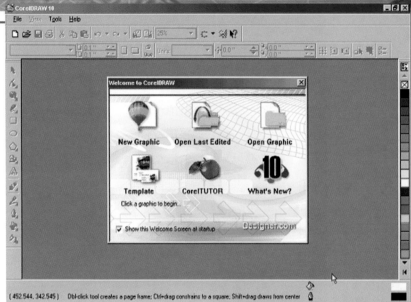

FIGURE 157
**CorelDRAW**

## New image

When you select the New Graphic icon, the default document is an A4 page. This can be changed by using the arrow keys on the toolbar

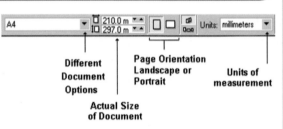

FIGURE 159
**Toolbar**

(Figure 159). You can select from a wide range of different documents (e.g. different page sizes, envelopes and postcards), change actual size of page, choose either landscape or portrait orientation and even alter the units of measurement of the page size (e.g. millimetres and inches).

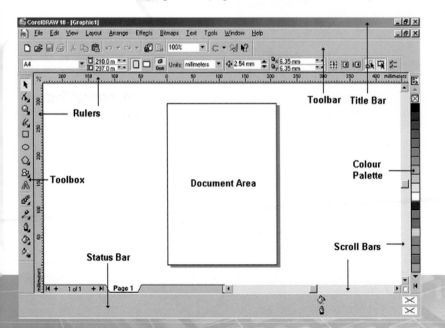

FIGURE 158
**CorelDRAW Application**

# Importing images

Pictures can be provided by:

scanning images

taking pictures using a digital camera

selecting from collections of clip art

drawing and painting your own graphics

FIGURE 160
**Importing an Image**

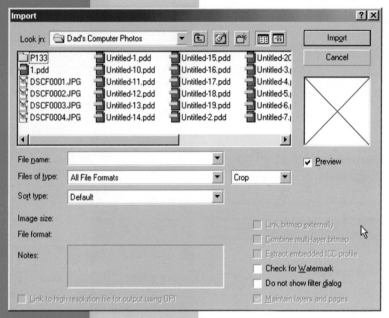

CorelDRAW can work with images from any source. Clip Art collections of many thousands of images can be bought and used. If you have access to a scanner or digital camera, you can use these resources to produce pictures. CorelDRAW can take these images in order to enhance and extend them. It is possible for the application to add captions to a digital picture explaining the different parts of the image.

CorelDRAW provides a straighforward way of importing images which allows you to:

crop the images (i.e. cut away parts of the picture you do not need)

resize images

precisely position imported images on your art work

FIGURE 161
**Crop and Resample**

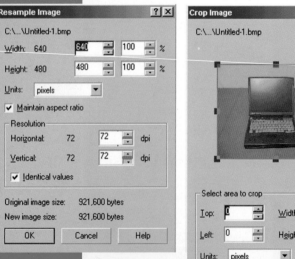

To import an image you need to select the File menu and the Import option. This reveals the Import window (Figure 160). The first step to importing an image is to locate the folder in which it is stored on your computer. This is undertaken by clicking on the down arrow at the end of the Look in box which will reveal a list of drives on which the folder could be stored.

If you select C: (the computer's internal hard disk) the work area will be filled with all the folders stored on that disk. To see what is in each folder you need to click on it. It will then open to show you its contents. This could be more folders and again, you need to click on them to reveal their contents.

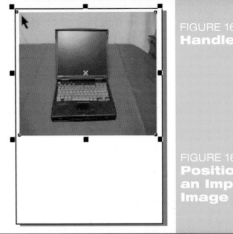

FIGURE 162
**Handles**

If you click on floppy, the work area will show you the contents of the disk. By clicking on D: you access the CD-Rom drive and if a CD-ROM is inserted you will be able to see its contents. Clip Art is often distributed on CD-ROMs since they can hold hundreds and in some cases thousands of images.

FIGURE 163
**Positioning an Imported Image**

Figure 160 shows a folder called Dad's Computer Photos which is stored on the hard disk (i.e. C:). These images are the result of taking digital photographs of computers and their components. It is good practice to set the Files of type to All File Formats using the down arrow button near the box. This will show you all the files available whereas other options will only reveal files of the type selected. This can sometimes confuse in that it can seem that the image you want has disappeared.

To identify the image, the window has a preview feature. If you click in the Preview radio button (a tick will appear) you can see every file that you have highlighted. This allows you to review the images until you find the one you want. When you have identified the correct picture you click on the Import button.

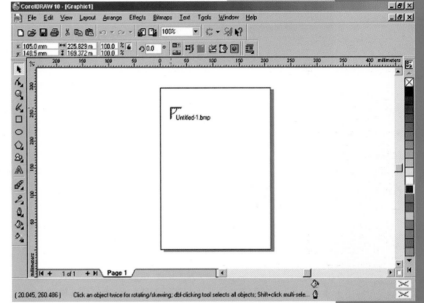

In the middle of the Import window is a small box which in Figure 160 has the word Crop placed in it. The down arrow next to the box, if clicked on, will reveal other options. These are:

**Full image –** this is the most straightforward option in that the chosen image is imported unchanged

**Crop –** this opens a further dialogue (window) box to allow you to identify what parts of the image you want to import (Figure 161). It provides you with a preview of the image

**Resample –** this allows you to change the resolution of an image and reduce its size (Figure 161)

**The Crop and Resample windows enable you to manipulate the image and**

when this has been done, the image is inserted into the document by clicking on the OK button.

When importing the image into the main application area, you need to choose where to place. This is done using a changed mouse pointer which allows you to position the top left-hand corner of the image precisely. Figure 163 shows the positioning of an image. The positioning pointer is placed at the desired point and the mouse button clicked. The image will now appear enclosed in a frame with a number of black squares (called handles). If the mouse pointer is placed on the handles it changes to a double headed arrow. If the mouse button is held down after the pointer has changed shape, you can drag the shape of the image around. The enclosure is removed by clicking away from the image and can be replaced by clicking on the image.

Figure 162 shows handles and internal handles. Internal handles are located at each corner of the image and let you skew the image using the mouse pointer which changes shape to that of a large arrowhead. At the centre of the image is a cross. If you place your mouse pointer over this cross it turns into a star. By holding down the mouse pointer, you can move the image to new positions.

# Exercise 48

## Importing an image

FIGURE 164
**Cropping**

**1.** CorelDRAW is opened by either selecting the Start button, highlighting Programs and clicking on the CorelDRAW item or by double clicking on the CorelDRAW icon on the Windows desktop.

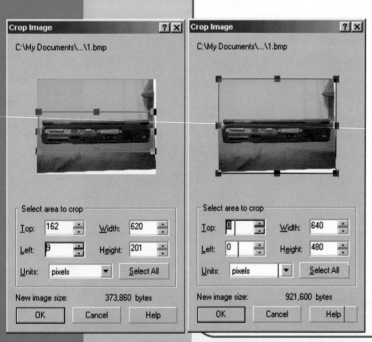

**2.** Select the New Graphics icon.

**3.** Select the File menu and Import option to reveal the Import window. Identify the folder in which the images are stored and use the preview facility to review the images. Select Crop options and double click on the picture's file name. The image will appear in the Crop window (Figure 161).

**4.** Use the enclosure handles to crop the chosen image. Figure 164 shows before and after cropping. You can use the handles for large crops and then select area to crop in detail.

**5.** When you are ready you click on the OK button and the positioning pointer will appear on the document for you to locate precisely. Locate the top left hand corner of the picture and click. The image of the laptop or your own picture will be placed on the document.

**6.** Figure 165 shows the image on the document and that it is too large for the document. Use the handles to resize the image.

**7.** By clicking on the centre handle you will see the handles change shape. If you place your mouse pointer on these handles it too will change shape (i.e. a partial circle with arrows on each end or parallel arrows facing opposite directions). The partial circle will allow you to rotate the image while the parallel arrows allow you to skew the image. Experiment with the two pointers by holding down the mouse button to move the image.

**8.** Skew the image. Turn it upside down and at right angles (Figure 166).

**9.** When the image is enclosed in its handles it is possible to copy or cut it using the functions on the Edit menu and the options Cut, Copy and Paste. These are also available on the Standard toolbar.

**10.** Select the Edit menu and the Copy option and then Paste. If you observe carefully you will see the image ficker. You now have two images of the laptop, one placed precisely on top of the other, so drag the top image down the page by clicking on the image and holding down the mouse button. You can paste as many copies of the laptop as you want.

FIGURE 165
**Cropped Image**

FIGURE 166
**Manipulating images**

FIGURE 167
**Edit Bitmap Image**

**11.** Delete the first image. You do this by clicking on it to enclose it and then you select the Edit menu and the Delete option. Or you can simply press the keyboard's delete key.

**12.** An alternative approach to manipulation is to use the Arrange menu and the Transformations option. This provides access to the Transformation window which is positioned alongside the graphic image. Explore the options (e.g. mirror to produce a

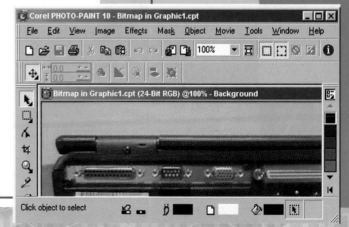

mirror image). To remove the window click on the cross in the top right-hand corner of the window.

**13.** Bitmapped images can also be edited. Click on the right mouse button to reveal a menu and select the Edit Bitmap option (Figure 167). This enables you to undertake detailed changes to the image.

**14.** Experiment with changing the image.

**15.** Save the image by selecting the File menu and the Save option. This will reveal the Save Drawing window. You need to decide where you will save your image. This is done by clicking on the down arrow near the Save in box. This will reveal a list of options. Select floppy disk and insert a disk into the drive. Click in the File name box and enter Imported Image. Click on the Save button. Your image is now saved as the file Imported Image.

**16.** Close the application by either selecting the File menu and the Exit option or clicking on the close button in the top right-hand corner of the window.

FIGURE 168
**Toolbox**

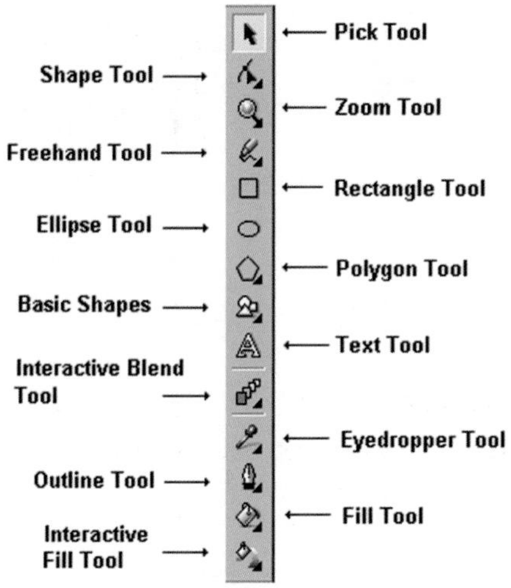

Shape Tool ⟶
Freehand Tool ⟶
Ellipse Tool ⟶
Basic Shapes ⟶
Interactive Blend Tool ⟶
Outline Tool ⟶
Interactive Fill Tool ⟶

← Pick Tool
← Zoom Tool
← Rectangle Tool
← Polygon Tool
← Text Tool
← Eyedropper Tool
← Fill Tool

## Create a graphic image

To create a graphic image you need to employ the tools available from the CorelDRAW toolbox which are available on the left edge of the application window (Figure 168 shows the different tools). They allow you to straighforwardly draw squares, circles, rectangles, ellipses, triangles, straight and curved lines as well as freehand drawings. Tools used to manipulate an imported image are also available for images drawn by yourself.

# Exercise 49

## Creating an image

**1.** CorelDRAW is opened by either selecting the Start button, highlighting Programs and clicking on CorelDRAW item or by double clicking on the CorelDRAW icon on the Windows desktop.

**2.** Select the New Graphics icon.

**3.** Click on the Freehand tool and try to draw a diagonal line across the page (top left to bottom right). The pointer takes the form of crosshairs to help position the start and finish of the line. You start by clicking where you want to begin and drag the line to opposite corner then click the button again when you want to finish.

**4.** The line will be surrounded by an enclosure of handles and a central cross. If you place the pointer over the centre you will see it change into a star. If you hold down the mouse button you can drag the line around. Try to move the line.

**5.** If you place the pointer over a handle it changes shape to a double-headed arrow and if you hold down the mouse button, you can reshape the line. Experiment with the different handles. You can use the undo and redo icons on the standard toolbar to retrace your steps.

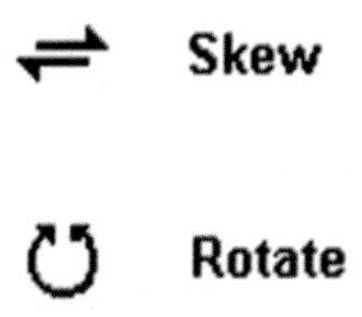

⇌ **Skew**

↺ **Rotate**

FIGURE 169
**Mouse Pointer Shapes**

**6.** If you click again on the centre or double click on the Pick Tool you will see the handles turn into curved arrows (Figure 170). These curved handles are used to rotate or skew the line using the mouse pointer. The mouse pointer turns into a partial circle and if you hold down the button, you can rotate the line or pointer turns into two parallel lines which you can use to skew the image. Experiment with rotating and skewing the line. Figure 169 shows the different mouse shapes.

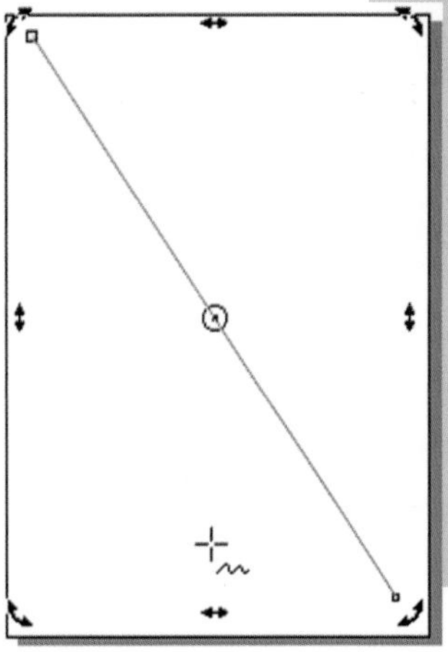

FIGURE170
**Rotational Handles**

**7.** Draw a curved freehand line by clicking where you want to start and releasing the button where you want to stop. Notice that along the curve are small squares or handles. If you place your pointer on one of these it will change shape into a large arrow. If you hold down your mouse pointer you can manipulate the shape of the line. Experiment with reshaping the line.

**8.** Click on the Pick tool and then on the shapes you have created. They will be enclosed and if you press the delete key, the shape will disappear. Clear all the shapes you have created.

**9.** Click on rectangle tool. The pointer will again change into a crosshair and you again start by clicking and holding down the tool. If you move diagonally you will see a rectangle appear. Draw a square using the rulers as a guide. The square will be enclosed and you can change the shape by moving the handles or move the square by using the central cross. You can even drag the image off the page into the surrounding area. This is a useful place to store objects until you are ready to use them. Again if you click on the centre cross or double click with the Pick tool you access the rotational handles. Experiment with rotating the square.

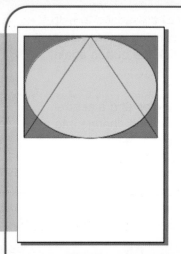

FIGURE 171
**Graphical Shapes**

**10.** Click on the Interactive Fill Tool and the colour palette (select red) and you will see the square fill with the red colour.

**11.** Click on the ellipse tool and attempt to draw an ellipse within the square. You will need to drag the ellipse handles to achieve the outcome.

**12.** Click on the Interactive Fill Tool and the colour palette (yellow red) and you will see the ellipse fill with the yellow colour.

**13.** Click on Freehand tool and draw a triangle within the square. Your picture should resemble something similar to Figure 171.

**14.** Continue to experiment with the different tools until you are confident that you can use them. If you find that the enclosure disappears and you cannot get it to reappear then you are probably clicking with the ordinary mouse pointer when you need to use the Pick tool.

**15.** Save the image by selecting the File menu and the Save option. This will reveal the Save Drawing window. You need to select the location where you will save your image. This is done by clicking on the down arrow near the Save in box. This will reveal a list of option. Select floppy disk and insert a disk into the drive. Click in the File name box and enter Graphical Shapes (Figure 172). Click on the Save button. Your image is now saved as a file entitled Graphical Shapes.

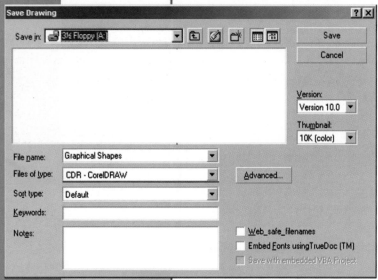

FIGURE 172
**Save**

**16.** Close the application by either selecting the File menu and the Exit option or clicking on the close button in the top right hand corner of the window.

## Line thickness

In the exercise we used quite thin lines but CorelDRAW allows you to vary line thickness using a toolbar option shown in Figure 173. You change the thickness of the lines by selecting the Freehand tool and then clicking on the down arrow next to the line thickness box to chose from the list of options. The thickness will be transferred to the other tools (e.g. rectangles will have the new line thickness). When you select the thickness, you may reveal a message which may not make a lot of sense to you at this point in time. Simply click on the OK button.

## Using text

The Toolbox provides you with a text tool, allowing you to enter text into your drawings. Use the tool to draw a rectangular area in which you can enter text from the keyboard. When you select the Text Tool, a new toolbar is inserted into the application (Figure 174) which allows you to select fonts, character sizes, embolden, write in italics and underline text. This is done either by clicking on the icons or on the down arrow to reveal lists of options.

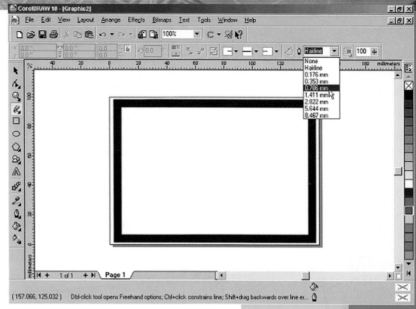

FIGURE 173
**Line
Thickness**

Layouts    Fonts    Character Sizes    Bold   Italics   Underline

FIGURE 174
**Text
Toolbar**

# Exercise 50

## Using text

**1.** CorelDRAW is opened by either selecting the Start button, highlighting Programs and clicking on the CorelDRAW item or by double clicking on the CorelDRAW icon on the Windows desktop.

**2.** Select the New Graphics icon.

**3.** Select the Text Tool and create a text rectangle on the document. Then select Ariel Black font and character size 48. The cursor flashes in the text rectangle to show you where the text is going to be inserted. Enter:

This is text

**4.** You can edit your word by using the backspace key to delete text or insert the cursor by clicking in the required place using the mouse pointer. Insert an 'a' between 'is' and 'Text' (i.e. This is a Text) and then the word rectangle after the work 'Text'. It should finally read:

This is a text rectangle

**5.** The text rectangle is enclosed in a similar way to the graphic images and if you place the mouse pointer over the handles you can resize it. The text remains unchanged. To change its size requires it to be highlighted using the mouse and a new character size chosen from the toolbar.

**6.** Change the text size to 36.

**7.** The text rectangle can be moved using the centre handle and the mouse pointer which changes into a star when placed over the centre handle. By holding down the mouse button you can drag the rectangle to a new position.

**8.** If you select the Pick tool and double click with it on the text rectangle you will see the rotational and skew handles appear. These allow you to rotate or skew the text. Explore the options.

**9.** You can enter coloured text by selecting the Text Tool and then clicking on your choice of colour in the palette on the right hand side of the application window. Enter:

This is coloured text

using an Arial Font, size 24 in red.

**10.** An alternative approach is to select the <u>A</u>rrange menu and the <u>T</u>ransformation option. Explore the options.

**11.** When the text rectangle is enclosed you can cut, copy and paste its contents or delete the whole rectangle. Experiment with making copies and deleting them. The options are available on the <u>E</u>dit menu.

**12.** When you are confident you can enter, amend and manipulate text then close the application by either selecting the <u>F</u>ile menu and the E<u>x</u>it option or clicking on the close button in the top right hand corner of the window.

FIGURE 175
**Print**

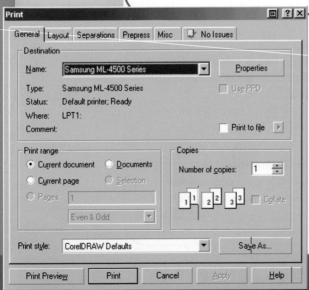

## Print

The quality of an image depends on its resolution. However, there are considerable differences between viewing an image on the screen and printing the graphic on to paper. The quality of monitors and printers varies considerably. A typical monitor may have a resolution of 72 dots per inch while a printer will often print using 300, 600 or 1200 dots per inch. To print a screen image using a high resolution may produce a larger or smaller print image compared with the display. It is not a matter of what you see is what you get (WYSIWYG) since the translation between screen and paper often means a change in size. However, CorelDRAW helps by presenting your image on a distinct size of page so that you can see how it will look when printed.

CorelDRAW shows you the size of the document on which you are creating your images and allows you to change its size using the toolbar. If you change the document size after creating an image you will see the page changes size but the image stays the same. This indicates that you need to resize the picture. When the image is enclosed by handles (highlighted) you can see the exact size of the graphic on the toolbar. If you move the handles to resize the image, the figures on the toolbar will change accordingly.

CorelDRAW provides you with tools to specify how your images are going to be presented. To print an image, select the File menu and the Print option to reveal the Print window (Figure 175). At the bottom of the Print window is a Print Preview button so you can see how the image will appear when printed. When you are statisfied, return to the Print window by clicking on the Close button and then clicking on the OK button to print.

## More Practice

# Exercise 51

## Design the artwork for a postcard

**1.** CorelDRAW is opened by either selecting the Start button, highlighting Programs and clicking on the CorelDRAW item or by double clicking on the CorelDRAW icon on the Windows desktop.

**2.** Select the New Graphics icon.

**3.** Select Japanese Postcard from the toolbar list and give the postcard a landscape orientation.

**4.** Click on the Freehand Tool and draw a straight line down the centre of the card using the rulers as a guide. Click on the Rectangle Tool and draw a rectangle to show where the stamp should be placed. Click again on the Freehand Tool to draw the four lines for the name and address to be written. If you draw one you can use the copy and paste to produce the others.

**5.** Click on the Text Tool and insert the word 'To' aligned with the bottom of the stamp. Use Ariel font and size 18 characters.

**6.** Click on the Freehand tool and change the line thickness to 0.706 . If a message appear simply click on the OK button. Click on the Rectangle Tool and draw a border around the other side of the postcard.

**7.** With the rectangle you have just created enclosed within its handles, select the File menu and the Import option. Import an image into the rectangle and using its handles, resize and position the image to fill the rectangle. In my case I have used a picture of an open laptop computer taken with a digital camera. You can use anything that is available (Figure 177).

**8.** If you want to make the image unusual you can flip the image using the Mirror buttons on the Toolbar (Figure 176) with the image enclosed. Try it and see what happens. You can retrace your steps using the undo icons or options on the Edit menu. This toolbar also shows you the exact dimensions of your image.

**9.** Save the image by selecting the File menu and the Save option. This will reveal the Save Drawing window. You need to select the location where you will save your image. This is done by clicking on the down arrow near the Save in box. This will reveal a list of options. Select floppy disk and insert a disk into the drive. Click in the File name box and enter Postcard. Click on Save button. Your image is now saved as the file Postcard.

**10.** Select the File menu and the Print option to reveal the Print window. Click on Print Preview button and check your postcard. If you are happy, click on the Close button to return to Print window and then on the OK button.

**11.** Close the application by either selecting the File menu and the Exit option or clicking on the close button in the top right hand corner of the window.

FIGURE 176
**Mirrow
Buttons**

FIGURE 177
**Postcard**

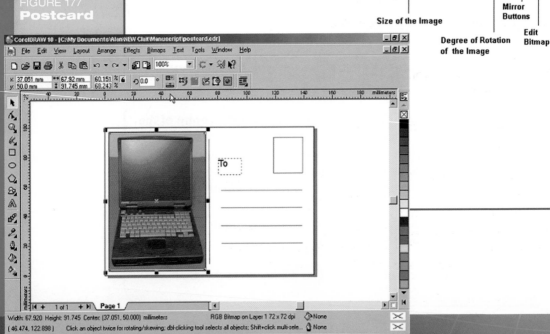

Size of the Image

Mirror
Buttons

Degree of Rotation
of the Image

Edit
Bitmap

# Exercise 52

## Design art work for a compact disc

**1.** CorelDRAW is opened by either selecting the Start button, highlighting Programs and clicking on CorelDRAW item or by double clicking on the CorelDRAW icon on the Windows desktop.

**2.** Select the New Graphics icon.

**3.** Insert a size of 430mm by 430mm by clicking in the size boxes on the toolbar and entering the new size. You are going to create the art work for a music CD.

**4.** Select the Freehand Tool, change the size of line to 0.706. Select Rectangle Tool and click on the red colour in the palette. Draw a rectangle inside the document leaving a small margin around the outside. You should see a red rectangle form.

**5.** Select the Ellipse Tool and draw a small circle outside the document area. It will be filled with red. However, while it is still enclosed, click on the yellow colour in the palette and you will see the circle change colour. Now copy the circle using the Copy and Paste functions on the Edit menu or the toolbar icons. When you have three circles move them to form a diagonal across the red rectangle.

**6.** Select the Text Tool and draw a text rectangle away from the document area and Enter:

Rock Music

using a font and character size of your choice.

**7.** Rotate the text until it is at a 45 degree angle. Copy the text twice more and drag it so that it rests diagonally across each circle. Your CD cover should look something like Figure 178.

**8.** Experiment with the design to improve its appearance (e.g. rotate the text so that it is at different angles)

**9.** Save the image by selecting the File menu and the Save option. This will reveal the Save Drawing window. You need to select the location where you will save your image. This is done by clicking on the down arrow near the Save in box. This will reveal a list of options. Select floppy disk and insert a disk into the drive. Click in the File name box and enter CD Cover. Click on Save button. Your image is now saved as the file CD Cover.

**10.** Select the File menu and the Print option to reveal the Print window. Click on Print Preview button and check your cover. If you are happy, click on the Close button to return to Print window and then on the OK button.

**11.** Close the application either by selecting the File menu and the Exit option or clicking on the close button in the top right-hand corner of the window.

FIGURE 178
**CD Cover**

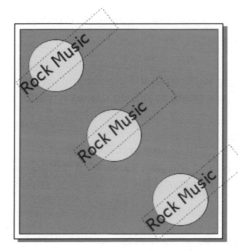

# Summary                                    Computer Art

**1. Open CorelDRAW** Select the Start button, highlight Programs and click on the CorelDRAW item or by double clicking on the CorelDRAW icon on the Windows desktop. Select the New Graphics icon.

**2. Close CorelDRAW** Select the File menu and the Exit option or click on the close button in the top right hand corner of the application window.

**3. New Image** Use the arrow buttons on the toolbar to select from options to choose page sizes, different types of documents, change actual size of page, have either landscape or portrait orientation and alter the units of measurement of page size (e.g. millimeters and inches)

**4. Import Images** Select the File menu and the Import option to reveal the Import window

**5. Crop or Resample Image** Select from full image, crop and resample by clicking on the down arrow to the right of box on the Import window. This will reveal the Crop and Resample windows which allow you to manipulate the image. Click on the OK button when ready.

**6. Edit Bitmaps** Right click on the image and select Edit Bitmap

**7. Manipulate Images** By clicking on the image you enclose it with handles. Using the mouse pointer you can resize and move images.

Click again on the centre or double click using the Pick Tool and the handles will turn into curved arrows. The curved handles allow you to rotate or skew the line using the mouse pointer. The mouse pointer turns into a partial circle and if you hold down the button you can rotate the line or pointer turns into two parallel lines which you can use to skew the image.
**Or**
Select the Arrange menu and the Transformation option

**8. Line Thickness** Select the freehand tool and then click on the down arrow next to the line thickness box on the toolbar to choose from the list of options.

**9. Draw a Graphic Image** Click on the various tools in the toolbox on the left edge of the application window. These allow you to draw squares, circles, rectangles, ellipses, triangles, straight and curved lines and freehand drawings.

**10. Print** Select the File menu and the Print option to reveal the Print window. Click on Print Preview button to see how the image will appear when printed. Click on the Close button and then on the Print button.

# Web Page Creation

This chapter will help you to create a web page including:

identifying and using appropriate software correctly

importing and placing text and image files

amending and formatting web pages

inserting relative, external and e-mail hyperlinks

managing and printing web pages

## Assessment

This unit does not assume any previous experience of creating web pages However, you may find it useful if you have previously undertaken Unit 1 (Using a Computer) and Unit 3 (Electronic Communication). After studying Unit 9 your skills and understanding are assessed during a 2-hour practical assignment. This is set by OCR and marked locally. However, the marking will be externally moderated by OCR. This ensures that the standard is being applied correctly across the many different providers of OCR New CLAIT.

## What is a web page?

When surfing the World Wide Web you read and interact with many different documents. These are known as web pages which when linked together, are called websites. A web page is created using a special language called the Hypertext Markup Language or HTML. This allows you to design the presentation of the pages information (e.g. text and images) so that anyone viewing the page using an application called a web browser can see the information. The HTML supplies the browser with the instructions to create a web page from different elements such as text, pictures, sounds and videos. The HTML code is simply a text document with special commands (i.e. HTML commands) embedded in the text. HTML commands are sometimes known as tags. These tell the browser to, for example, show an image, underline text or enclose an area in a border. The images, text and sounds are not HTML. They are separate files which the code locates and presents in the browser. HTML is a language which organises information into an attractive, interesting and readable form.

A web page can be as long as you want it to be. It can contain a vast amount of information or only a single item. The designer decides on the contents and the length of the page. Many web pages need their users to scroll down them to access their contents. It is good practice to limit the length of a page to no more than four A4 sheets. This minimises the possibility of users getting lost and confused within the page. This is increased when web pages are linked to others using hypertext links. These are places on the page which, when clicked on with a mouse pointer cause the browser to jump to a new page. Links can be single words or phrases, pictures, icons and almost anything else you decide to make a link. There are a number of common conventions in designing links and possibly the most well known is the underlined word which signals that it is a link to another page.

## HTML applications

Originally to design a web page you had to understand the HTML language in depth. However, several HTML editors using a WYSIWYG (What You See Is What You Get) approach are now available. You can visually create a page so that you can see how it appears as you design it. This is obviously easier than writing lines of code and having to visualise mentally the resulting page which normally leads to the final appearance being different to that you intended and your being forced to amend the code.

Word processors (e.g. Microsoft Word) and desktop publishing applications can convert their documents into HTML automatically. This is a useful productivity tool when you want to place a document you have created quickly onto a web page. However, the precise presentation of the information is often different in a browser to that created in the word processor. You are converting between two different formats and there is often a need for a degree of compromise between them. If you rely on using a word processor to develop all the content for a web page it will rapidly come to look like an office noticeboard while a professional HTML editor will add quality and impact to the raw information.

FIGURE 179
**FrontPage**

This chapter is based on Microsoft FrontPage which is an editor capable of developing complex web sites with many different web pages. We will only be considering a limited range of its capabilities but it will provide you with the foundation to develop your knowledge and skills later.

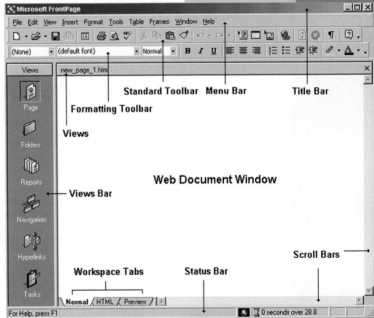

## Microsoft FrontPage

FrontPage is loaded either by clicking on the Start button, highlighting <u>P</u>rograms and then selecting the Microsoft FrontPage item or by double clicking on the FrontPage icon on the windows desktop. Figure 179 shows the FrontPage application. This consists of:

menu and toolbars – these provide the many functions available to you and are similar to those in other Office applications

**web Document Area –** this is the area in which you create, view and edit your page

**views Bar –** this provides you with access to the different views available to you and, in our case, the view of the web page

**workspace Tabs –** these three tabs provide you with access to the different modes of the FrontPage operation:

**Normal –** to edit the page in WYSIWYG mode
**HTML –** to edit the HTML code directly
**Preview –** to see what the page looks like in a browser

# Exercise 53

## Explore FrontPage

**1.** Load FrontPage either by clicking on the Start button, highlighting Programs and then selecting the Microsoft FrontPage item or by double clicking on the FrontPage icon on the windows desktop.

**2.** Maximise the application window to fill the display using the maximise button in top right-hand corner if the application is displayed in a window.

FIGURE 180
**HTML
Code**

**3.** Turn the view to page by clicking on the Page icon in the Views Bar if this is not already set. Turn the workspace tab to Normal by clicking on the tab.

**4.** The web document area should be clear now. The top of the area should show new_page_1.htm indicating that you are working on the first page. Htm is the extension of the hypertext markup language.

```
new_page_1.htm

<html>

<head>
<meta http-equiv="Content-Type" content="text/html; charset=windows-1252">
<meta name="GENERATOR" content="Microsoft FrontPage 4.0">
<meta name="ProgId" content="FrontPage.Editor.Document">
<title>New Page 1</title>
</head>

<body>

<p><font FACE="Arial">This is a new Page.</font></p>

</body>

</html>
```

**5.** The cursor will be flashing on the top line of the area. Enter:

This is a new page.

**6.** If you click on the HTML workspace tab you will see the code to present this simple text. Figure 180 shows the HTML code.

**7.** This shows some of the HTML tags such as:

<html> marks the start of the HTML commands
</html> marks the end of the HTML commands

<head> marks the beginning of an HTML document
<body> shows the start of the main body of a document
</body> shows the end of the main body of a document
<p> start of a paragraph

other tags are <b> and </b> bold and <a href> and <a/> hypertext links.

If you are interested in creating a simple page using HTML then try the optional exercise at the end of the chapter.

**8.** Click on the Normal workspace tab.

**9.** Explore the different options comparing menus and toolbar layouts with other Office applications. Try to locate:

the Insert menu and the File and Picture options

the File menu and the Open, Save, Print and Exit options

the Format menu and Background option

**10.** Continue to explore the application until you are confident that you can find your way around the interface.

**11.** Close the application by selecting the File menu and Exit option or by clicking on the close button in top right-hand corner of the window. You may be asked if you want to save your work on this occasion click on the No button.

# Designing a web page

Before you begin to design a page it is useful to consider what you are trying to achieve and who will be reading its contents. FrontPage provides you with many different options and the main error new designers make is to use too many of them. You could display a page with dozens of different fonts, a wide range of character sizes, lots of colour, several pictures and lots of emphasis. In practice the overuse of the different design elements will result in a poor page which is difficult to read and understand. It is good practice to keep your designs simple.

For example

1. Colour adds interest so a background colour is a useful device to enhance your web pages.

2. Varying character sizes helps to draw the reader's attention to the content of the page but should not be overused.

3. Pictures add interest to a page but are best used when they relate to the text.

4. The use of bold and italics to emphasise particular pieces of text is effective so long as it is not overused.

## Entering and emphasising text

FIGURE 181
**Format
Toolbar**

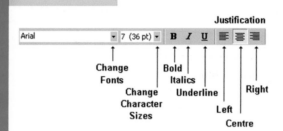

FrontPage provides you with two ways of picking fonts and character sizes. These are to select the down arrow button to the right of the font or character size box (Figure 181) to reveal a list of options from which you can choose. This is done by clicking on the item. When you then enter text it is in the font and size you have chosen. However, you can also change them by highlighting the text and then selecting the font and size.

In a similar way you can enter text which is bold, in italics or underlined by either selecting the option initially and then entering the text or by highlighting and changing them later.

You can justify text and pictures on your page by using the justification

FIGURE 182
**Justification**

options on the toolbar. Again this can be done prior to inserting the text or picture or after by highlighting the object and then making the selection. Figure 182 shows the different justification options.

Although Figure 182 shows the justification of a whole page you are free to vary the justification down the page so you can have a heading and a picture which is centred, while the main body of words is left justified.

# Exercise 54

## Creating a web page

**1.** Load FrontPage either by clicking on the Start button, highlighting, Programs and then selecting the Microsoft FrontPage item or by double clicking on the FrontPage icon on the windows desktop.

**2.** Maximise the application window to fill the display using the maximise button in top right-hand corner if the application is displayed in a window.

**3.** Turn the view to page by clicking on the Page icon in the Views Bar if this is not already set. Turn the workspace tab to Normal by clicking on the tab.

**4.** We are going to create a simple web page for a company called First Generation.

**5.** Select Arial font and a character size of 36 (using the format toolbar) and enter the main heading as First Generation Company. Centre this heading by highlighting the text and clicking on the centre justification icon.

**6.** Press enter twice to move the cursor down the page.

**7.** The next step is to insert a suitable picture to gain the attention of the users. Do this by selecting the Insert menu, highlighting the Picture option and clicking on Clip Art item. This will reveal the Clip Art gallery which is divided into many categories. If you click on a category you will locate many individual images to chose from. Explore the options and identify a suitable image for the page. The picture is inserted by clicking on the image to reveal a short menu of options (Figure 183). The top option is Insert Clip. Click on Insert Clip and your image will be placed on the page. You may get a message telling you that the clip art requires you to insert the Office master CD-ROM into the appropriate drive since the clip art is stored on this disk. You must insert the CD-Rom into the appropriate drive to access that image. You also insert your own pictures by selecting From File instead of Clip Art option and then direct FrontPage to the folder containing your images.

**8.** Since you last chose centre justification, your image will be placed in the centre of the page. The cursor will be flashing alongside the image so that if you select left, centre or right justification the image will move to relate to that justification. Explore the different justifications and position the image where you feel is best.

**9.** If you click on the picture you will see the image enclosed with a series of squared dots. If you place your pointer on these dots then the pointer will change shape and if you hold down the mouse button you can change the shape of the image. Experiment with this to resize your picture.

**10.** Press enter to move the cursor down the page. We will next enter the links to the rest of the site.

**11.** Enter:

<u>Contacts</u>　　<u>Products</u>　　<u>Prices</u>　<u>News</u>　　there are five spaces between each word.

**12.** Underline each word separately and centre them all. To underline, highlight each word individually and then click on the underline icon on toolbar. Once they are all underlined then highlight them all and select centre justification. Underlined words are frequently used to indicate links to other pages.

FIGURE 183
**Insert Clip**

**13.** You have created a simple page. Preview the page and consider the HTML code for this page.

**14.** Insert a floppy disk into the computer's drive. To save your web page select the File menu then the Save option to reveal the Save As window. You need to choose the location in which to store your page by clicking on the down arrow at the end of the Save in box. This will reveal a list. Click on the floppy disk option. You will then see this appear in the box. Now click in the File name box and enter from the keyboard the name 'First_Generation_ Company.htm" and click on the Save button. You will hear the drive and the publication will be saved on the floppy disk as a file called First_Generation_Company.htm.

**15.** You may be presented with a second window asking if you want to save the embedded files. In this case it means the Clip Art image. Click on the OK button and window will clear.

**16.** Now Print the page by selecting the File menu and the Print option to reveal the Print window. Click on the OK button to print the page using the printer default settings.

**17.** Change the workspace tab to HTML and print the code using the same procedure. You will now have printouts of the code and the visual presentation of the page.

**18.** Close the application by selecting the File menu and Exit option or by clicking on the close button in the top right-hand corner of the window.

## Standard Toolbar

The Standard Toolbar provides a range of tools (Figure 184) which include alternative ways of inserting pictures, printing and saving using the toolbar icons. In addition the undo and redo icons allow you to recover from making a mistake. You can reverse what you have done by clicking on undo. If you

FIGURE 184
**Standard Toolbar**

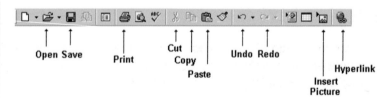

make an error in using undo, then you can turn the clock back with redo.

As with other Office applications you can cut, copy and paste text and pictures around a web page or between Office applications and FrontPage. These functions operate by highlighting the text or picture and then selecting the cut or copy icon. The cut function removes the highlighted area and you can paste it (relocate) into a new position by placing the cursor at the desired location and clicking on the paste icon. The copy function works in the same way but does not remove the original text or picture.

## Inserting text files

Although you can enter text from the keyboard, it is also possible to import text as files or to paste text from other Office applications into your web page. To import a text file you need to position the cursor at the location on the page you want the text to be inserted. The Insert menu and the File (Figure 185) option provides the means of importing text into the page. Once the file option is selected the Select File window is opened which allows you to choose the file to be inserted (Figure 186).

In order to select a file you need to know where it is located within your computer or on your floppy disk. To find the location, click on the down arrow button to the right of the Look in box. A list of drives will appear (Figure 186) such as floppy disk and C:. C: is normally the designation for the computer's internal hard disk in which most files are stored within folders. In Figure 186 you will see that below C: is a folder called My Documents. This folder is one of the many stored on the hard disk.

If you click on C: then you will see the folders stored on the disk appear in the work area. To discover what each folder contains you need to double click on it. Its contents will then appear in the work area. When you locate the text file you want to include you can either double click on it or single click to insert its name in the File name box and then on the Open button. The text file will then be opened on the web page.

FIGURE 185
**Insert Menu**

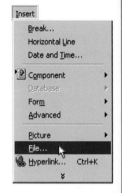

FIGURE 186
**Select File**

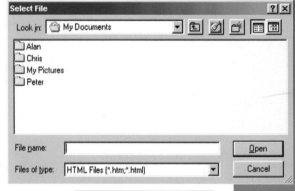

# Exercise 55

## Insert a text file

**1.** Load FrontPage either by clicking on the Start button, highlighting Programs and then selecting the Microsoft FrontPage item or by double clicking on the FrontPage icon on the windows desktop.

**2.** Maximise the application window to fill the display using the maximise button in the top right-hand corner if the application is displayed in a window.

**3.** Turn the view to page by clicking on the Page icon in the Views Bar if this is not already set. Turn the workspace tab to Normal by clicking on the tab.

**4.** We are going to insert a text file into a simple web page.

**5.** If you have undertaken the word processing unit you will have created some text files which you will have saved to a floppy disk. This exercise is based on inserting one of them. However, you can use any text file you like.

**6.** Insert the floppy disk containing the file in the drive. Position your cursor three lines down the new page by using the enter key. Select the Insert menu and the File option to reveal the Select File window. Choose the floppy disk option in the Look in box and double click on the text file of your choice. We are going to select the Invasion of Russia. If your disk appears blank this may be due to the 'Files of type' box containing a type not present on the disk. You will need to change it by clicking on the down arrow button at end of the box and selecting All Files (*.*) which will look for files of all types. It is good practice to always set the box to this option.

**7.** Observe what happens. You should briefly see a message saying that the file is being converted into HTML code and then the file will appear on the page. You are now free to enhance its appearance but before we attempt that, look at the file in the HTML workspace. See if you can identify the paragraph breaks from the HTML code (<p>).

**8.** Highlight the title Invasion of Russia and change its font to Arial and size 24.

**9.** Highlight the rest of the passage and change the font to Times New Roman and size 12.

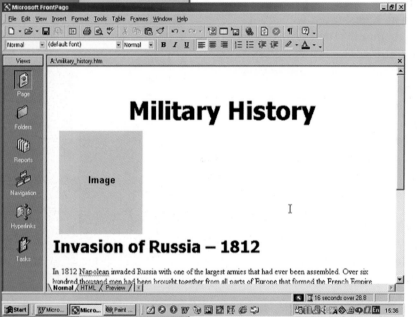

FIGURE 187
**Invasion of Russia**

**10.** Above the title Invasion of Russia insert the page heading 'Military History' using Arial but in size 36. Centre the text and embolden it.

**11.** Insert an appropriate clip art image between the page heading and the passage title. Left justify the picture. Experiment with resizing the image to get the best effect.

**12.** You have created another simple page. Preview the page and consider its HTML code.

**13.** Insert a floppy disk into the computer's drive.To save your web page select the File menu then the Save option to reveal the Save As window. You need to chose the location in which to store your page by clicking on the down arrow at the end of the Save in box. This will reveal a list. Click on the floppy disk option. You will then see this appear in the box. Now click in the File name box and enter from the keyboard the name Military_History.htm and click on the Save button. You will hear the drive and the publication will be saved on the floppy disk as a file called Military_History.htm.

**14.** You may be presented with a second window asking if you want to save the embedded Files. In this case this means the Clip Art image. Click on the OK button and window will clear.

**15.** Now print the page by selecting the File menu and the Print option to reveal the Print window, click on the OK button to print the page using the printer default settings. Figure 187 shows the web page.

**16.** Change the workspace tab to HTML and print the code using the same procedure. You will now have printouts of the code and the visual presentation of the page.

**17.** Close the application by selecting the File menu and Exit option or by clicking on the close button in the top right-hand corner of the window.

## Background colours and images

FIGURE 188
**Background Colour and Pictures**

Colour is very helpful in creating attractive and interesting designs. FrontPage provides the tools to change the background colour of your page or to use a picture as the background. Your text is thus presented on top of the picture or colour. A key factor when selecting a colour is to ensure that it provides a contrast to the text colour (or foreground colour) and thus makes the text legible.

The background colour or picture is set using the Format menu and the Background option. This will reveal the Page Properties window (Figure 188). The background settings can be seen on the Background tab display.

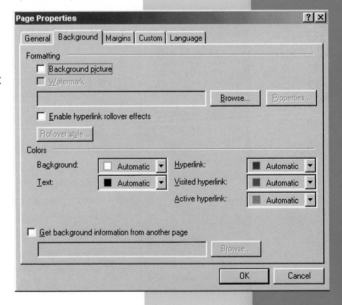

At the top of the display is an item called Background picture. This is activated by clicking in the small blank square in front of the item. A small tick will appear in the square and the box alongside the Browse button becomes white. You can insert the source of the picture in the box (e.g. A:\Picture.gif) which will become the background image. If you cannot remember the exact location of the image you can browse the hard disk or floppy disk to locate it by clicking on the Browse button. This opens the Select Background Picture window from which the image can be selected. This window also provides access to the Clip Art gallery which can be used as a background picture.

Below this area of the window is the section dealing with colour. There are five options to choose from:

1. Background – the default is white

2. Text – the default is black

3. Hyperlink – this shows the colour of the underlining of a text link with the default blue

4. Visited Hyperlink – this shows the colour of the underlining when a link has been used in the past with the default of purple

5. Active Hyperlink – this shows the colour of the underlining when a link is currently active with the default of red

Items 3, 4 and 5 are fairly standard and should not be changed. The normal text colour is black and should also not often need to be changed, unlike background colours. If the down arrow to the right of the Background Automatic box is clicked then a palette of colours is revealed. To select a new background colour you need to click on it and it will then appear in the automatic box.

# Exercise 56

## Change background colours

**1.** Load FrontPage either by clicking on the Start button, highlighting Programs and then selecting the Microsoft FrontPage item or by double clicking on the FrontPage icon on the windows desktop.

**2.** Maximise the application window to fill the display using the maximise button in the top right-hand corner if the application is displayed in a window.

**3.** Open the file First Generation Company by inserting the floppy disk into the drive then selecting the File menu and Open option to reveal the Open File window. Change the Look in box to floppy disk and you should see the file in the work area. If it is not visible then check that the Files of type box reads All Files (*.*) and change it to this option. The file should now be visible and you can load it by double clicking on its name. The First Generation Company page should now appear in FrontPage.

**4.** Explore the different background colours, checking the effects the colour has on the image and text. In particular make sure the text is legible.

**5.** When you are confident, save the revised page and close FrontPage.

# Hyperlinks

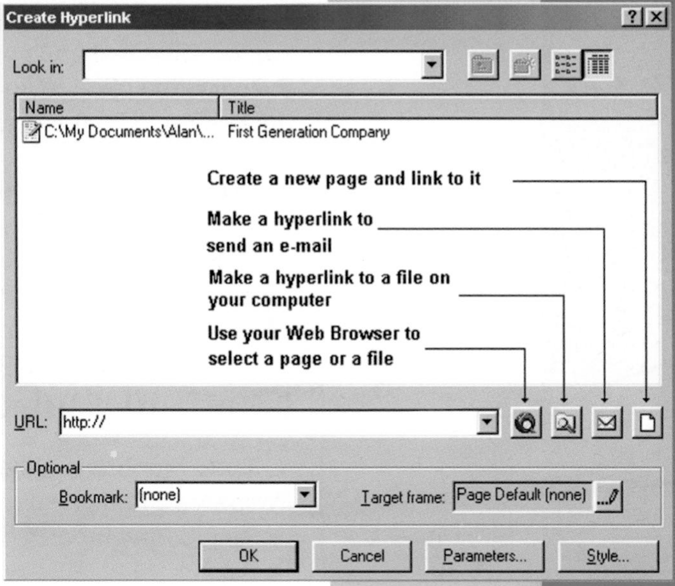

An important feature of web pages is their ability to be connected or hyperlinked both to other pages within the same site and to other sites. The word hyperlink is often shortened to link. There are four main types of link available to you when you are designing a web page. These are:

1. A simple link between two pages you have created. This will allow you to design a route through the site you are building

2. A link to a file stored on your computer so that you have access to extra material on your page. You could load a Powerpoint presentation to explain an idea or subject to your users

Create a new page and link to it

Make a hyperlink to send an e-mail

Make a hyperlink to a file on your computer

Use your Web Browser to select a page or a file

FIGURE 189
**Hyperlinks Window**

3. A link to a web page which is part of another site on the World Wide Web. This is a widely used link and most sites have many of this type

4. A link to an e-mail editor to allow you to send an e-mail to a chosen location. You could use this link to let your users comment on the design of the page or to order products advertised on the page or any other communication need

Links are activated by clicking on them and usually take one of two main forms. An underlined word or phrase or a picture. The picture can be an icon, a large image or even the whole screen.

FrontPage gives you access to the hyperlinks though selecting the Insert menu and the option Hyperlink to reveal the Create Hyperlink window (Figure 189). Across the work area of the screen you will be able to see the location and name of the web page you are working on. In this example it is the First Generation Company stored on the hard disk with a folder called Alan within another folder called My Documents. If you wanted to change the page you would use the Look in box, employing the same method you have used to save or open a file.

The window provides you with the means of creating four types of link. These are shown as four icons alongside the URL box. URL stands for Uniform Resource Locator which is the technical term for a web page address on the World Wide Web. From left to right the icons are:

1. To establish a link with a page somewhere on the World Wide Web using your browser

2. To link the page to a file stored on your computer or on a floppy disk. The

file can be another page you have already created

3. To link the page to send an e-mail to a particular location (i.e. e-mail address)

4. To link the page to a new page you have not yet created

# Exercise 57

## Creating and testing hyperlinks

**1.** Load FrontPage either by clicking on the Start button, highlighting Programs and then selecting the Microsoft FrontPage item or by double clicking on the FrontPage icon on the windows desktop.

**2.** Maximise the application window to fill the display using the maximise button in the top right-hand corner if the application is displayed in a window.

**3.** Open the file First Generation Company by inserting the floppy disk into the drive and selecting the File menu and Open option to reveal the Open File window. Change the Look in box to floppy disk and you should see the file in the work area. If it is not visible then check that the Files of type box reads All Files (*.*) and change it to this option. The file should now be visible and you can load it by double clicking on its name. The First Generation Company page should now appear in FrontPage.

**4.** When we designed this page we provided four potential links at the bottom of the page. These are:

Contacts
Products
Prices
News

**5.** We will create links to each of these words.

**6.** The contacts link is intended to allow users of the page to e-mail the company to ask for information, ask questions or comment on the page.

**7.** Highlight the word Contacts to identify it as the link you are going to create. Select the Insert menu and the Hyperlinks option to open the Create Hyperlinks window.

**8.** The First Generation page should be identified in the Create Hyperlinks window. Click on the icon to create an e-mail link – this is the third from the left and if you rest your pointer on the icon it identifies itself. This will open

Create E-mail Hyperlink (Figure 190).

**9.** Enter webmaster@firstgeneration.co.uk in the window and click on the OK button. You will see the address appear in the URL box in the Create Hyperlink window. It reads:

mailto:webmaster@firstgeneration.co.uk

This shows you have created an e-mail link. Click on the OK button and you will return to the First Generation Company page.

**10.** Observe the Contacts link and you will see that it has changed colour to blue which indicates that it is a link. Change the workspace tab to Preview and we will test the link.

**11.** Click on the Contacts link in the Preview mode. You should see the e-mail system that is set up on the computer that you are using appear. In my case this is Outlook Express. It is important to test each link to ensure it does what you intend.

**12.** Return to Normal mode by clicking on the workspace tab. Highlight Products and again access the Create Hyperlinks window and then create a link to a file on your computer icon. This will reveal the Select File window (Figure 191).

**13.** You are going to link the First Generation Company page to the Military History page you created earlier, although you could link to other files if you prefer. Insert the floppy disk in the drive and change the Look in box to Floppy and you should see the files on the disk appear in the work area. Double click on the Military_History.htm file. You will hear the floppy drive. Return to the Normal workspace of the page.

**14.** You should see the word 'Products' has changed colour to blue, indicating a link has been established.

**15.** Test the link by changing to the Preview workspace and click on the Products link and you will see the Military History page appear if the link has been correctly established. Click on the Normal workspace tab to return to the First Generation page.

**16.** Observe the two links (Contacts and Products) and you will notice that they have changed from blue to Purple indicating that they have been used.

**17.** Highlight Prices and again access the Create Hyperlinks window. You

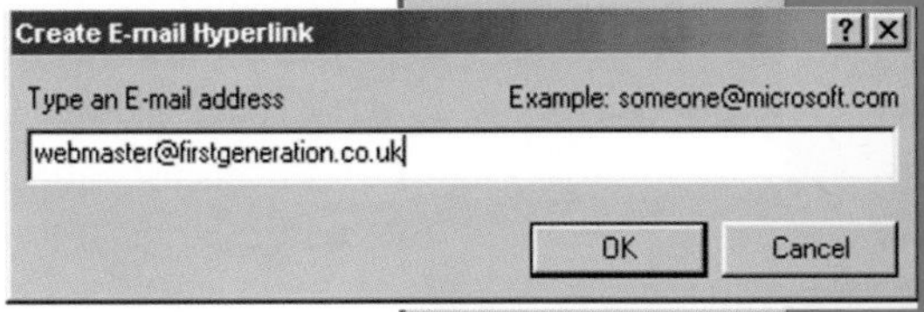

FIGURE 190
**Creating an e-mail link**

FIGURE 191
**Select File Window**

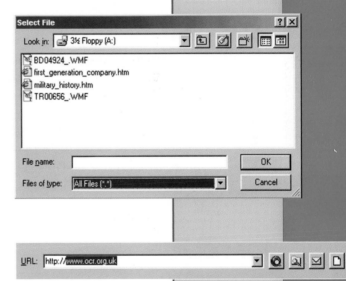

FIGURE 192
**URL**

are going to create a link to another web page. You can do this in two ways. Either enter the address of the web page into the URL box directly (Figure 192) or use the icon to create a link to a web page on a site in the World Wide Web. If you click on this icon it will open your browser. Figure 193 shows the Internet Explorer Browser.

**18.** Enter  http://www.ocr.org.uk  into the URL box and click on OK. You have established a link to the web page.

**19.** To establish a link using the browser you need to surf the World Wide Web for the page you want to link to and then return to FrontPage. You will see the URL (web page address) in the box. To confirm this is the correct page you click on OK but this will only work if you are connected to the Internet so that you can browse.

**20.** The link you have established must be tested. After selecting the Preview workspace, click on Prices to see what happens. If your computer is linked to the Internet it should open a browser and take you to the selected site. However, if you are not connected then the message will depend on the configuration of your system. A browser may open and simply tell you it is unable to access your chosen page.

FIGURE 193
**Browser**

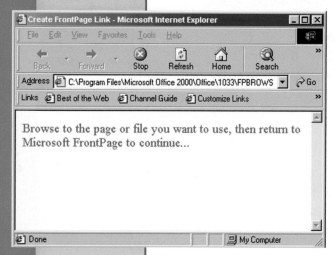

**21.** The last link is to a new page. This is useful when you are creating a whole group of pages since you can insert the links as they are developed. In this case the link is from News to a new page, so highlight News and access the Create Hyperlinks window. Click on the link to new page icon. This will open the New window to start the process of creating a new page. Click on Normal Page and you will find a blank new page appear in the web document window.

**22.** The link you have established must be tested, so select the Preview workspace and click on News to see what happens. You should be linked to the blank new page.

**23.** Insert a floppy disk into the computer's drive. To save your web page, select the File menu then the Save As option to reveal the Save As window. You need to choose the location in which to store your page by clicking on the down arrow at the end of the Save in box. This will reveal a list. Click on the floppy disk option. You will then see this appear in the box. Now click in the File name box and enter from the keyboard the name Links.htm then click on the Save button. You will hear the drive and the publication will be saved on the floppy disk as a file called Links.htm.

**24.** You may be presented with a second window asking if you want to save the embedded files. In this case this means the Clip Art image. Click on the OK button and window will clear.

**25.** We are going to explore the effects of editing the HTML code. Click on the HTML workspace tab which will reveal the code. Experiment with changing the code and use the Preview to see the effects of the change.

Try removing <p align="center"> from the line <p align="center"><font face="Arial" size="7">First Generation Company</font></p> by highlighting it and pressing the
delete key.

In the Preview you will see that the title is now left justified.

If you are interested in creating a simple page using HTML then try the optional exercise at the end of the chapter.

**26.** When you are finished close the page by selecting the File menu and Close. You will asked if you want to save the changes. Click on No since you do not want to save your changes to the code. Load the First_Generation_Company.htm page so that you return to the original code.

**27.** When you edit code it sometimes will not take effect since FrontPage is still working from the original code. It is therefore necessary to reload pages after saving the changes to refresh the code in Frontpage.

**28.** Now Print the page by selecting the File menu and the Print option to reveal the Print window. Click on the OK button to print the page using the printer default settings.

**29.** Change the workspace tab to HTML and print the code using the same procedure. You will now have printouts of the code and the visual presentation of the page.

**30.** Close the application by selecting the File menu and Exit option or by clicking on the close button in the top right-hand corner of the window.

## Link resources

When you are creating links you have to remember that the resources you are linking to must be available when the web page is part of the website. There is no point linking to a file which, when the page is on the World Wide Web, is not available.

All the linked resources must therefore be retained and it is good practice to save everything to the same folder or floppy disk. In our exercises you have been asked to save everything to a floppy disk. When you were saving your pages you were prompted to save the embedded files. This is a function of FrontPage that tries to help you retain all the data required for the web page

# Exercise 58

## More Practice 1

**1.** Load FrontPage by either clicking on the Start button, highlighting Programs and then selecting the Microsoft FrontPage item or by double clicking on the FrontPage icon on the windows desktop.

**2.** Maximise the application window to fill the display using the maximise button in the top right-hand corner if the application is displayed in a window.

**3.** Turn the view to page by clicking on the Page icon in the Views Bar if this is not already set. Turn the workspace tab to Normal by clicking on the tab.

**4.** We are going to create a simple web page about the hobby of collecting stamps.

**5.** Enter the heading Stamp Collecting in a font of your own choice in size 36.

**6.** Centre the heading and insert a clip art image suitable for the subject, centred on the page. Resize the image as appropriate.

**7.** Below the picture enter, in a font of your choice and in size 12, the following text.

Stamp Collecting is the largest collecting hobby in the world. It attracts people of all ages and backgrounds. This site aims to help people discover more about stamp collecting. The links below provide access to more information about the hobby. You can e-mail me by clicking on E-mail link. To link to the introduction page click on Introduction. If you click on the picture you will be linked to other sites about stamp collecting.

**8.** Establish links from the word e-mail to sending an e-mail link, from the word Introduction to a new page and from the picture to web site http://www.stampcollecting.co.uk. In all cases, highlight the text or picture and select Insert menu and Hyperlink option to reveal the Create Hyperlinks window. The link text should be size 14.

**9.** Test your links using the Preview workspace tab.

**10.** Change the background colour to yellow

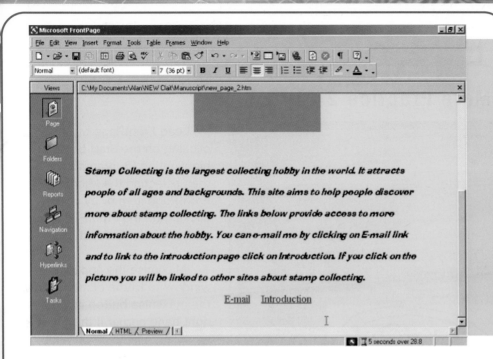

FIGURE 194
**Stamp
Collecting**

**11.** Figure 194 shows our attempts at this page.

**12.** Insert a floppy disk into the computer's drive. To save your web page, select the File menu then the Save option to reveal the Save As window. You need to choose the location in which to store your page by clicking on the down arrow at the end of the Save in box. This will reveal a list. Click on the floppy disk option. You will then see this appear in the box. Now click in the File name box and enter from the keyboard the name Stamp_Collecting.htm and click on the Save button. You will hear the drive and the publication will be saved on the floppy disk as a file called
Stamp_ Collecting.htm.

**13.** You may be presented with a second window asking if you want to save the embedded files. In this case this means the Clip Art image. Click on the OK button and the window will clear.

**14.** Now Print the page by selecting the File menu and the Print option to reveal the Print window. Click on the OK button to print the page using the printer default settings.

**15.** Change the workspace tab to HTML and print the code using the same procedure. You will now have printouts of the code and the visual presentation of the page.

**16.** Close the application by selecting the File menu and Exit option or by clicking on the close button in the top right-hand corner of the window.

# Exercise 59

## More Practice 2

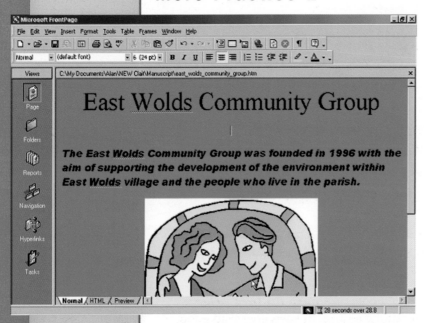

**1.** Load FrontPage by either clicking on the Start button, highlighting <u>P</u>rograms and then selecting the Microsoft FrontPage item or by double clicking on the FrontPage icon on the windows desktop.

**2.** Maximise the application window to fill the display using the maximise button in the top right hand corner if the application is displayed in a window.

**3.** Turn the view to page by clicking on the Page icon in the Views Bar if this is not already set. Turn the workspace tab to Normal by clicking on the tab.

**4.** We are going to create a simple web page about a community group.

**5.** Enter the heading East Wolds Community Group in a font of your own choosing in size 36. Leave one blank line and then enter the text below in a font of your choice but in size 14:

The East Wolds Community Group was founded in 1996 with the aim of supporting the development of the environment within East Wolds village and the people who live in the parish.

**6.** Left justify this text.

**7.** Change the background colour to green.

**8.** Insert a suitable clip art image appropriate to the subject centred on the page. Resize the image as appropriate.

**9.** Leave two blank lines below the image and insert the text below to act as links using a font of your choice and a character size of 18. Centre them and embolden the text.

East Wolds                    Contact

**10.** Establish links from the words East Wolds to a new page and from the word Contact to sending an e-mail link. In both cases, highlight the text or picture and select the Insert menu and Hyperlink option to reveal the Create Hyperlinks window.

**11.** Test the links using the Preview workspace tab.

**12.** Figure 195A shows our attempts at this web page.

**13.** Insert a floppy disk into the computer's drive. To save your web page select the File menu then the Save option to reveal the Save As window. You need to choose the location in which to store your page by clicking on the down arrow at the end of the Save in box. This will reveal a list. Click on the floppy disk option. You will then see this appear in the box. Now click in the File name box and enter from the keyboard the name East_Wolds.htm and click on the Save button. You will hear the drive and the publication will be saved on the floppy disk as a file called East_Wolds.htm.

**14.** You may be presented with a second window asking if you want to save the embedded files. In this case this means the Clip Art image. Click on the OK button and the window will clear.

**15.** Now Print the page by selecting the File menu and the Print option to reveal the Print window. Click on the OK button to print the page using the printer default settings.

**16.** Change the workspace tab to HTML and print the code using the same procedure. You will now have printouts of the code and the visual presentation of the page.

**17.** Close the application by selecting the File menu and Exit option or by clicking on the close button in the top right-hand corner of the window.

# Optional exercise

## HTML page

**1.** HTML files are simply plain text files and can be created by many text editors including Notepad which is supplied as part of Microsoft Windows.

**2.** To load Notepad select Start button, highlight Programs, Accessories and ckick on Notepad.

**3.** Enter the text below:

```
<html>
<head>
<TITLE>A Basic Page</TITLE>
</head>
<body>
<H1>This is the first heading of the Page</H1>
<P>This starts the first paragraph</P>
<P>A new paragraph</P>
<P>Yet another paragraph</P>
</body>
</html>
```

**4.** This uses only a few tags. These were:

```
<html> marks the start of the HTML commands
</html> marks the end of the HTML commands
<head> marks the beginning of the HTML document
</head> marks the end of the heading
<body> shows the start of the main body of a document
</body> shows the end of the main body of a document
<H1> marks the start of first heading
</H1> marks the end of first heading
<P> marks the start of a paragraph
</P> marks the end of a paragraph
```

FIGURE 195B
**Simple Web Page**

**5.** Insert a floppy disk in the computer's drive. To save your web page select the File menu then the Save As option to reveal the Save As window. You need to choose the location in which to store your page by clicking on the down arrow at the end of the Save in box. This will reveal a list. Click on the floppy disk option. You will then see this appear in the box. Now click on the File name box and enter from the keyboard the name HTMLexample.htm and click on the <u>S</u>ave button. You will need to add the extension .htm and this is vital or your browser will not recognise the code. You will hear the drive and the publication will be saved on the floppy disk as a file called HTMLexample.htm.

**6.** Close the application by selecting the <u>F</u>ile menu and E<u>x</u>it option or by clicking on the close button in the top right-hand corner of the window.

**7.** Without connecting to the Internet open Internet Explorer or another browser either by clicking on the Start button, highlighting <u>P</u>rograms and then selecting the Internet Explorer item or by double clicking on the Internet Explorer icon on the Windows desktop.

**8.** Click on the address box and enter A:\HTMLexample.htm and press enter. Your page will be displayed (Figure 195B).

**9.** Close the application by selecting the <u>F</u>ile menu and <u>C</u>lose option or by clicking on the close button in the top right hand corner of the window.

# Summary

**1. Load Microsoft FrontPage** Click on the Start button, highlight Programs and then select the Microsoft FrontPage item or double click on the FrontPage icon on the windows desktop.

**2. Close FrontPage** Select the File menu and Exit option or click the close button in top right hand corner of the window.

**3. Justification** Highlight the text and select the respective icons (i.e. left, right or centre) from the format toolbar.

**4. Select Fonts and Character Size** Highlight the text. Select the small down arrow button to the right of the character size box to reveal a list of sizes. Click on the size of your choice.

Select the small down arrow button to the right of the font box to reveal a list of fonts. Click on the font of your choice.

**5. Bold, Italics and Underline** Highlight the text and select the respective icons (i.e. bold, italics or underline) from the format toolbar.

**6. Insert Clip Art Images** Select the Insert menu, highlight the Picture option and click on the Clip Art item. The Clip Art gallery categories are revealed. Select a category to show the individual images. Insert your chosen image to reveal a short menu of options. Click on the top option, Insert Clip.

**7. Insert Files** Select the Insert menu and the File option to reveal the Select File window

**8. Background Colours and Images** Select the Format menu and Background option. This will reveal the Page Properties window

**9. Creating Hyperlinks** Highlight the word or image which will form the link. Select the Insert menu and the option Hyperlink to reveal the Create Hyperlink window. Ensure the web page you are working on is identified and select the icon related to the type of link you want to establish.

**10. Save on a Floppy Disk** Insert a floppy disk into the computer's drive. Select the File menu and the Save option to reveal the Save As window. Click on the down arrow at the end of the Save in box. This will reveal a list. Click on the floppy disk option. Now click in the File name box and enter from the keyboard the name of the file then click on the Save button.

**11. Print Page** Change the worspace tab to Normal. Select the File menu and the Print option to reveal the Print window. Click on the OK button to print the page using the printer default settings.

**12. Print Code** Change the workspace tab to HTML. Select the File menu and the Print option to reveal the Print window. Click on the OK button to print the code using the printer default settings.

# Presentation Graphics

This chapter will help you to:

identify and use presentation graphics software correctly

set up a slide layout

select fonts and enter text

format slides

manage and print presentation files

## Assessment

This unit does not assume any previous experience of presentation graphics. However, you may find it useful if you have previously undertaken Unit 1 (Using a Computer). After studying Unit 10 your skills and understanding are assessed using a 2-hour practical assignment. This is set by OCR and marked locally. However, the marking will be externally moderated by OCR. This ensures that the standard is being applied correctly across the many different providers of OCR New CLAIT.

## Presentation applications

Microsoft Powerpoint is a presentation application. It provides the resources to create presentations in the form of overhead projector slides, computer presentations and handouts. It is used extensively in both business and education. A sales manager may develop a presentation to persuade customers to buy a new product, a teacher may use it as a visual aid to make a subject more understandable and a manager may employ the application to explain changes in the organisation.

This chapter is based on Microsoft PowerPoint 2000 and Figure 196 shows the PowerPoint interface. It is an application with many functions to assist you to produce exciting and interesting presentations by providing a wide range of templates, graphic images and text tools.

When you load Microsoft PowerPoint is starts by showing a dialogue window overlaying the interface. This provides you with four choices. These are:

open an Existing Presentation

create a new Blank Presentation

create a new presentation using the AutoContent Wizard

## create a new presentation using Design Templates

We are going to create a new blank presentation so we need to click on the radio button for this option and then on the OK button. When you click on the radio button then a dot will appear to indicate it is the chosen item. When you click on the OK button, Figure 197 will appear. This again shows an overlaid dialogue window with a variety of templates that you can use to design your slides. You can select a template either by single clicking on the template which is then enclosed in a blue rectangle and then on the OK button, or by double clicking on the template.

Figure 198 will appear as soon as the template has been selected. In this case we have chosen the title template which is used to begin a presentation. At the moment the slide is transparent. PowerPoint provides you with a variety of tools to add background colours and an overall design to your slides. These are available within the Design Template function which is in the first dialogue window (Figure 196) and from the Format menu and Apply Design Template option.

When the Apply Design Template is selected, Figure 199 will appear. The different designs can be reviewed by single clicking on the different options shown in the list on the left-hand side of Figure199. A preview of the design then appears in the right-hand side of the window. When you have located the design you wish to use, click on the Apply button. This will result in the design being applied to the layout template already selected (Figure 200).

In common with the other Microsoft Office applications, it is possible to achieve this result in a variety of ways. For example if you select Create a new presentation using Design Template from the opening window, you first choose the design template and then overlay it with the layout template.

Once you have established the design of the slides you can then add the text that forms the message of your presentation. The title slide offers you two text boxes in which you can add text. These are the title and sub-title. By clicking in the boxes, you simply enter text from the keyboard.

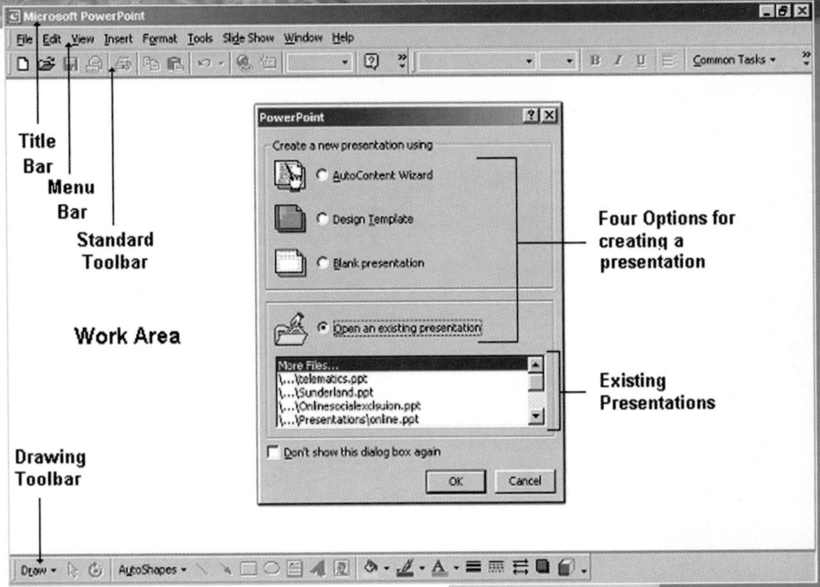

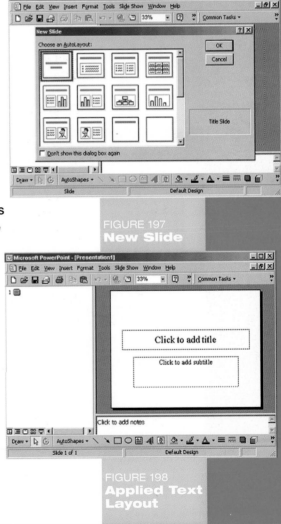

FIGURE 196
**Microsoft PowerPoint**

FIGURE 197
**New Slide**

FIGURE 198
**Applied Text Layout**

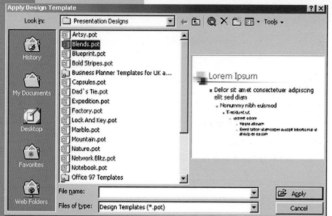

FIGURE 199
**Design Template Options**

A presentation consists of several slides. Once you have completed the title slide, you then need to add a new blank slide. This is done by selecting the Insert menu and then the New Slide option (Figure 201). This will open the layout window (Figure 197) and again you can select the layout of the next slide. The Design layout (e.g. background colours) remains the same as the first slide. It is important in any presentation that the slides are consistent, as this helps the audience to understand the presentation. If each slide is different, with multiple designs and colours employed, there is the danger that the people listening to the presentation will be distracted from the message.

The new slide text layout is chosen in the same way as previously discussed (i.e. double click on the selected template). Figure 202 illustrates some of the possible templates. These allow you to present information in several different ways and to include illustrations in the slide.

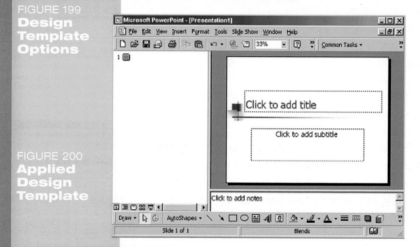

FIGURE 200
**Applied Design Template**

The rest of the presentation can be developed in this way by adding slides one by one. PowerPoint lets you edit your slide so it is possible to rapidly develop a presentation by outlining each slide and then completing the presentation later.

Although New CLAIT does not require you to use its more advanced features, PowerPoint does provide you with the means of animating slides so that your text can appear to fly on to the slide from

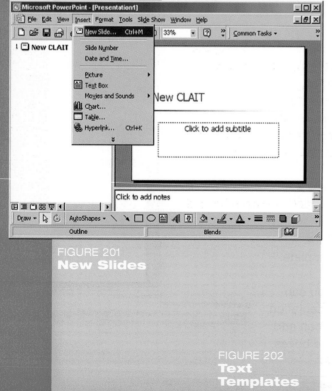

FIGURE 201
**New Slides**

FIGURE 202
**Text Templates**

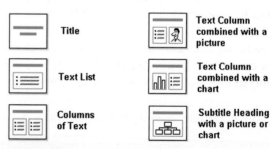

202

almost any direction. The transition from one slide to the next can be made interesting by a variety of means. Some of these features are available in the Slide Show menu.

Many organisations have developed standard house styles for all presentations carried out by their staff. Organisations have often produced their own design templates including features such as company logos and colour schemes. It is useful to find out if your employer has a house styles since you will be expected to follow it and also it may save you a lot of preparation time.

# Exercise 60

## Create a presentation

**1.** Load Microsoft PowerPoint using either the Programs menu or the PowerPoint icon on the desktop.

**2.** Select Create a new Blank Presentation and select the title text layout and the Blends.pot Design template. Enter New CLAIT as the title.

**3.** Create a second new slide using the Insert menu and enter the following bullet points:

Level 1 Qualification
Certificate – 5 units

and the Title – New CLAIT. You can insert new bullet points by pressing the enter key at the end of the previous line (e.g. after entering Qualification).

If you make a mistake you can delete the text by using the backspace key if you identify it immediately. If you do not notice it until the slide is finished then click in the text where the error is. This will move the cursor to the new location and you can now delete or insert text at the new position.

An alternative way of dealing with mistakes is to use the undo function on the Standard Toolbar (Figure 203). This removes the last action you have carried out. You can use undo repeatedly so that you can remove several actions. You can effectively undo the undo action by using the function redo on the standard toolbar. Practise using undo and redo.

To move to another slide you can use the scroll bar on the right of the display or click on the slide list to the left-hand side of the display. Practise by returning to first slide and then to your new second slide.

**4.** Create a third slide using the Insert menu, entering the following bullet points under the same title of New CLAIT:

Mandatory unit
Optional units

**5.** Create a fourth and final slide, entering the following bullet points under the same title of New CLAIT:

Thank you
Insert your name

**6.** Save the presentation you have created on to a floppy disk. This procedure is the same in all Windows applications - you save a presentation, spreadsheet, database or graphic image in exactly the same way.

insert a floppy disk into drive A:
click on the File menu item and a menu will open showing a list of options. Select Save and a window will open.

**7.** Click in the box File name and Enter A:\New CLAIT. Now click on the Save button on the right of the window. You have now saved your presentation as a file called New CLAIT. You may hear the drive A: work during this process.

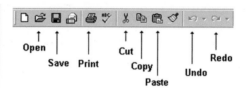

**8.** To run the slide show you have created select the view menu and then click on the slide show option. The presentation will fill the screen and you can move between slides by clicking the left mouse button. When the presentation is over you will return to PowerPoint. Alternatively select the Slide Show menu and the View show otion.

**9.** You can close PowerPoint now by either clicking on the File menu item and a menu will appear with a list of options. At the bottom of the list is the option Exit. If you click on Exit then PowerPoint will close. An alternative way is to click on the close button in the top right-hand corner of the application window.

## Edit your presentation

As you can with other Microsoft Office applications, you are able to add, delete and replace parts of your presentation using functions such as:

Cut, copy and paste (Figure 203)
Search and replace (Figures 204 and 205)

Cut, copy and paste work by using the mouse pointer to highlight the text or object you want to edit. Highlighting is undertaken by clicking the mouse pointer at the chosen location and holding down the left mouse button while dragging it over the text or object. The text is shown to be highlighted by the background darkening. When the selected text is highlighted you can release the mouse button. To cut or copy the highlighted area you click on the Standard toolbar icon (Figure 203). These functions are also available on the Edit menu (Figure 204).

The Cut function removes the highlighted area completely and you can then move it to a new location by using the mouse pointer. A new location is selected by positioning the pointer and clicking. The new position is identified by the cursor being moved (i.e. in the same way as the cursor is moved in Word). Now click on the Paste icon and the cut section is placed back into the presentation. The Copy function operates in the same way except that the original highlighted area is not removed.

Cut and copy are very useful functions since a key element in any presentation is consistency. These functions allow you to ensure quickly and effectively that identical elements are present on all slides (e.g. titles, company logos etc.).

Presentations often consist of many slides and if you need to change some text on every slide it can be a long and tedious process. PowerPoint provides a way of finding a particular section of text of any length and replacing it with an amended phrase. This is not only fast but also free from errors such as spelling mistakes caused by having to enter replacement text from the keyboard.

Search and replace is available as an option on the Edit menu called Replace (Figure 204).

By selecting Edit and then Replace, a window will appear (Figure 205) with two text boxes. By clicking in the top box you can enter the words you wish to find and by clicking in the lower box, the words you want to replace them with. There are also two options shown by the radio button in the bottom left-hand corner of the window:

Match case
Find whole words only

Match case means that the search will only locate phrases which are identical in case (e.g. capitals) to the text entered in the window. Find whole words only restricts the search to matches which are entire words, otherwise the search finds words which are parts of longer words (e.g. a search for car will match with carton, care and careless). This option is important if you are searching for a single word.

FIGURE 204
**Edit menu**

FIGURE 205
**Search and Replace**

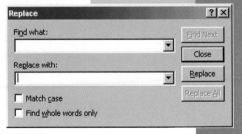

Once you have completed the two text boxes you can start the search by clicking on the Find Next button. The search starts from the location of the cursor and proceeds through the presentation. Whenever a match is located you have the choice of replacing it by clicking on the Replace button which changes that single entry. You then need to click on Find Next again to continue the search. An alternative is to click on Replace All which will change all the matches to the new text. You should only use this option if you are completely certain that you want to change them all.

# Exercise 61

## Edit New CLAIT

**1.** Load Microsoft PowerPoint using either the Programs menu or the PowerPoint icon on the desktop.

**2.** Select the option Open an existing presentation and either double click on the New CLAIT file shown in the list or single click on the file and then on the OK button. In either case the New CLAIT presentation will be loaded, but remember to have your floppy disk inserted in the A: drive.

**3.** Using the Replace function in the Edit menu change the title text from New CLAIT to NEW CLAIT on all four slides.

**4.** Using the cut function, move the text Level 1 Qualification from the second slide to the subtitle box on slide one.

**5.** Save the presentation you have created on to a floppy disk. This procedure is the same in all Windows applications you save a presentation, spreadsheet, database or graphic image in exactly the same way.

insert a floppy disk into drive A:
click on the File menu item and a menu will open showing a list of options. Select Save and a window will open

**6.** Click in the box File name and Enter A:\NEW CLAIT revised. Now click on Save button on the right of the window. You have now saved your presentation as a file called NEW CLAIT revised. You may hear drive A: work during this process.

**7.** To run the slide show you have created, select the View menu and then click on the slide show option. The presentation will fill the screen and you can move between slides by clicking the left mouse button. When the presentation is over you will return to PowerPoint. Alternatively select the Slide Show menu and the View show option.

**8.** You can close PowerPoint now by clicking on the <u>F</u>ile menu item and a menu will appear with a list of options. At the bottom of the list is the option E<u>x</u>it. If you click on E<u>x</u>it then PowerPoint will close. An alternative way is to click on the close button in the top right hand corner of the application window.

# Enhance your presentation

Microsoft PowerPoint has a variety of functions which allow you enhance your presentation. Many of these functions are similar to those available in other Microsoft Office applications (e.g. Microsoft Word) and include:

bold, italics and underline
justification (left, right and centre)
bullet points
change fonts and character size
indenting text (i.e promoting and demoting text)
insert graphics (i.e. pictures and charts)

The Format Toolbar (Figure 206) provides access to the functions which allow you to embolden text, write in italics, underline, justify, change fonts and alter the size of characters. Microsoft Office provides you with a wide range of fonts and character sizes to choose from. If you click on the small down arrow alongside the font and size boxes on the toolbar a menu of options will drop down. Click on the selected option. You can do this before you enter text so that the words you enter will appear in the font and size of your choice or you can change the text you have already entered.

To change already entered text you must first highlight it and then make your choice from the drop down menus. The font and size of your text is critical for an effective presentation since you are seeking to capture your audience's attention. The font must be attractive and interesting to the audience but must not distract from the message you are presenting. The size of characters must be selected carefully to ensure that the slides are visible from the back row of the room. You will need to test your slides in the room. It is also important to check the legibility of your slides since colour combinations which appear very effective on the screen are often poor when projected or printed onto an Overhead Projector slide.

FIGURE 206
**Format Toolbar**

Powerpoint provides tools to promote and demote text. This essentially means that you can structure you bullet points so that you can enhance the main points and show the difference between main and subsiduary issues. By highlighting the text and selecting either the promoting or demoting icons on the Format toolbar you can add an indent or remove an indent. This is

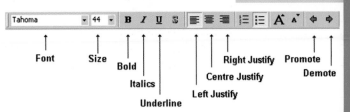

essentially the same as using the tab key to indent your text.

Figure 207 illustrates three different fonts called Arial, Tahoma and Algerian using different combinations of size, bold, italics and underlining. These options provide you with a variety of ways of emphasising your message and drawing the attention of your audience to the critical points. Bold, italics and underlining all make text stand out.

FIGURE 207
**Enhancing your text**

Arial Font – size 10          **Arial Font – size 10          - Bold**
*Arial Font – size 10          - Bold and italics*
<u>*Arial Font – size 10          - Bold, italics and underlined*</u>

Tahoma Font – size 12          Tahoma Font – size 12 – Bold
*Tahoma Font – size 12 – Bold and Italics*
<u>*Tahoma Font – size 12 – Bold, italics and underlined*</u>

**ALGERIAN FONT – SIZE 14    ALGERIAN FONT – SIZE 14 – BOLD**
***ALGERIAN FONT – SIZE 14 – BOLD AND ITALICS***
<u>***ALGERIAN FONT – SIZE 14 – BOLD , ITALICS AND UNDERLINED***</u>

FIGURE 208
**Justification**

AAAAAAAAAAAAAAAA
BBBBBBBBBB
CCCCCCCCCCCCC
DDDDDDDDD
EEEEEEEEEEEEEEEE          LEFT

AAAAAAAAAAAAAAAA
BBBBBBBBBB
CCCCCCCCCCCCC
DDDDDDDDD
EEEEEEEEEEEEEEEE          RIGHT

AAAAAAAAAAAAAAAA
BBBBBBBBBB
CCCCCCCCCCCCC
DDDDDDDDD
EEEEEEEEEEEEEEEE          CENTERED

Another useful function is justification. You can align your text so that it is left, centre or right justified. Left justified means that the text starts parallel to the left margin and is uneven on the right edge (i.e. the normal way text is presented). Right justified means that text is aligned parallel to the right margin and is uneven on the left. This is an unusual way to present text and is rarely used in a presentation. Centre justified means that the text is centred down the middle of the slide. Figure 208 illustrates the three options. In presentations, centred is frequently used since it is a slightly unusual way of showing text and draws the audience's attention to the words. Left is also used since it is the most readable way of presenting text.

In a similar way to the use of bold, italics and underline, you can choose to select the justification before entering the text by clicking on the icon on the Format toolbar or you can change the

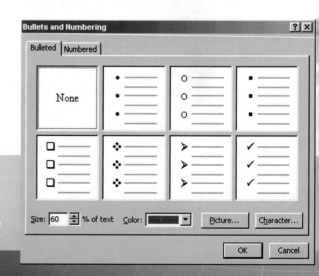

FIGURE 209
**Format Menu**

FIGURE 210
**Bullets**

justification later. By highlight the words you wish to justify and click on the appropriate justification icon. You can justify a single word, a sentence, a paragraph, a slide or indeed the entire presentation in a single justification style or you can combine all three ways.

An important device in a presentation is the bullet pointed list. This is a simple list of items beginning with a symbol (e.g. numbers or geometric symbols) to differentiate it from the rest. It is useful since during a presentation you will be using the slides to indicate the key points of the topic which can be shown as individual bullet points.

PowerPoint provides you with a selection of bullet points to choose from, accessed from the Format menu (Figure 209). By clicking on the Format menu item, the drop down menu is revealed and you can click on Bullets and Numbering option to show the bullets and numbering window (Figure 210). Figure 210 shows some bullet symbol options and the buttons Picture and Character provide a wider variety. The tab Numbered reveals styles of numbering which can be used as bullets. You need to explore the wide range of options.

The PowerPoint templates assume you are using bullet points so will automatically provide lists. However, you can change the default setting by clicking on the Format menu, selecting Bullets and Numbering and choosing a bullet style. Your chosen style will then appear as you enter the text. However, you can alter the bullet at any time by highlighting the item and choosing a new style. You can change a single item or a whole list.

Pictures can make a presentation more interesting. Use the Picture options on the insert menu (Figure 211) to insert images into your presentations. They can be placed anywhere you want them. However, when you are selecting the layout of each slide there are several which include pictures.

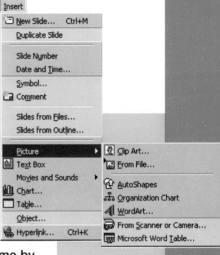

FIGURE 211
**Insert Menu**

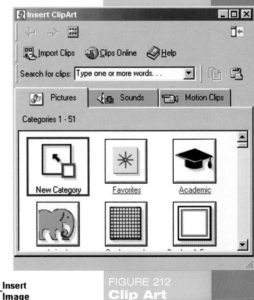

FIGURE 212
**Clip Art**

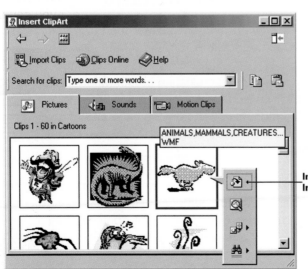

Insert Image

FIGURE 213

To insert a picture into a slide you need to click on Insert menu item, highlight Picture option and a second menu will appear to the right of Insert. This provides you with two choices:

Clip Art
From File

Clip Art images are provided with PowerPoint to help you design presentations. From File allows you to select images you have created yourself or have bought. We will only consider the Clip Art option. By clicking on Clip Art you open a library of pictures to select from (Figure 212). Figure 212 shows you the Clip Art window which is initially displayed. The images are categorised by type so your initial task is to select a category by single clicking on it to open a new window with the actual images. Then select the actual picture, you need to click on it and a short menu of options will appear (Figure 213). The top option will place the image on your slide. However, at this point you may get an error message telling you the pictures are on another disk. This is the Microsoft Office installation disk and if you have it, you need to place this disk in the CD-ROM drive.

The image will either be placed at the cursor or, if your slide has no cursor showing, in the middle of the slide. A frame surrounds the image and, if you move the mouse pointer over the image, causes it to change to a star shape. By holding down the left mouse button when it is over the image you can drag it around the slide and position it. You fix the image by releasing the mouse button and clicking away from the graphic. However, if you click on the graphic image again, the frame will reappear and you can move it to a new position.

# Exercise 62

## Enhancing your presentation

1. Load Microsoft PowerPoint using either the Programs menu or the PowerPoint icon on the desktop.

2. Select the option Open an existing presentation and either double click on the NEW CLAIT revised file shown in the list or single click on the file and then on the OK button. In either case the NEW CLAIT revised presentation will be loaded, but you must have your floppy disk inserted which contains the presentation file.

3. During this exercise you are going to use the various PowerPoint functions to enhance your presentation. The first step is to emphasise the titles on each slide and in particular on the opening one so on the initial slide, change the title font to Algerian, the character size to 60 and embolden it. You

need to highlight the title and then select the font, character size and the bold option. Once you have made your selections, simply click away from the highlighting to see the changes made.

**4.** Next change each title on the other slides to Algerian but only with character size 48.

**5.** The slide bullet points were produced using the default options so you need to change them to a bullet symbol of your choice. Systematically highlight each list of bullet points and select another bullet symbol (i.e. Format menu, Bullets and Numbering option). It is worth exploring the different options to identify one you like and feel is appropriate.

**6.** Now change all the other text to a font and character size different from the title (e.g. Algerian). Explore the different options until you find a font which looks good. Remember to highlight the text and use the font and character options on the Format toolbar.

**7.** Centre your bullet points (e.g. justification icons on Format toolbar) and check to see if you feel this is appropriate way of presenting the text. If you do not like the way it appears, change the justification to left justified.

**8.** Insert a graphic image on the opening slide to provide interest. Remember to move to this slide by using the scroll bar and then select the Insert menu, highlight the Picture option and click on Clip Art. Try to pick an image which is appropriate to the study of an information and communication qualification. The image will need to moved around the slide until you place it in an appropriate spot.

**9.** While the image is enclosed within its frame, placing the mouse pointer over an edge will change its shape to a double-headed arrow. If you hold down the left mouse button you can change the shape of the picture. Try to alter the size of the image. You will need to pull two sides to keep it symmetrical or the corner.

**10.** Save the presentation you have created on to a floppy disk. This procedure is the same in all Windows applications: you save a presentation, spreadsheet, database or graphic image in exactly the same way.

insert a floppy disk into drive A:
click on File menu item and a menu will open showing a list of options. Select Save and a window will open.

**11.** Click in the box File name and Enter A:\NEW CLAIT revised2. Now click on the Save button on the right of the window. You have now saved your presentation as a file called NEW CLAIT revised2. You may hear drive A: work during this process.

**12.** To run the slide show you have created select the <u>V</u>iew menu and then click on the slide sho<u>w</u> option. The presentation will fill the screen and you can move between slides by clicking the left mouse button. When the presentation is over you will return to PowerPoint. Alternatively select the Sli<u>d</u>e Show menu and the <u>V</u>iew show option.

**13.** You can close PowerPoint now by clicking on <u>F</u>ile menu item and a menu will appear with a list of options. At the bottom of the list is the option E<u>x</u>it. If you click on E<u>x</u>it then PowerPoint will close. An alternative way is to click on the close button in the top right-hand corner of the application window.

## Printing your presentation

So far, we have considered how to create a presentation which appears on the computer screen or which could be projected using a data or video projector. However, in many cases you will want to print your slides to provide a set of handouts or to be able to project them on an overhead projector (OHP), which involves printing them on transparencies. There are different types of transparencies depending on your printer (i.e. laser and inkjet). It is important to check that you are using the correct type since it may result in poor slides or may even damage your printer.

To print your slides you need to click on the File menu and the option <u>P</u>rint. This will reveal the Print window shown in Figure 214. The Print window is divided into areas. These are:

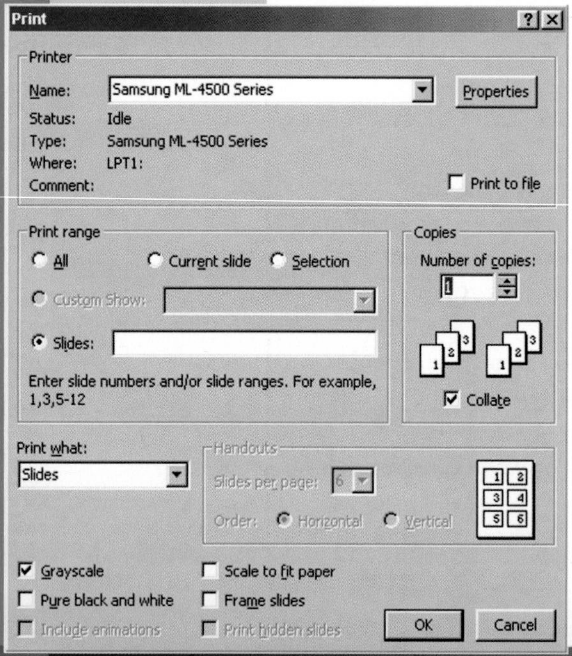

**Printer** – this shows you the name of the printer which will be used

**Print Range** – there are a variety of options which you select by clicking in the radar buttons (e.g. <u>A</u>ll, Curr<u>e</u>nt, <u>S</u>election and Sli<u>d</u>es). The <u>A</u>ll option prints the whole presentation. Curr<u>e</u>nt prints only the slide being viewed at that moment. <u>S</u>election prints the area of the slide which has been highlighted and Sli<u>d</u>es allows you to select some of the slides by entering their numbers in the text box alongside

**Copies** – this allows you to print more than one copy and to collate them

**Print <u>w</u>hat** – by clicking on the small down arrow at the end of the box, a list of options is revealed allowing you to print slides (transparencies), handouts, notes pages and outline view. Figure 215 shows the different options. You select the option by clicking on it.

FIGURE 214
**Printing**

The different Print what options are:

**slides –** prints the images on to transparencies

**handouts –** prints the slides on to paper so that each person in your audience has a copy of your presentation to take away with them

**notes pages –** you can add notes to your slides so that the audience gets a copy of the slides and your speaking notes

**outline view –** this is a list of all the text on the whole presentation. It is useful to help you check that you have not left out any important points

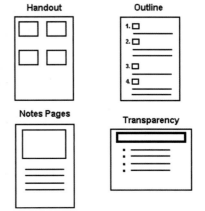

FIGURE 215
**Print What**

# Exercise 63

## Printing

**1.** Load Microsoft PowerPoint using either the Programs menu or the PowerPoint icon on the desktop.

**2.** Select the option Open an existing presentation and either double click on the NEW CLAIT revised2 file shown in the list or single click on the file and then on the OK button. In either case the NEW CLAIT revised2 presentation will be loaded.

**3.** You are going to print your slides and produce audience notes (e.g. a handout).

**4.** Print your slides on to paper initially to check how they look. Transparency film is quite expensive so it is worth checking before you waste it. Transparencies are loaded into the printer in the same way as paper but make sure you are using the correct type of transparency for the printer (e.g. inkjet or laser transparencies). It can damage your printer if you use the wrong type. Read the instructions on the transparency box as you may need to insert them in a particular way.

**5.** All printers have default settings and you will be using these to print. PowerPoint defaults to printing slides as landscape images but handouts, notes pages and outlines as portrait images (Figure 215). Defaults can be changed.

**6.** Print your slides (File menu, Print, change Print what to slides (it may already be set to this option) and OK button). The printer defaults to printing all your slides so you do not need to change the Print dialogue box settings.

**7.** Print handouts (File menu, Print, change Print what to handouts and OK button). The printer defaults to printing six thumbnail images on each page and therefore since your presentation comprises four slides, four thumbnail images of the slides will be printed. If you look to the right on the Print dialogue box you will see how the thumbnails will appear.

**8.** Print the notes pages (File menu, Print, change Print what to notes pages and OK button). In this case your presentation is printed on four sheets with a copy of the slide at the top and a space below for any notes you may have added.

**9.** Print outline view (File menu, Print, change Print what to outline view and OK button). The outline is printed on a single sheet.

**10.** Take a moment to consider the different printer outputs. You can close PowerPoint now by clicking on File menu item and a menu will appear with a list of options. At the bottom of the list is the option Exit. If you click on Exit then PowerPoint will close. An alternative way is to click on the close button in the top right hand corner of the application window.

## Master slides

There is a special tye of slide called a Master Slide. This allows you to define the fonts, character sizes, colour and layout which will be used throughout your presentation. This is very helpful in ensuring that you provide a consistent appearance to your slides. Anything you place on the master slide will appear on all the slides.

FIGURE 216
**Master slide**

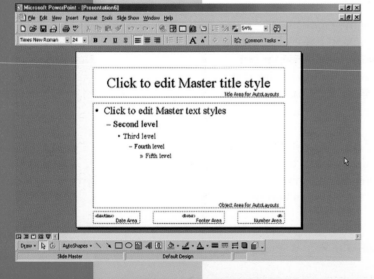

When you start a new presentation you create a master slide by selecting the View menu, highlight the Master option and clicking on Slide Master. The master slide appears (Figure 216). To define fonts click on the area and then change the font, character sizes and other features (e.g. insert picture). These features will be reproduced throughout the presentation.

Once you have defined your master you simply go ahead with designing each slide and you will see the standard features appear on each of them. If you want to make a change then by altering the master slide you can change all the slides.

# Exercise 64

## More Practice 1   Sell a product

**1.** Load Microsoft PowerPoint using either the Programs menu or the PowerPoint icon on the desktop.

**2.** You are going to develop a presentation to sell the Wireless Laser Printer (WLP). PowerPoint is often used for sales presentations.

**3.** Select Blank presentation and the title template.

**4.** Select a design template (Format, Apply Design Template and select Apply button). Review the different styles and select one you feel is appropriate for a sales presentation.

**5.** Insert the title Wireless Laser Printer – explore the different fonts and character size.

**6.** Insert your own name in the subtitle box again exploring the different fonts and character sizes but remember it is important to be consistent and not use to wide a range of fonts.

**7.** Insert a new slide (Insert, New slide and select a template) and a new layout template – select one which includes a picture image.

**8.** Insert a picture by double clicking on the picture area of the slide. Select a picture which you feel is appropriate (e.g. Office category provides several cartoons of printers). Insert Wireless Laser Printer on the title bar and then add the following bullets to the text column in italics:

No cables
Radio communication
Under £200

Select bullet types, font and character size which you feel are effective.

**9.** Insert a new slide (Insert, New slide and select a template) and a new layout template – select one which is text only.

**10.** Insert Wireless Laser printer as the title and the following bullets in italics:

10 pages per minute
600 dots per inch
Quiet operation
Design life 100,000 pages
3 year warranty

Select bullet types, font and character size which you feel are effective.

**11.** Insert a new slide (Insert, New slide and select a template) and a new layout template – select one which is text only.

**12.** Insert Wireless Laser Printer as the title and the following bullets in italics:

Acme Printer Company
234 New Way, Birmingham
Info@acmestar.co.uk
Your name, Sales Representative

Select bullet types, font and character size which you feel are effective.

**13.** Save the presentation you have created on to a floppy disk.

insert a floppy disk into drive A:
click on File menu item and a menu will open showing a list of options. Select Save and a window will open.

**14.** Click in the box File name and Enter A:\Sales. Now click on the Save button on the right of the window. You have now saved your presentation as a file called Sales. You may hear drive A: work during this process.

**15.** Print your slides and a handout (File, Print option and OK button).

**16.** To run the slide show you have created select the View menu and then click on the slide show option. The presentation will fill the screen and you can move between slides by clicking the left mouse button. When the presentation is over you will return to PowerPoint. Alternatively select the Slide Show menu and the View show option.

**17.** You can close PowerPoint now by clicking on File menu item and a menu will appear with a list of options. At the bottom of the list is the option Exit. If you click on Exit then PowerPoint will close. An alternative way is to click on the close button in the top right-hand corner of the application window.

# Exercise 65

## More Practice 2   Explain a hobby

**1.** Load Microsoft PowerPoint using either the Programs menu or the PowerPoint icon on the desktop.

**2.** You are going to develop a presentation to explain why collecting postcards is interesting and fun. PowerPoint is often used to explain a subject to an audience.

**3.** Select Blank presentation and the title template.

**4.** Select a design template (Format, Apply Design Template and select Apply button). Review the different styles and select one you feel is appropriate for this subject.

Insert the title Postcard Collecting in bold – explore different fonts and character size.

**5.** Insert your own name in the subtitle box again exploring the different fonts and character sizes but remember it is important to be consistent and not to use too wide a range of fonts.

**6.** Insert a new slide (Insert, New slide and select a template) and a new layout template – select one which includes a picture image.

**7.** Insert a picture by double clicking on the picture area of the slide. Select a picture which you feel is appropriate (e.g. People category provides several cartoons of people who might be collectors). Insert Postcard Collecting in bold on the title bar and then add the following bullets to the text column:

Postcards are over 100 years old
1896 in Great Britain
Thousands of collectors
All ages and backgrounds
Many different themes (e.g. local history)

Select bullet types, font and character size which you feel are effective. These bullets can be indented to show their relation to each other. Indent (demote) 1896 in Great Britain to show it relates to Postcards are over 100 years old by highlighting the text and clicking on the demote icon on the Format toolbar. Demote (indent) All ages and backgrounds as well. If you want to reverse this process (i.e. remove an indent) then highlight the text and use the promote icon on the toolbar. It is also good practice to use a different bullet symbol.

Your layout should be similar to:
Postcards are over 100 years old
    1896 in Great Britain
Thousands of collectors
    All ages and backgrounds
Many different themes (e.g. local history)

Experiment with promoting and demoting text.

**8.** Insert a new slide (Insert, New slide and select a template) and a new layout template – select one which includes a picture image.

**9.** Insert a picture by double clicking on the picture area of the slide. Select a picture which you feel is appropriate (e.g. Gestures category provides several cartoons of new ideas). Insert Postcard Collecting in bold as the title and the following bullets:

Wider price range
from 10p to many pounds
Photographic to artist-drawn cards
Local history
Many books to explain the hobby

Indent the bullets 'from 10p to many pounds' and 'Local History' using the demote icon on the toolbar. To achieve a result similar to:

Wider price range
    from 10p to many pounds
Photographic to artist-drawn cards
    Local history
Many books to explain the hobby

**10.** Insert a new slide (Insert, New slide and select a template) and a new layout template – select one which is text only.

**11.** Insert Postcard Collecting in bold as the title and the following bullets:

Many collectors' fairs
Postcard clubs
Monthly magazine
Dealers
Websites

Select bullet types, font and character size which you feel are effective.

**12.** Insert a new slide (Insert, New slide and select a template) and a new layout template – select one which is text only.

**13.** Insert Postcard Collecting in bold as the title and the following bullets:

Visit the postcard display
Ask any questions

Select bullet types, font and character size which you feel are effective.

**14.** Save the presentation you have created on to a floppy disk.

insert a floppy disk into drive A:
click on File menu item and a menu will open showing a list

of options. Select <u>S</u>ave and a window will open.

**15.** Click in the box File <u>n</u>ame and Enter A:\Postcards. Now click on the <u>S</u>ave button on the right of the window. You have now saved your presentation as a file called Postcards. You may hear the drive A: work during this process.

**16.** Print your slides and a handout (<u>F</u>ile, <u>P</u>rint option and OK button).

**17.** To run the slide show you have created select the <u>V</u>iew menu and then click on the slide sho<u>w</u> option. The presentation will fill the screen and you can move between slides by clicking the left mouse button. When the presentation is over you will return to PowerPoint. Alternatively select the Sli<u>d</u>e Show menu and the <u>V</u>iew show option.

**18.** You can close PowerPoint now by either clicking on <u>F</u>ile menu item and a menu will appear with a list of options. At the bottom of the list is the option E<u>x</u>it. If you click on E<u>x</u>it then PowerPoint will close. An alternative way is to click on the close button in the top right-hand corner of the application window.

## Other ideas

If you would like to practise then the following list of ideas for presentations might be useful. Design presentations to:

1. introduce new employees to your workplace
2. explain why you deserve a pay rise
3. explain a hobby or interest (e.g. collecting postcards, keeping guinea pigs or walking)
4. help new computer users understand the uses of information and communication technology
5. help people new to the Internet to search for information
6. experiment with using a Master Slide.

## Final tip

When making a presentation, you do not want to use slides which contain spelling mistakes and PowerPoint provides you with a spell checker similar to Microsoft Word. Before printing your slides, use the spell checker to make sure there are no errors.

# Summary

Presentation Graphics

**1. Load Microsoft PowerPoint** Use either the Start button and the Programs menu or double click on the PowerPoint icon on Windows desktop

**2. Close** Click on the File menu item and the Exit option or click on the close button in the top right hand corner of the application window.

**3. Save a file on a floppy disk** Insert a floppy disk into drive A: and click on File Menu and Save. Select the drive (floppy Disk A:) and enter file name.

Having saved a file once, you can update it by clicking on File Menu and Save without the Save As window appearing again. It simply overwrites the original file.

**4. Start a new presentation** Select the option Create a new Blank Presentation from the initial dialogue box which appears when PowerPoint is loaded.

**5. Select New layout** Select a layout by double clicking on the desired template

**6. Delete Text** You have two different keys (i.e. backspace and delete) which both work from the position of your cursor.

Backspace key – this removes text, character by character, to the left of the cursor position.

Delete key - this removes text, character by character, to the right of the cursor position.

There is also undo and redo. Undo removes the last action you have undertaken, while redo carries out the actions removed by undo. They can be used to remove text.

**7. Select Design Template** Select the Format menu and the Apply Design Template option to access the dialogue box then use the Apply button when you have chosen a design.

**8. Insert Graphics** If you have used a graphics template then you need to double click on the image area to access the clip art. Select a category and a picture then select Insert from the pop-up menu.

Select the Insert menu, highlight the Picture option and choose Clip Art from the new menu. Select a category and a picture, then select Insert from pop-up menu.

You may see an error message telling you the pictures are on another disk. This is the Microsoft Office installation disk and you need to place this disk if you have it in the CD-ROM drive.

## 9. Move the Image
Place the mouse pointer over the image and the pointer will change to indicate that the picture can be dragged by holding down the left mouse button.

## 10. Change the Font, character size and text characteristics (bold, italics and underline)
Highlight the text you want to change. Change the font and/or character size by selecting the item in the drop down list on the Formatting Toolbar. Change the text characteristics (i.e. bold, italics and underline) by selecting the icon on the formatting toolbar.

## 11. Change the text justification
Highlight the text you want to change. Select the justification option by clicking on the icon on the Formatting toolbar.

## 12. Replace text
Edit Menu and the Replace option. Replace window appears. Enter the text you want to replace in the Find what: box and the replacement text in Replace with: box.

## 13. Bullets
Select the Format menu and the Bullets and Numbering option. The dialogue box gives you a range of styles to choose from.

## 14. Printing
Select the File menu and the option Print.

# chapter 11

# BBC Becoming WebWise

This chapter will provide you with an introduction to Unit 11 BBC Becoming WebWise course. The chapter does not give full coverage of the unit simply because, unlike other CLAIT units, you have to complete Becoming WebWise online at the BBC site. The aims of the BBC course are to:

identify the current range of digital technologies for Internet access and their functions

use Internet navigation software, user interfaces and software applications

develop understanding and awareness of the range of Internet services and tools

identify the potential application of the Internet for an individual's circumstances

## Assessment

This unit does assume that you already have basic IT desktop and browser navigation skills. The Unit overlaps with Unit 2: Electronic Communications so you cannot offer both Units as part of New CLAIT. The assessment for Becoming WebWise is undertaken through the BBC website (http://www.bbc.co.uk/webwise/learn/). The assessment consists of 12 multiple-choice questions and three practical tasks. These involve e-mail, browsing and searching. You must correctly answer 7 questions and complete all the tasks. If you are unsuccessful you can retake the assessment which takes place in a supervised assessment centre and lasts an hour.

You must be registered with both OCR and the BBC in order to gain recognition for this unit. In practice, this means that you will be undertaking New CLAIT with your learning provider offering you the opportunity to undertake the BBC Becoming WebWise course. However, you can undertake BBC Webwise on your own, independently of New CLAIT.

The BBC website provides an explanation of the assessment process.

## Online Course

BBC has undertaken several major programmes to encourage people to learn about information and communication technology. The first initiative was Computers Don't Bite which provided many colleges, Adult Education Services, libraries and training providers with an introduction to computers on a CD-ROM. This was followed by WebWise which offered an introduction to communication technologies, also on a CD-ROM. Both CD-ROMs are still in use and your college, adult education service or training provider may have access to the material. They are both excellent introductions to computers and the Internet.

Becoming WebWise is the latest development of the BBC's efforts to encourage people to learn about ICT. It is an online course whereas you undertake the learning through studying the content and taking part in the activities available on the BBC's website. The course should take about 10 hours to complete but people learn at different speeds so treat this timescale as a guide. It may take you longer or you may be able to complete the course faster.

The course consists of eight sections called trips. Each trip has three landmarks which are chunks of information and tests that you can study. The trips provide an introduction to the Internet, browsers, multimedia, searching the World Wide Web, using e-mail, web pages design, legal and security aspects of the Internet and alternative ways of accessing the Internet.

If you are interested in undertaking Becoming WebWise as part of New CLAIT, please ask your course provider for details and visit the BBC's website (http://www.bbc.co.uk/webwise/learn/).

# Glossary

**Application** - an application is a software program designed to perform a task such as desktop publishing, designing a database or designing a web page.

**Bar Chart** – is a chart which represents numerical information as bars of different length.

**Bitmap** – A bitmap image is composed of many dots called pixels. The more pixels in a given amount of space (i.e. a square inch) the clearer the image or the higher the resolution of the picture.

**Boot** – this is the process that occurs when you switch on the computer. It involves the loading of the operating system (e.g. Windows 98) and checking of the equipment to ensure that everything is ready for you to use.

**Browser** – A browser is an application which allows you to access a World Wide Web page. Each page has a unique address which is called a URL (Uniform or Universal Resource Locator) which, when entered into the browser, allows it to find the site and view its contents.

**Byte** – the basic measure of memory. A byte is sufficient memory to store one character (e.g. a letter or a number).

**Column Charts** – is a chart which represents numbers and columns of different length.

**CPU** – Central Processing Unit is a silicon chip which controls the operation of the computer.

**Database** – this is a way of storing information so that its contents can be extracted in many different combinations and ways.

**Desktop** – this is the main display of the operating system and is normally the first display you see after the computer has loaded the operating system (i.e. Windows).

**Desktop Publishing** – an application which allows text and image to be combined in many different ways so that many different forms of printed document can be designed (e.g. newsletters and posters).

**Directory** – a directory is a list of World Wide Web addresses related to a particular topic or subject.

**DTP** – see Desktop Publishing

**E-mail** – a message which is sent electronically through the Internet or over a local network.

**Field** – an individual piece of information stored on a database usually as part of a record.

**File** – a collection of digital (computer) information. There are many types of file such as word-processing, graphic and spreadsheet files.

**Floppy Disk** – a floppy is a small magnetic disk on which you can store a small amount of information in the form of files.

**Folder** – this is a location on the computer in which you can store files.

**Font** – characters can be printed and displayed in many different styles. These styles are known as fonts.

**Format** – a way of structuring the computer information stored in a file on a disk or drive. There are many different types of file format.

**Formula** – a method of calculating parts of a spreadsheet automatically.

**Greyscale** – a way of describing an image which is shown in a range of shades of grey rather than in different colours.

**GUI** – a Graphical User Interface is a Windows 95 type display in which icons, windows and a mouse pointer interact to produce an easy to use environment.

**Hard disk** – large magnetic disk which is located inside the computer on which a large amount of information can be stored.

**Hardware** – the physical components which make up the computer.

**HTML** – Hypertext Markup Language is a specialist language which is used to design World Wide Web pages so that they can be read using a browser.

**HTTP** – Hypertext Text Transfer Protocol which moves documents around the World Wide Web (e.g. http://www.bbc.org.uk)

**Hypertext** – Pages of a web site are linked together through a number of hypertext connections. These are shown by underlined words, coloured words, icons and graphic pictures. The links allow the user to jump between different parts of the site or even between sites.

**Icon** – a small picture which represents a computer function or operation.

**Internet** – a super network of networks which links millions of computers throughout the world.

**ISP** – Internet Service Providers are commercial companies who provide connections to the Internet for individuals and companies.

**Justification** – a way of laying out text, e.g. left justification means that text is aligned so that its left edge is parallel with the papers edge when it is printed.

**Kb** – a Kilobyte is a measure of memory (i.e. 1024 bytes).

**Laptop** – a laptop is a portable computer with a screen built into its cover.

**Line Graphs** – a graphical way of comparing two or more sets of numerical information.

**Mb** – a Megabyte is a measure of computer memory (approximately a million bytes).

**Memory** – a meaure of the computer capacity to perform tasks and to store information.

**Menu** – a method of displaying options.

**Operating system** – software provides the instructions to make the hardware work. It allows specific tasks to be performed such as communicating with the Internet or word–processing. Computers need to match hardware and software together, and to ensure that the match is exact, a special software program is needed. This is the Operating System.

**Password** – a series of alphanumeric characters that limits access to a computer system.

**Personal Computer** – an individual computer which is normally used by one person at a time.

**Pie chart** – a graphical representation of information by showing it as slices of a circle so that the size of each slice is proportional to the data.

**Pixel** – graphic images are made up of many small rectangular areas which are called pixels.

**Port** – a way of connecting peripheral devices (e.g. printers) to a computer.

**Query** – this is a way of asking a database of information a particular question. Normally, this takes the form of identifying particular combinations of information (e.g. all customers who have ordered more than £100,000 during the last three months).

**QWERTY** – this is the order of the top line of alphabetical keys on the keyboard.

**RAM** – Random Access Memory is the computer's working memory in which the computer carries out its functions once it is switched on. It only exists while the machine is on. If the power is switched off, so is the memory.

**Record** – a group of related fields of information which you normally find in a database.

**Resolution** – this is a way of describing the quality of an image, monitor or printer. The quality is described in terms of the dots which make up the image. That is, the more dots the higher the quality of the image, monitor display or printer output.

**ROM** – Read Only Memory is the computer's permanent memory and is built into the structure of the silicon chips inside it. It is not lost if the power is switched off.

**Search Engine** – a search engine is an application that allows you to search the World Wide Web for a web page containing information on a specific topic or to search within a website for a particular item of information.

**Software** – computer programs written to allow you or the computer to carry out certain tasks such as constructing databases.

**Sort** – a way of presenting information in a spreadsheet or database (e.g. alphabetical).

**Surfing** – this is the process of wandering around the World Wide Web in search of interesting information.

**Table** – a table is part of a database on which information is stored as a series of records and fields.

**URL** – Uniform Resource Locators is the unique address of a World Wide Web site that allows a browser to locate the site.

**Vector** – an image that is defined by mathematical formula rather than pixels. This defines the start and finish of the line and allows it to be easily changed. Vector image can be resized and it will stay in perfect proportion.

**Virus** – a virus is a computer program designed to cause harm to a computer.

**Web page** – a document which forms part of a website.

**Web site** – A web site is a collection of pages on the Internet.

**Word Processor** – an application which allows you to create and manipulate documents.

**WWW** – the World Wide Web is a collection of millions of web sites and documents spread across the world as part of the Internet.

**Window** – a window is a rectangular area of the screen in which computer applications and information is displayed.

**Wizard** – Many Windows 95/98 applications include a Wizard. Wizards are used to perform complex tasks more easily by allowing the user to choose between options.

# Index

## A

**Access**

## B

## C

## M
**Monitor** 9
**Mouse** 7, 9, 14–17, 34

## O
**Operating System** 8
**Outlook Express**
Address book 73–74, 78
E-mail
Addresses 68–69
Copy 70–71, 78
Delete 71
Forward 70, 72, 77
Open 66–67
Organize 70–71
Print 78
Receive 70–72
Reply 70, 72, 77
Save 67–68
Send 68–70, 77

## P
**Paint** 22
**Passwords** 31, 35
**Personal Computer** 7, 8, 9
**Pixels** 158
**Ports** 7, 8, 34
**Powerpoint**
Background 201, 202
Bullets 203, 207, 208–9, 211, 216, 217, 221
Character Font and Size 207–8, 211, 221
Close 207
Create 201–4
Cut, Copy and Paste 204, 206
Delete 203, 220
Edit 204–7
Format 207–12
Graphics 209–10, 211, 215, 217, 218, 220–21
Justify 208–9, 211, 221
Master Slides 214
Open 200, 206
Print 212–14, 221
Promote and Demote 207–8, 217